Mathematics
for
Business

Gary Bronson
College of Business
Fairleigh Dickinson University,
Madison Campus

Richard Bronson (Emeritus)
University College
Fairleigh Dickinson University,
Metropolitan Campus

Maureen Kieff
College of Business
Fairleigh Dickinson University,
Metropolitan Campus

Natalie Yang
College of Business
Fairleigh Dickinson Universit
Madison Campus

D1472657

ISBN-10: 1986065731
ISBN-13: 978-1986065733

Dedication

To Oliver, Benjamin, and Serafina

Gary Bronson

To Casley, Sarah, Asher and Max

Richard Bronson

To Richard, Kristen, Annie, and My Parents

Maureen Kieff

To Hong, Rachel, Benjamin, and My Parents

Natalie Yang

Acknowledgements

With many students finding current textbooks out of their financial reach, the motivation for this edition, as for the first edition, is to provide a college level text, written by established and successful authors, at an affordable price.

Making this objective a reality, however, required the help of many people. In this regard, our most heartfelt acknowledgment and appreciation for this edition go to the instructors and students who found the prior edition helpful in their quest to teach and learn the fundamentals of the basic mathematical tools required in business. In particular, Prof. Sapna Shah did an extraordinary job of proofing the prior edition, and special thanks are due her. Additionally, three students went through the prior editions, making many suggestions and noting both typographical and solution errors; as such, we want to thank them by name. Saadiq Muhammad, Cara Dell Cioppa, and Rob Barker. As always, any errors or mistakes in the current edition are our responsibility.

We also deeply appreciate the efforts of the technical staff at CreateSpace, who have been extremely helpful in guiding us through the production phase of the book.

Finally, we are very grateful for the direct encouragement, support, and positive academic climate provided by our campus provosts, Dr. Peter Woolley and Robert Vodde, our dean, Dr. Andy Rosman, and our department chairman, Dr. Zhaobo Wang.

A Word About Trademarks ....

CONTENTS

4. Rates of Change: The Derivative

5. Applications of the Derivative   189

6. Curve Fitting and Trend Lines   235

PREFACE

Quantitative methods have become essential to business and business decision making in almost all areas of modern businesses These include economic forecasting, allocation of resources, capital budgeting, portfolio analysis, inventory analysis, marketing, data-mining, and new and innovative solutions to a myriad of social media businesses.

The aim of this book is to introduce and provide a basic and necessary understanding of these methods to business students. We understand that the average business major knows that mathematics is a powerful tool for solving problems, but may feel uneasy, sometimes fearful, about the subject matter. Our primary concern in writing this text is to present the material in a clear, understandable, and non-intimidating manner. By numerous examples we relate each new mathematical concept to a practical commercial problem, so that the student never loses sight of the ultimate goal: to develop mathematical tools to solve business problems. We are not interested in mathematics as an end unto itself. Additionally, because many of the topics are now solved using spreadsheets, we show where, when, and how to apply these increasingly necessary toots .

The book assumes student familiarity with algebraic concepts but not facility in using them. As such, Chapter 1 is a review of elementary concepts typically covered at the secondary school level. Students with strong mathematical backgrounds are encouraged to skim this chapter and begin the text with Chapter 2.

Chapter 2 deals with mathematical equations and their application to a variety of business concerns. In this chapter the traditional material on polynomial equations and their graphs is presented.

Interest rates, cash flows, and annuities are purposely treated near the beginning of this book, in Chapter 3. This serves as both motivation and introduction to applying mathematical equations to areas typically of interest to students. Here, mortgages, consumer loans, annuities and their relationship to pension plans, bond payments, and lottery winnings paid over time are presented. The subject matter is relatively easy to grasp and since most students find it interesting, it provides an opportunity for early success in using mathematical methods.

The next two chapters (4 and 5) bring the student to an appreciation and awareness of differential calculus as a powerful mathematical approach for analyzing and modeling commercial systems. The applications in these chapters were developed with this philosophy in mind. They provide a setting for introducing mathematical models and exposing students to realistic applications of average and instantaneous rates of change. Although we do not expect the reader of the book to become an expert in modeling, we do hope that these applications develop an understanding of how differential calculus can be used.

The material in Chapter 6, on least-squares analysis, is included to answer the usual question asked by students as to the origin of the equations they have been using. An integral part of this chapter is the use of spreadsheets to create trend lines and their associated equations.

We are indebted to a number of people for helping to make this book a reality. First, our appreciation goes to our students, who used most of the material in this book in prepublication form. We sincerely hope this text provides a very low cost alternative to the otherwise extremely expensive texts they have been required to purchase in the past, with the same quality that has characterized all of our published texts. Finally, and most importantly, we owe our deep appreciation and thanks to our spouses, Rochelle, Evelyn, Richard, and Hong.

Chapter

The Basics: A Review

This chapter is a review of the topics in algebra that are used throughout the text. Readers who already have a working knowledge of this material are advised to skim over the chapter and go directly to Chapter 2. Others are advised to spend as much time as is necessary to master this material before proceeding further.

1.1 Signed Numbers

Many people have no difficulty performing the basic arithmetic operations (addition, subtraction, multiplication, and division) on positive numbers, but find similar operations on negative numbers mind–boggling. These operations typically are much easier to understand as they relate to profit and loss in commercial settings

In business, among many other uses, positive numbers represent profits, and negative numbers represent losses. In particular, −$5.00 denotes a loss of $5.00, −$10.25 denotes a loss of $10.25, and +$3.00 denotes a profit or gain of $3.00. By convention, a number without a sign is considered positive. Therefore, 3 = + 3, ,5 = + 5, and 9.75 = +9.75.

In the context of profits and losses, the addition sign is read "followed by." Then, −3 + 5 is a $3 loss *followed by* a $5 gain; the result is a net gain of $2, so −3 + 5 = 2. For some, the process is clarified when viewed in the context of betting at a horse race. If a person loses $3 on the first race and then wins $5 on the second race, he or she will have a net gain of $2. Again, −3 + 5 = 2.

To calculate 3 + (−7), we reason similarly. A $3 profit followed by a $7 loss results in a net loss of $4. Alternatively, if a person wins $3 on the first race but loses $7 on the second race, he or she will then be behind by $4. Either way, 3 + (-7) = -4.

The same reasoning is valid when adding two negative numbers. The quantity (-10) + (-8) denotes a $10 loss followed by an $8 loss. Or it can be viewed as a person losing $10 on the first bet and then losing $8 on the second bet. The end result is the same, a total loss of $18. Therefore −10 + (−8) = -18.

Viewed as profits and losses, the following results should be straightforward:

$$5 + 7 = 12$$
$$-9 + 3 = -6$$
$$2 + (-4) = -2$$
$$8 + (-5) = 3$$
$$-7 + (-8) = -15.$$

The multiplication of signed numbers is a two–step operation. The first step is to multiply the numbers disregarding any negative signs (treat all numbers as positive). The second step is to determine the appropriate sign for the result. Here the following rules apply:

Multiplication Rules:

- The product of two positive numbers is positive.
- The product of two negative numbers is positive.
- The product of two different signed numbers is negative.

Thus, when both numbers have the same sign (either both positive or both negative); the result is positive. When both numbers have different signs (one positive and one negative), the result is negative. For the multiplication of more than two numbers, the following rules apply:

- The product of an even number of negative numbers is positive.
- The product of an odd number of negative numbers is negative.

To calculate -5 times +2, we first multiply 5 by 2 (disregarding all negative signs) and obtain 10. To determine the appropriate sign for −5 times 2, we note that both numbers have different signs (a negative 5 and a positive 2), so the result is negative. Accordingly −5 times + 2 is-10.

Mathematically, two sets of parentheses next to each other denote multiplication. We write (3)(7) for 3 times 7, (8)(−4) for 8 times −4, and (−3) (−6) for −3 times −6. In particular, (−5)(2) denotes −5 times 2, which was just found to be (−5)(2) = -10.

To calculate (8)(−½), we first disregard the negative sign and multiply the positive numbers, obtaining (8)(½) = 4. Because +8 and −½ have different signs, their product is negative. Accordingly, (8)(−½) = −4.

To calculate (-3)(-6), we first calculate (3)(6) = 18. Because −3 and−−6 have the _same_ sign (both negative), we conclude that (-3)(-6) = 18. Similarly,

$$(3)(-4) = -12$$
$$(-3)(4) = -12$$
$$(-3)(-4) = 12$$
$$(5.1)(-0.2) = -1.02$$
$$\left(-\frac{1}{3}\right)\left(-\frac{5}{2}\right) = \frac{5}{6}$$

Division follows the same pattern as multiplication. First divide the two numbers disregarding signs and assuming all numbers to be positive. Then determine the appropriate sign of the result exactly as in multiplication. Thus, the following division rules apply:[*]

---

[*] Division by 0 is not defined and 0 divided by any non-zero number is 0. That is, for any real number a, a/0 is not defined and 0/a = 0 for any number a ≠0.

Division Rules:

- The quotient of a division problem is positive if both the numerator and denominator have the same signs.
- The quotient of a division problem is negative if the numerator and denominator have opposite signs.

Thus, to calculate $-6 \div 3$ for example, or equivalently, $-6/3$, first divide $+6$ by $+3$, obtaining 2. Because -6 and $+3$ have different signs, the quotient is negative. Thus, $-6/3 = -2$. To calculate $-12/-3$, we first find $12/3 = 4$. Because both -12 and -3 have the same sign, their quotient is positive and $-12/-3 = +4$. Similarly,

$$8/-4 = -2$$
$$4/-8 = -0.5$$
$$-11/-5 = 2.2$$
$$2.1/-3.2 = -0.65625.$$

The most difficult operation for many is subtraction. For subtraction, the following rule applies:

For any real numbers a and b, $\ a - b = a + (-b)$.

That is, subtraction can be converted to addition and the standard addition rules will then apply. The key step is to introduce a plus sign before the subtraction sign and then incorporate the minus sign into the second number. We write $8 - 10$ as $8 + (-10)$; we write $-7 - 11$ as $-7 + (-11)$; we write $-3 - (-8)$ as $-3 + [-(-8)]$. Each subtraction then becomes an addition. If, as a result, there are two negative signs next to each other, such as $-(-8)$, the following rule applies:

The negative of a negative number is the number itself; that is, $\ -(-a) = a$.[†]

Thus, the expression $-(-8) = +8$

To calculate $-7 - 11$, we rewrite the expression as $-7 + (-11)$. This can be considered as a \$7 loss followed by a \$11 loss, which results in a net, which results in a net loss of \$18. That is,

$$-7 - 11 = -7 + (-11) = -18. \text{ Similarly,}$$

[†] This follows because every negative sign can be considered as a -1. Therefore, $-(-a) = (-1)(-a) = +a$ from the multiplication rules previously provided.

$$8 - 10 = 8 + (-10) = -2$$
$$-3 - (-8) = -3 + [-(-8)] = -3 + 8 = 5$$
$$-9 - (-2) = -9 + [-(-2)] = -9 + 2 = 7$$
$$7 - 4 = 7 + (-4) = 3$$
$$-3 - 4 = -3 + (-4) = -7$$

Occasionally, one is faced with a series of operations such as $(-8)(-3 + 5)$. The procedure is to combine two numbers at a time. Because $(-8)(-3 + 5)$ is -8 times the quantity $-3 + 5$, we first calculate the sum $-3 + 5$, which equals 2. Then,

$$(-8)(-3 + 5) = (-8)(2) = -16$$

A more complicated expression is $7[-3 - 2(8 - 10)]$. When calculating any expression having more than two numbers, the following order of operations must be followed:

Order of Operations:

1. Parenthesis – calculate all expressions within parentheses first, starting with the innermost parentheses, or brackets and then systematically working toward the outermost parentheses or brackets. If there is only one set of parentheses, calculate the expression within the parentheses before proceeding with the remaining operations.

2. Exponents – perform all exponents[‡]

3. Perform all multiplications and divisions – left to right

4. Perform Addition and subtraction – left to right

Thus, in the expression $7[-3 - 2(8 - 10)]$, we first compute $(8 - 10)$ within the innermost parentheses and then multiply this result by 2. Accordingly,

$$7[-3 - 2(8 - 10)] = 7[-3 - 2(-2)]$$
$$= 7[-3 + (-2)(-2)]$$
$$= 7[-3 + 4] = 7[1] = 7$$

Similarly,

$$5[3(2 - 8) - 4(5 - 6)] = 5[3(-6) - 4(-1)]$$
$$= 5[-18 + (-4)(-1)]$$

[‡] Exponents are presented in Section 1.3.

$$= 5[\,-18 + 4]$$
$$= 5[\,-14]$$
$$= -70$$

and

$$[5 + (-3)][2 - 7] = [2][2 - 7]$$
$$= 2[2 + (-7)]$$
$$= 2(\,-5)$$
$$= -10$$

All signed numbers obey specific properties of arithmetic. For example, the order in which addition is performed is immaterial. In particular, $5 + 7 = 7 + 5$, $-2 + 8 = 8 + (-2)$, $5 + [8 + (-3)] = [5 + 8] + (-3)$, and $-6 + [-7 + 4] = [-6 + (-7)] + 4$. The only requirement is that each number in a sum be added once. If we let a, b, and c denote any signed numbers, either positive or negative, we can state these rules formally as

$a + b = b + a$ (commutative law for addition)
$(a + b) + c = a + (b + c)$ (associative law for addition)

Similar rules hold for multiplication; the order in which multiplication is performed is irrelevant. Clearly, $(5)(7) = (7)(5)$, $(-2)(8) = (8)(-2)$, $(5)[(8)(-3)] = [(5)(8)](-3)$, and $(-6)[(-7)(4)] = [(-6)(-7)](4)$. Again, the only requirement is that each number in a product be multiplied once. Formally,

$(a)\,(b) = (b\,)(a)$ (commutative law for multiplication)

$(a)\,[(b)\,(c)] = [(a)\,(b)]\,(c)$ (associative law for multiplication)

The left side of the last equation indicates that first b and c are multiplied together and the result then multiplied by a. The right side indicates that first a and b are multiplied together and the result then multiplied by c. The equality indicates both procedures yield the same result. Specifically, with $a = -3$, $b = -2$, and $c = 8$, $(-3)[(-2)(8)] = (-3)(-16) = 48$ and $[(-3)(-2)](8) = [(6)](8) = 48$, which are indeed equal.

Other rules are useful if the operations of addition and multiplication are mixed. They are

$(a)(b + c) = (a)(b) + (a)(c)$ (left distributive law)
$(b + c)(a) = (b)\,(a) + (c)(a)$ (right distributive law).

If, as an example, $a = -3$, $b = -2$, and $c = 8$, the left side of the equation for the left distributive law becomes $(-3)(-2 + 8) = (-3)(6) = -18$, while the right side becomes $(-3)(-2) + (-3)(8) = 6 + (-24) = -18$.

    Note that each side of the equations for the distributive laws is arithmetically different. On the left side, two numbers are first added and the result then multiplied by a. On the right side, two pairs of numbers are first multiplied and the results then added. The final results on both sides, however, are equal.

Section 1.1 Exercises

Evaluate the following expressions.

1. $3 + (-6)$
2. $-4 + 7$
3. $19.7 + (-18.1)$
4. $-6.2 +) + (-8.1)$
5. $-9 + (-1/2)$
6. $-4.1 + 7$
7. $9(18)$
8. $9(-8)$
9. $(-9)(18)$
10. $(-9)(-18)$
11. $(2)(-1/3)$
12. $(-5)(-1/6)$
13. $(-6.1)(2.3)$
14. $(-8)(-1.4)$
15. $(-8)/(-2)$
16. $8/(-2)$
17. $-8/2$
18. $-2/8$
19. $4/(-5)$
20. $(-5)/(-4)$
21. $-22/4$
22. $8 - 4$
23. $4 - 8$
24. $-4 - 8$
25. $-4 - (-8)$
26. $-8 - 4$
27. $-8 - (-4)$
28. $2.1 - 5.6$
29. $-5.6 - 2.1$
30. $1/10 - 1/5$
31. $2[5 + (-3)]$
32. $-2[1 + (-6)]$
33. $-4(1 - 3) + 2(2 - 5)$
34. $6[2(-1 + 7) - 3]$
35. $(1.6)(1.9 - 2.1) - 6.3$
36. $4\{(-1)(2-9) + 7(3 - 4)]$

37. $\dfrac{8[1-(-8)]-2[7-1]}{2}$

38. $\dfrac{[(8-12)/4]+4(9-3)}{5-9}$

39. $\dfrac{(5-11)(8-14)+42(2+3)}{7[2(1+30)-3(2-5)]}$

40. $\dfrac{8[-3(4-1)-6(4-8)]}{2[-8-(-7)]}$

1.2 Solving Equation Having One Unknown Quantity

One major use of arithmetic operations on signed numbers is solving a single equation for its unknown quantity. Any signed number that satisfies the equation (makes it true) is called a *solution* to the equation. For example, a value of x that satisfies the equation $-2x = 10$ is a solution to the equation. Similarly, a value of y that satisfies the equation $2 - y = 4$ is a solution to the equation.

An equation that has a solution is called a **conditional equation**, while one that does not have a solution is called an **inconsistent equation**. An equation, such as $x = x$, for which any number is a solution is called an **identity equation**.

In finding solutions (that is, one or more values that satisfy the equation), you should be aware of two notational conventions that are universally followed when writing equations with unknowns. First, parentheses are omitted for the product of a known number and an unknown quantity. For example, $(8)(y)$ is written as $8y$ and $(-3)(x)$ is written as $-3x$. Secondly, if the product involves a 1, the 1 is omitted and simply understood. Accordingly, both $(1)y$ and $1y$ are written as y, both $(1)x$ and $1x$ are written as x, both $(1)p$ and $1p$ are written as p, and so on. The same convention holds for -1. Thus, for example, both $(-1)y$ and $-1y$ are written as $-y$, and both $(-1)x$ and $-1x$ *are* written as $-x$.

A numerical value for an unknown quantity in an equation is a *solution* for the equation if that value, when substituted for the unknown, makes the equality valid. For example, to determine whether $x = 4$ is a solution of $-2x = 10$, substitute $x = 4$ into the equation. Because $-2x = -2(4) = -8$, which does not equal 10, the value 4 is not a solution to the equation.

Example 1 Determine whether or not $x = 2$ is a solution of the equation

$$\frac{5x + 3(x - 7)}{2x + 4} = -3.$$

Solution Substituting $x = 2$ into this equation, the left side becomes

$$\frac{(5)(2) + 3(2 - 7)}{2(2) + 4} = \frac{10 + 3(-5)}{4 + 4} = \frac{10 + (-15)}{8} = -\frac{5}{8}$$

Because this does *not* equal -3, which is the right side of the original equation, the proposed value of $x = 2$ is not a solution.

Example 2 Determine whether or not $p = \frac{5}{9}$ is a solution of the equation
$7 - p = 2 + 8p$.

Solution When $p = \frac{5}{9}$ is substituted into this equation, the left side becomes

$$7 - \frac{5}{9} = \left(\frac{63}{9} - \frac{5}{9}\right) = \frac{58}{9}$$

and the right side becomes

$$2 + 8\left(\frac{5}{9}\right) = \frac{18}{9} + \frac{40}{9} = \frac{58}{9}$$

Because these values *are* equal, $p = \frac{5}{9}$ is a solution.

One method for solving an equation for an unknown is trial and error. Guess a solution and then substitute it into the equation to see if it is valid. If not, guess again and continue guessing solutions until the correct one is found. Clearly this method is time consuming. It could take many guesses before the correct value is found. It also could take forever; one may never guess the correct value.

A more systematic procedure is to use the arithmetic operations developed in Section 1.1 to isolate the unknown on one side of the equation. The correct value for this unknown will then be on the other side of the equation. The key is remembering that the unknown is really a number and should be treated as such. Remember that

$$1x = x$$

and

$$0x = 0.$$

Furthermore, the associative laws and distributive laws remain valid. For example,

$$5 + (7 + y) = (5 + 7) + y = 12 + y \quad \text{(associative law for addition)}$$
$$(-2)(8y) = [(-2)(8)]y = -16y \quad \text{(associative law for multiplication)}$$
$$7p + 5p = (7 + 5)p = 12p \quad \text{(right distributive law)}$$
$$5a + (-5a) = [5 + (-5)]a = 0a = 0 \quad \text{(right distributive law)}.$$

Suppose we have the quantity $x + 5$ and we want to isolate x. By adding -5 to this quantity, we obtain $(x + 5) + (-5)$. One application of the associative law for addition yields $(x + 5) + (-5) = x + [5 + (-5)] = x + 0 = x$, and the unknown is isolated . If we have the quantity $-7y$, we can isolate y by either dividing by -7 or multiplying by -1/7.

In general, additive factors such as $+5$ in $x + 5$ can be removed by adding their negatives, and multiplicative factors such as -7 in $-7y$ can be removed by dividing by the number in front of the unknown quantity. In doing so, however, we must remember the following fundamental rule:

Fundamental Rule: *Whenever an arithmetic operation is performed on one side of an equation, an identical operation must be performed on the other side of the equation.* **There are no exceptions to this rule.**

This rule is frequently stated as the following two principles:

The Addition/Subtraction Principle:

For an equation A = B and any real number c,
$$A + c = B + c$$

Notice that if c is a negative number, the same number is effectively subtracted from both sides of an equation.

The Multiplication/Division Principle:

For an equation A = B and any real, non-zero, number c,

$$c \cdot A = c \cdot B$$

and

$$\frac{A}{c} = \frac{B}{c}$$

It is important to emphasize that the value c either multiplies *every* term on *both sides* of the equation, or divides *every* term on *both sides* of the equation., depending on which principle is used. For example, consider the equation $7x - 3 = 4x + 12$. Using the Multiplication Principle with c = 2 yields

$$2(7x - 3) = 2(4x + 12)$$

which becomes

$$14x - 6 = 8x + 24$$

One of the most useful applications of the Addition/Subtraction and Multiplication/Division principles is in finding solutions, if they exist, to equations with one unknown quantity

Example 3 Solve the equation $-2x = 10$ for x.

Solution The goal is to isolate x on one side of the equation. Here, this is accomplished by removing the multiplicative factor -2 in front of the x on the left side of the equation. This is easily accomplished using the multiplication/division principle and dividing both sides of the given equation by -2. Then,

$$\frac{-2x}{-2} = \frac{10}{-2}$$

which yields

$x = $ -5.

Example 4 Solve the equation $x + 7 = 5$ for x.

Solution The goal is again to isolate x on one side of the equation. This is accomplished here by removing the additive factor +7 from the left side of the equation. By adding -7 to both sides of the equation (or, equivalently, by subtracting 7 from both sides of the equation, we obtain

$x + 7 + (-7) = 5 + (-7)$

which yields

$x = -2.$

Example 5 Solve the equation $2 - y = 4$ for y.

Solution We first remove the 2 from the left side, thereby leaving only y terms on that side of the equation. This is done by adding -2 to both sides of the equation (or, equivalently, by subtracting 2 from both sides of the equation). Then,

$-2 + 2 - y = -2 + 4$

which yields

$-y = 2$

We do not have y yet, but we are close. If we multiply both sides of the equation by -1, we obtain

$(-1)(-y) = (-1)(2)$

or

$y = -2.$

Example 6 Solve the equation $7 - p = 2 + 8p$ for p.

Solution We begin by grouping all the p terms on the same side of the equation. One way is to add p to both sides. Then,

$7 - p + p = 2 + 8p + p$
$7 = 2 + 9p$

Next we isolate the p terms on the right side by subtracting 2 from both sides of the equation

$7 - 2 = 2 + 9p - 2$

which yields

$5 = 9p$

Finally, we divide both sides of this equation by 9 to isolate p by itself. Thus,

$\frac{5}{9} = p$, which can be rewritten as $p = \frac{5}{9}$

Example 7 Solve the equation $3(x - 7) = \frac{5x+9}{4}$ for x.

Solution To eliminate the fraction, we multiply both sides of the equation by 4. Then,

$4[3(x - 7)] = 4\left[\frac{5x + 9}{4}\right]$

$12(x - 7) = 5x + 9$

$12x - 84 = 5x + 9$

Now, subtracting 5x from both sides, which eliminates the x term on the right side of the equation, yields

$7x - 84 = 9$

To isolate the x term, we now add 84 to each side of the equation, which yields

$7x = 93$

Finally, dividing both sides of the equation by 7 yields

$x = 93/7$

Example 8 Solve the following equation for x.

$$\frac{5x + 3(x - 7)}{2x + 4} = -3$$

Solution To eliminate the fraction we multiply both sides of the equation by the quantity $(2x + 4)$, which yields

$$(2x + 4)\left[\frac{5x+3(x-7)}{2x+4}\right] = (2x + 4)(-3)$$

which can be simplified to

$$5x + 3(x - 7) = -6x - 12$$

Then, multiplying the $(x - 7)$ term through by 3, we have

$$5x + 3x - 21 = -6x - 12$$

Adding the $5x$ to the $3x$ yields

$$8x - 21 = -6x - 12$$

Adding $6x$ to both sides yields

$$14x - 21 = -12$$

Adding 21 to both sides yields

$$14x = 9$$

Finally, dividing both sides by 14 yields the solution $x = 9/14$

Section 1.2 Exercises

In Exercises 1 through 6 determine whether or not the proposed values of the unknowns are solutions of the given systems.

1. $2x+3=1$; $x = -1$
2. $y + 4 = 2y$; $y = 1$
3. $2(p + 7) = 3p + 4$; $p = 1$
4. $x + 3 = 2(x + 1) + 1$; $x = 0$

5. $\dfrac{(s+3)(s-2)}{2s+1} = s + 7;$ $s = 1$

6. $\dfrac{(2t+3)(t-1)+1}{2(t+3)+1} = 3t - 4;$ $t = 2$

7. Determine whether or not $x = 1$ is a solution of the following equation if it is known that $y = 2$ and $z = 0$:

$$\frac{x(y-1) + yz}{y(x-z)} = \frac{x}{y}$$

For Exercises 8 through 26, solve each equation for the unknown quantity.

8. $x + 7 = 2$

9. $7 = 2 + x$

10. $y - 8 = -2$

11. $8x = \text{-}16$

12. $2p = 30$

13. $\text{-}4p = 16$

14. $s + 10 = 2s$

15. $t - 10 = 4 - t$

16. $2t + 1 = t - 5$

17. $2x = 3(x + 1)$

18. $5y - 1 = 4(y - 2)$

19. $8(p - 2) = 7(2p + 1)$

20. $7p + 1 = 7(p - 1) + 3p$

21. $2(a + 7) - 4 = 3(a - 1) + 2a$

22. $\dfrac{(x-1)+5(x-4)}{8} = 2x + 1$ 23. $\dfrac{2(y-1)+4}{y} = 8$

24. $\dfrac{(t-4)}{5} = \dfrac{3t+1}{8}$ 25. $\dfrac{3(2t-6)+4(t-8)}{7(6+t)-8(t-4)} = -3$

26. $\dfrac{8t+9(1-t)+7}{3} = \dfrac{2(t-8)-5(t+1)}{2}$

1.3 Exponents

Exponents provide a convenient notation for representing the product of a number times itself many times. For example, consider the following, which are valid for any signed number a (either positive or negative)

$$a^2 = (a)(a)$$

$$a^3 = (a)(a)(a)$$

$$a^4 = (a)(a)(a)(a)$$

The definition of a number, denoted as a, raised to the nth power, where n denotes a nonnegative integer (whole number) is given by

$$a^n = (a)(a)(a)(a).......(a) \quad \leftarrow n \text{ values of a multiplied together}$$

The quantity a^n is typically read as either "the nth power of a," or "a to the nth." For example,

$$5^2 = (5)(5) = 25 \qquad \text{("5 squared is 5 times 5, which equals 25")}$$

$$(-4)^3 = (-4)(-4)(-4) = -64 \quad \text{("-4 cubed is -4 times -4 times -4, which equals -64")}$$

$$(-1/3)^4 = (-1/3)(-1/3)(-1/3)(-1/3) = 1/81 \quad \text{("-1/3 to the 4}^{\text{th}}\text{ power, equals 1/81")}$$

and

$$2^{10} = (2)(2)(2)(2)(2)\ (2)(2)(2)(2)(2) = 1024 \quad \text{("2 to the 10}^{\text{th}}\text{ power, equals 1024")}$$

Notice that it is much easier to write 2^{10}, than list 2 ten times. Additionally, as most calculators have an exponential function (usually with keys having either a y^x or $^\wedge$ notation) it is easier to calculate the final numerical value using the designated exponential key than entering and multiplying the given number n times.

One consequence of the exponential definition is the property

$$(a^n)(a^m) = a^{n+m} \qquad \text{(Eq. 1.1)}$$

where n and m are positive integers. For example,

$$(6^2)(6^3) = [(6)(6)][(6)(6)(6)] = (6)(6)(6)(6)(6) = 6^5 = 6^{2+3}$$

$$(-2)^4(-2)^3 = [(-2)(-2)(-2)(-2)][(-2)(-2)(-2)] = (-2)^7 = (-2)^{4+3}$$

and

$$\left(-\frac{1}{3}\right)^4\left(-\frac{1}{3}\right)^2 = \left[\left(-\frac{1}{3}\right)\left(-\frac{1}{3}\right)\left(-\frac{1}{3}\right)\left(-\frac{1}{3}\right)\right]\left[\left(-\frac{1}{3}\right)\left(-\frac{1}{3}\right)\right] = \left(-\frac{1}{3}\right)^6 = \left(-\frac{1}{3}\right)^{4+2}$$

Equation 1.1 is valid only if the left side of the equation is a number raised to a power times that *same number* raised to a power. The formula is not valid if one a in Equation 1.1 is replaced by another number b. For example, Equation 1.1 is *not* applicable to the product $(2)^5(3)^4$.

A second useful property of powers is

(Eq. 1.2)

$$\boxed{(a^n)^m = a^{nm}}$$

That is, any number a raised to a power n, which is itself raised to a power m, is equal to a raised to the power n times m. For example, note that

$$(2^2)^3 = (2^2)(2^2)(2^2) = [(2)(2)][(2)(2)][(2)(2)] = 2^6 = 2^{(2)(3)}$$

and

$$\left[\left(-\frac{1}{3}\right)^3\right]^3 = \left[\left(-\frac{1}{3}\right)\left(-\frac{1}{3}\right)\left(-\frac{1}{3}\right)\right]^3$$

$$= \left[\left(-\frac{1}{3}\right)\left(-\frac{1}{3}\right)\left(-\frac{1}{3}\right)\right]\left[\left(-\frac{1}{3}\right)\left(-\frac{1}{3}\right)\left(-\frac{1}{3}\right)\right]\left[\left(-\frac{1}{3}\right)\left(-\frac{1}{3}\right)\left(-\frac{1}{3}\right)\right]$$

$$= \left(-\frac{1}{3}\right)^9 = \left(-\frac{1}{3}\right)^{(3)(3)}$$

Using Equations 1.1 and 1.2 together, we have

$$(2^4)^3(2^2)^4 = 2^{12}2^8 = 2^{12+8} = 2^{20}$$

and

$$[(-4)^3]^5[(-4)^2]^3 = (-4)^{15}(-4)^6 = (-4)^{21}$$

Be careful not to confuse these two properties. A common error is to write $(a^n)^m = a^{n+m}$ or $(a^n)(a^m) = a^{nm.}$ Both of these are *incorrect and lead to wrong answers*.

Equations 1.1 and 1.2 can be extended to negative powers if we first give meaning to what a negative exponent means. Accordingly, for any nonzero signed number a and any positive integer, we define

$$a^{-n} = \frac{1}{a^n}$$

(Eq. 1.3)

Therefore,

$$5^{-2} = \frac{1}{5^2} = \frac{1}{25}$$

$$(4)^{-3} = \frac{1}{(4)^3} = \frac{1}{64}$$

$$(-4)^{-3} = \frac{1}{(-4)^3} = \frac{1}{-64} = -\frac{1}{64}$$

$$\left(-\frac{1}{3}\right)^{-4} = \frac{1}{\left(-\frac{1}{3}\right)^4} = \frac{1}{\left(\frac{1}{81}\right)} = 81$$

and

$$2^{-10} = \frac{1}{2^{10}} = \frac{1}{1024}.$$

It follows from Equations 1.1 and 1.2 that the expression, $27 2^{-3} = 2^{7+(-3)} = 2^4$, and that $(4^{-6})^{-5}$, for example, equals $4^{(-6)(-5)} = 4^{30}$.

It is also useful to define

$$a^0 = 1$$

(Eq. 1.4)

for every nonzero signed number a.[§] Accordingly, $5^0 = 1$, $(-4)^0 = 1$, and $(-5/8)^0 = 1$.

Using Equations 1.1 and 1.3, we have

[§] Note that 0^0 is not defined as 1, as it would lead to contradictions in more advanced mathematics.

$$\frac{a^n}{a^m} = a^n \left[\frac{1}{a^m}\right] = a^n a^{-m} = a^{n+(-m)} = a^{n-m}$$

Therefore,

$$\boxed{\frac{a^n}{a^m} = a^{n-m}}$$

(Eq. 1.5)

Equation 1.5 is applicable for every real number a and all integers n and m. Thus, for example, using Equation 1.5,

$$\frac{5^7}{5^4} = 5^{(7-4)} = 5^3 = 125$$

$$\frac{2^6}{2^8} = 2^{(6-8)} = 2^{-2} = \frac{1}{2^2} = \frac{1}{4}$$

and

$$\frac{(-\frac{1}{3})^2}{(-\frac{1}{3})^5} = (-\frac{1}{3})^{2-5} = (-\frac{1}{3})^{-3} = \frac{1}{(-\frac{1}{3})^3} = \frac{1}{-(\frac{1}{27})} = -27$$

Equations 1.1 through 1.5 can be used to simplify tedious multiplication and division operation when each factor can be expressed as *the same number* raised to a power. For example, if one recognizes that $8 = 2^3$, $512 = 2^9$, $64 = 2^6$, and $1024 = 2^{10}$, then

$$\frac{8(512)}{(64)(1024)} = \frac{2^3 2^9}{2^6 2^{10}} = \frac{2^{3+9}}{2^{6+10}} = \frac{2^{12}}{2^{16}} = 2^{(12-16)} = 2^{-4} = \frac{1}{2^4} = \frac{1}{16}$$

Although Equations 1.1 through 1.5 were defined for any signed number a and all integers (whole numbers) n and m, they actually are also valid for non-integer exponents. To understand why this is so we first have to give meaning to fractional exponents such as ½, 1/3, and 1/10 in expressions such as $4^{1/2}$, $8^{1/3}$, and $120^{1/10}$. This is accomplished by defining the exponent $1/n$ as the nth root of the number a, which is frequently written as $\sqrt[n]{a}$. **

Calculators that have exponential capabilities can also calculate fractional exponents if the fraction is first converted to a decimal value; the decimal value is then used as the exponent.

Numbers raised to more complicated fractional exponents, such as $4^{7/2}$ and $27^{5/3}$ also can be defined mathematically, which we do now for completeness, noting beforehand that such numbers have very limited applications to business problems. In general $a^{p/q} = (a^{1/q})^p$ when a is a positive number and both p and q are positive integers. Therefore, $4^{3/2} = (4^{1/2})^3 = 2^3 = 8$. Note that $a^{p/q}$ can also be defined as $(a^p)^{1/q}$ Using this definition, $4^{3/2} = (4^3)^{1/2} = (64)^{1/2} = 8$, which is, of course the same result as obtained using the first definition. Using a calculator, for fractional exponents is accomplished in the same manner as integer exponents. First calculate the decimal value of the exponent, and then use this value as the exponent using the calculator's exponentiation capability.

Table 1.1 summarizes the exponential rules for *all* positive real numbers a, n, and m. Additionally, if both n and m are integers, these properties are also true for negative values of a.

TABLE 1.1

Definition	Example
$a^n a^m = a^{n+m}$	$2^3 2^5 = 2^8$
$(a^n)^m = a^{nm}$	$(3^5)^4 = 3^{20}$
$a^{-n} = 1/a^n$	$4^{-2} = 1/4^2 = 1/16$
$a^0 = 1$ (for any $a \neq 0$)	$25^0 = 1$
$a^n/a^m = a^{n-m}$	$5^7/5^3 = 5^4$

There is one last property of exponents that is useful; it involves the product of two different positive numbers raised to the *same* exponent:

$$a^n b^n = (ab)^n$$

(Eq. 1.6)

** By convention, the second root of a number, which is its square root, is written as $\sqrt{a}$, rather than as $\sqrt[2]{a}$.

For example,

$$(5.2)^3(2)^3 = [(5.2)(2)]^3 = (10.4)^3 = 1{,}124.864$$

$$(4)^{3.1}(7)^{3.1} = (28)^{3.1} = 30{,}633.02583$$

and

$$(1.2)^{-3.4}(1.1)^{-3.4} = [(1.2)(1.1)]^{-3.4} = (1.32)^{-3.4} = 0.38908871$$

Like the other properties, Equation 1.6 is also valid for negative values of a and negative b.

We conclude this section with a warning. Most other properties of exponents that are ingeniously invented at times of stress, for example, during an examination, are usually not valid. In particular, as previously noted

$$a^n a^m \neq a^{nm}$$

$$(a^n)^m \neq a^{n+m}$$

Additionally,

$$a^n b^m \neq (ab)^{n+m}$$

The safest procedure is to understand and memorize the six properties provided in Table 1.1 and to *assume* that all other properties are not valid unless *you* can prove them.

Section 1.3 Exercises

In Exercises 1 through 9, simplify each of the given expressions into one exponent. Make sure that each solution is given with a positive exponent.

1. $\dfrac{3^5 3^4}{3^2 3^3}$

2. $\dfrac{7^2 7^{-3} 7^4}{7^8 7^{-2}}$

3. $\dfrac{\pi^4 (\pi^2)^3}{(\pi^{-2})^4 \pi^3}$

4. $\left[\left(-\frac{1}{2}\right)^2\right]^4 \left[\left(-\frac{1}{2}\right)^{-3}\right]^2 \left[\left(-\frac{1}{2}\right)^{-4}\right]^{-5}$

5. $\dfrac{(1.7)^{8.1}(1.7)^{-3.4}}{(1.7)^{-4.1}(1.7)^{3.7}}$

6. $\dfrac{x^3(x^2)^4(x^{-3})^7}{(x^{-3})^{-4} x^5}$

7. $\dfrac{(y^{-3})^{-2} y^4 y^{-1}}{y^2 (y^3)^{-1}}$

8. $\dfrac{(x^4)^2 (1/x)^{-3}}{(1/x)^2}$

9. $\{[(3.1)^{-2}]^{-4}\}^3$

Using a calculator, determine the values of the quantities given in Exercises 10 through 21.

10. $9^{3/2}$

11. $16^{-5/4}$

12. $27^{2}/3$

13. $100^{-3/2}$

14. $(3^{1/2})(12^{1/2})$

15. $(3^{1/3})(9^{1/3})$

16. $(5)^{-1/2}(20)^{-1/2}$

17. $(2^{-3/2})(32)^{-3/2}$

18. $\sqrt{9/4}$

19. $\sqrt{\dfrac{8}{18}}$

20. $\sqrt{\dfrac{(49)(16)}{25}}$

21. $\sqrt[3]{\dfrac{(27)(8)}{125}}$

1.4 Solving Quadratic Equations using the Quadratic Formula

Equations of the form $x^n = c$, where n and c are known numbers, are easily solved for the unknown, which in this case is x, using the properties of exponents. Examples of such equations are:

$x^4 = 16$ (here, $n = 4$ and $c = 16$)

$x^7 = 5$ (here, $n = 7$ and $c = 5$)

$x^{1.3} = \pi$ (here $n = 1.3$ and $c = \pi = 3.1417...$)

and

$y^3 = 27$ (here the unknown is y, $n = 3$ and $c = 27$)

Equations of this form are solved by raising both sides of the equation to the $1/n$ power. This is accomplished by taking the nth root of both sides of the equation. Thus, if we raise both sides of the equation $x^n = c$ to the $1/n$ power, we obtain the solution $x = c^{1/n}$, which can also be written as $\sqrt[n]{c}$.[††]

[††] Note that if the number n in the equation $x^n = c$ is an even integer ≥ 0 ($n = 2$, $n = 4$, $n = 6$, and so on), there are two real solutions to the given equation. One solution is $x = c^{1/n}$; the second solution is $x = -c^{1/n}$. The two solutions are usually given together as $x = \pm c^{1/n}$.

Example 1 Solve the equation $x^2 = 16$ for x.

Solution Raising both sides of the equation to the ½ power yields $x = 16^{1/2} = \sqrt{16}$. Thus, the solution is $x = \pm 4$ (see footnote on page 19).

Example 2 Solve $y^3 = 27$ for y.

Solution Raising both sides of this equation to the 1/3 power, we obtain $y = (27)^{1/3}$. This can be written as $\sqrt[3]{27}$, which is the cube root of 27. Either using a calculator or knowing that the cube root of 27 is 3, we have that the solution is $y = 3$.

Example 3 Solve $x^{1.3} = \pi$.

Solution Raising both sides of this equation to the 1/1.3 power yields $x = \pi^{\left(\frac{1}{1.3}\right)}$. Using a calculator, we find $x = 2.412$ rounded to three decimal places.

A more difficult problem arises when the unknown quantity appears more than once in a given equation, each time raised to a different power. For example, finding the solution for x in the equation $2x^5 + 3x^2 - 1 = 0$, or finding the solution for y in the equation $y^{10} + 2y^8 - y^3 + 7 = 0$. For most equations of this form, the solutions cannot be obtained algebraically. Solution methods do not exist. One of the few exceptions is the quadratic equation.

A *quadratic equation* has the form $ax^2 + bx + c = 0$, where a, b, and c are all known numbers and $a \neq 0$. Examples of quadratic equations are:

$2x^2 + 5x - 7 = 0$ (here $a = 2$, $b = 5$ and $c = -7$)

$7x^2 - 2x - 1 = 0$ (here $a = 7$, $b = -2$ and $c = -1$)

As usual, the letter used to denote the unknown is not important. Thus, both of the following are also quadratic equations, with the first being quadratic in y and the second quadratic in p.

$4y^2 - 2y - 3 = 0$ ($a = 4$, $b = -2$ and $c = -3$)

$3p^2 + p + 2 = 0$ ($a = 3$, $b = 1$ and $c = 2$)

The important feature of a quadratic equation is that the unknown only appears raised to the second and first powers.

We prove at the end of this section that the solutions to equations of the form $ax^2 + bx + c = 0$ are given by the *quadratic formula*

$$x = \frac{-b \pm \sqrt{b^2 - 4ac}}{2a}$$

(Eq. 1.7)

To solve any quadratic equation, substitute the values of its coefficients a, b, and c into the quadratic formula and simplify.

Caution: Before using the quadratic formula to solve for x, make sure that the given equation is in the form: $ax^2 + bx + c = 0$.

Note that

If $b^2 - 4ac = 0$, then there is only one real solution: $x = \frac{-b}{2a}$.

If $b^2 - 4ac > 0$, then there are two distinct real solutions.

If $b^2 - 4ac < 0$, then there are no real solutions.

Example 4 Solve the equation $x^2 + 2x - 3 = 0$ for x.

Solution This is a quadratic equation with $a = 1$, $b = 2$, and $c = -3$. Substituting these values into the quadratic formula, we obtain

$$x = \frac{-2 \pm \sqrt{2^2 - 4(1)(-3)}}{2(1)} = \frac{-2 \pm \sqrt{4 + 12}}{2} = \frac{-2 \pm \sqrt{16}}{2} = \frac{-2 \pm 4}{2}$$

Using the plus sign, we obtain one solution as $x = (-2 + 4)/2 = 1$. Using the minus sign, we find a second solution as $x = (-2 - 4)/2 = -3$.

Example 5 Solve the equation $4y^2 - 2y = 3$ for y.

Solution We first rewrite this equation in the form as $4y^2 - 2y - 3 = 0$, which is a quadratic equation with $a = 4$, $b = -2$, and $c = -3$. Substituting these values into the quadratic formula, we have

$$y = \frac{-(-2) \pm \sqrt{(-2)^2 - 4(4)(-3)}}{2(4)} = \frac{2 \pm \sqrt{4 + 48}}{8} = \frac{-2 \pm \sqrt{52}}{8} = \frac{2 \pm 7.21}{8}$$

The solutions are then $y = (2 + 7.21)/8 = 1.15$ and $y = (2 - 7.21)/8 = -0.65$, with all calculations rounded to two decimals.

The quadratic formula does not always yield two solutions. If $b^2 - 4ac = 0$, the formula reduces to

$$x = \frac{-b \pm \sqrt{0}}{2a} = -\frac{b}{2a}$$

In these cases the quadratic equation has only one solution. If $b^2 - 4ac$ is negative, the square root cannot be taken, and no real solutions exist. Readers familiar with complex numbers will note that complex solutions exist. Because complex numbers have no use in commercial situations, we do not consider them here.

Example 6 Solve the equation $x^2 - 2x + 1 = 0$ for x.

Solution Here $a = 1$, $b = -2$, and $c = 1$. Substituting these values into the quadratic formula, we obtain

$$x = \frac{-(-2) \pm \sqrt{(-2)^2 - 4(1)(1)}}{2(1)} = \frac{2 \pm \sqrt{4 - 4}}{2} = \frac{2 \pm 0}{2} = 1.$$

The only solution is $x = 1$.

Example 7 Solve the equation $2p^2 + p + 1 = 0$ for p.

Solution Substituting $a = 2$, $b = 1$, and $c = $ into the quadratic formula, yields

$$p = \frac{-1 \pm \sqrt{(1)^2 - 4(2)(1)}}{2(2)} = \frac{-1 \pm \sqrt{1 - 8}}{4} = \frac{-1 \pm \sqrt{-7}}{4}.$$

Because $\sqrt{-7}$ is not defined; the given equation has no real solutions.

Proof of the Quadratic Formula

To prove the quadratic formula, we first rewrite $ax^2 + bx + c = 0$ as $ax^2 + bx = -c$, and then divide both sides of the equation by a, obtaining

$$x^2 + \frac{b}{a}x = -\frac{c}{a}.$$

Using a method known as completing the squares, we add the quantity

$\dfrac{b^2}{4a^2}$ to both sides of this equation, which yields

$$x^2 + \frac{bx}{a} + \frac{b^2}{4a^2} = -\frac{c}{a} + \frac{b^2}{4a^2}$$

By the completion of squares, the left side of this equation can be rewritten as

$$x^2 + \frac{bx}{a} + \frac{b^2}{4a^2} = \left(x + \frac{b}{2a}\right)^2$$

and by using a common denominator, the right side can be rewritten as

$$-\frac{c}{a} + \frac{b^2}{4a^2} = \frac{-4ac + b^2}{4a^2} = \frac{b^2 - 4ac}{4a^2}$$

Thus the original equation becomes

$$\left(x + \frac{b}{2a}\right)^2 = \frac{b^2 - 4ac}{4a^2}.$$

Taking the square root of both sides, we have

$$x + \frac{b}{2a} = \pm\sqrt{\frac{b^2 - 4ac}{4a^2}} = \pm\frac{\sqrt{b^2 - 4ac}}{\sqrt{4a^2}} = \pm\frac{\sqrt{b^2 - 4ac}}{2a}$$

By subtracting $\dfrac{b}{2a}$ from both the left hand and right hand sides of the last equation, and using the term 2a as a common denominator, we obtain the solution for x as

$$x = \frac{-b \pm \sqrt{b^2 - 4ac}}{2a},$$

which is the quadratic formula.

Section 1.4 Exercises

Solve the following equations for the unknown quantity (note: factoring can be used wherever it is appropriate).

1. $x^3 = 8$.
2. $x^3 = 125$.
3. $y^4 = 81$.
4. $p^6 = 64$.
5. $b^{-2} = \frac{1}{4}$.
6. $b^3 = 9$.
7. $p^5 = 1.3$.
8. $y^\pi = 8$.
9. $t^{9.3} = 9.3$.
10. $p^{-1.2} = 3.1$.
11. $x^2 - 5x + 6 = 0$.
12. $2y^2 - 3y - 2 = 0$.
13. $2p^2 + 6p - 4 = 0$.
14. $c^2 - c - 1 = 0$.
15. $x^2 + 6x + 9 = 0$.
16. $y^2 - y - 2 = 0$.
17. $3n^2 + 2n - 1 = 0$.
18. $4n^2 - 2n + 1 = 0$.
19. $5t^2 - t = 1$.
20. $x^2 - 8x = -16$.
21. $x^2 - 2x = 0$.
22. $3b = b^2 - 1$.

1.5 The Cartesian Coordinate System

Consider the map illustrated in Figure 1.1 with streets running in either a north–south direction or an east–west direction. By using the center of Broad and Market Streets as a reference (perhaps a motorist has stopped there for directions), it is easy to locate any other point on the map. The intersection of Elm Lane and Maple Street is two blocks west and one block south of the reference point. The light at Freeman Street and Valley Road is three blocks east and two blocks north of the reference point.

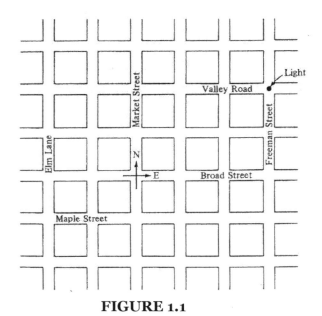

FIGURE 1.1

In each case, the new point on the map is uniquely determined from the reference point by two numbers and their directs

The *Cartesian coordinate system*, which is also known as the *Rectangular coordinate system*, is a generalized version of the previous map. To construct this system, two intersecting perpendicular lines (forming an angle of 90 degrees with each other) are first drawn, as illustrated in Figure 1.2. The horizontal line is often called the *x*-coordinate axis (or just the *x*-axis for short), while the vertical line is often called the *y*-coordinate axis (or *y*-axis for short). The intersection of these two axes is the *origin,* and it represents the reference point of the system.

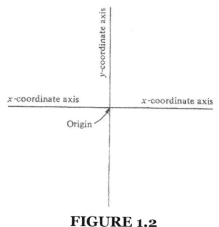

FIGURE 1.2

Each axis is marked in fixed units of length, as illustrated in Figure 1.3. Units to the right of the origin on the axis and units above the origin on the *y*-axis are assigned positive values. Units to the left of the origin on the *x*-axis and units below the origin on the *y*-axis are assigned negative values. The complete system is the *Cartesian* (or rectangular) *coordinate* system.

Note that arrows have been appended to the positive portions of the *x*- and *y*-axes in Figure 1.3. These arrows simply indicate, visually, the direction of increasing values of *x* and *y*. We can think of the *x*-axis as representing the east–west direction on a map, and the *y*-axis as representing the north–south direction. The arrows then indicate the directions east and north. Moving in a positive *x* direction corresponds to moving east. Moving in a negative *y* direction corresponds to moving south. Motion in the directions of north and west is defined by moving in the positive *y* and negative *x* directions, respectively.

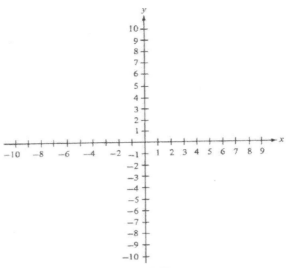

FIGURE 1.3

The usefulness of the Cartesian coordinate system is that any point on the plane can be located from the origin by two numbers. Directions need not be specified, since they are inherent in the signs of the numbers. As an example, consider the point P shown in Figure 1.4. To reach this point from the origin, one must move 6 units along the x-axis in the positive direction and then 4 units in the positive y direction along a line segment parallel to the y-axis beginning at $x = 6$. The point P is located by the two numbers 6 and 4, if we agree that the first number, 6 denotes moving 6 units along the x-axis and the second number, 4, denotes moving 4 units in the y direction.

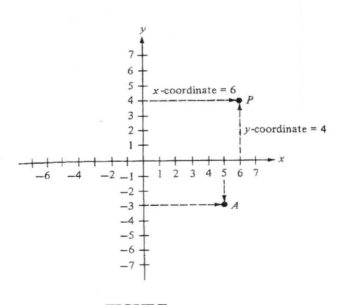

FIGURE 1.4

Every point on the plane can be uniquely located by two numbers. By convention, the first number always indicates movement along the x-axis, while the second number always indicates movement parallel to the y-axis. Positive numbers denote movement in the positive direction (in the direction of the arrows); negative numbers indicate movement in the negative direction. The two numbers defining the point of interest are separated by a comma and enclosed in parentheses. Point P in Figure 1.4 is given by (6, 4), and point A is given by (5, -3) To reach A from the origin (our reference point), we move 5 units along the x-axis in the positive x direction (the first number is +5), and then we move 3 units in the negative y direction (the second number is –3).

The two numbers defining a given point are called the *coordinates* of the point. Not surprisingly, the first number is often called the *x-coordinate* and the second number the *y-coordinate*. For point A in Figure 1.4, the x-coordinate is 5, and the y-coordinate is -3.

Example 1 Using a Cartesian coordinate system, locate and plot the point having coordinates (3, –5).

Solution The point of interest is reached by first moving 3 units along the   x-axis in the positive direction from the origin and then moving 5 units in the negative y direction. The point is plotted as Q in Figure 1.5.

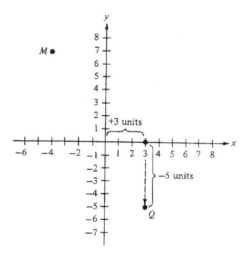

FIGURE 1.5

Example 2 Determine the coordinates of the point M shown in Figure 1.5.

Solution To reach M from the origin, we must move 4 units in the negative x direction (which implies an x-coordinate of -4) and then 7 units in the positive y direction (which implies a y-coordinate of $+7$). The coordinates are $(-4, 7)$. Recall that the x-coordinate is always given before the y-coordinate.

A Cartesian coordinate system divides the plane into four sections. Each section is called a *quadrant,* labeled I, II, III, or IV, as illustrated in Figure 1.6. A point in the first quadrant has both a positive x- and a positive y-coordinate. A point in the second quadrant has a negative x-coordinate and a positive y-coordinate, while a point in the third quadrant has a negative x-coordinate and a negative y-coordinate. A point in the fourth quadrant has a positive x-coordinate but a negative y-coordinate.

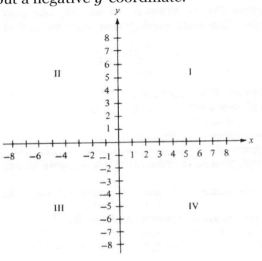

FIGURE 1.6

In practice two modifications are often made in the Cartesian coordinate system as we have defined it. First, the letters used to label the axes need not be x and y but can be any other two letters that are convenient. In a problem dealing with the price and demand of a certain product, it may be more revealing to label the axes P for price and D for demand. Regardless of the letters used, the first component of a point always refers to movement along the horizontal axis (i.e. the conventional x-axis), while the second component refers to movement in a direction parallel to the vertical axis (i.e, the conventional y-axis).

The second modification is that the same scale need not be used on both coordinate scales. The scale on the horizontal axis can, and frequently does, differ from the scale used on the vertical axis. Figure 1.7 illustrates this, where each axis uses a different scale. The coordinates of point B on this Figure are $(2, 25)$. *The only restriction in this modification, is that each scale, individually, once chosen, must be marked off consistently in equal units.*

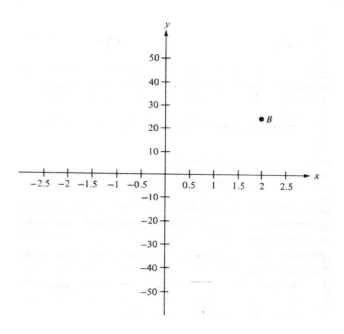

FIGURE 1.7

Section 1.5 Exercises

1. Consider the points labeled *A* through *K* in Figure 1.8
   a. Determine the coordinates of each point.
   b. Which points are located in quadrant I?

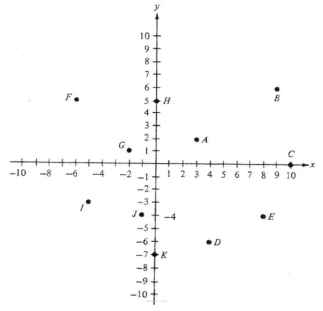

FIGURE 1.8

2. Redo Exercise 1 for the points A through H in Figure 1.9.

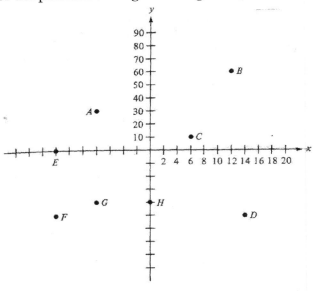

FIGURE 1.9

3. Consider the points shown in Figure 1.10.
   a. Draw a coordinate system that places A in quadrant I, B in quadrant II, and C in quadrant IV.
   b. Draw a coordinate system that places $A, B,$ and C in quadrant I and D in quadrant IV.
   c. Draw a coordinate system that places all points in quadrant III.

     •B •A

         •C

  •D

FIGURE 1.10

4. Plot each of the following points on the same coordinate system:
   a. (3, -1)   b. (2, 5)   c. (-5, 2)   d. (-6, -6).

5. Plot each of the following points on the same coordinate system:
   a. (3, -10)   b. (2, 50)   c. (-5, 20)   d. (-6, -60).

6. Plot each of the following points on the same coordinate system:
   a. (250, 45)   b. (500, -10)   c. (400, 20)   d. (-6, -60).

7. a. Determine the value of the y-coordinate of every point on the x-axis.

32

b. Determine the value of the *x*-coordinate of every point on *the y*-axis.

8. Construct a Cartesian coordinate system with each axis scaled the same. Draw a straight–line segment between the origin and the point having coordinates (10, 10). Determine the angle this line makes with the positive *x*-axis.

9. Construct a Cartesian coordinate system and draw a line parallel to the *x*-axis. What do all points on this line have in common?

1.6 Graphical Solutions to Equations in Two Unknowns

Section 1.2 provided methods for solving one equation in one unknown. In this section, we show how to solve a single equation that has two unknowns. As you might expect, finding all of the solutions becomes more complicated. This is because two values, one for each unknown, must be determined, so that when they are used together, simultaneously, they solve the given equation.

For example, consider the problem of finding numerical values for x and y that satisfy the equation $y = 2x^2 + 1$. As another example, find values for x and y that satisfy the equation $y = 3x - 2$. The difficulty is that such equations generally have not one, but infinitely many solutions.

Some of the solutions can be found by arbitrarily selecting values for one of the unknowns and substituting these values into the given equation. The result is one equation in one unknown, which often can be solved for the remaining unknown.

As an example, consider the equation $y = 3x - 2$. Arbitrarily setting $x = 1$ and substituting it into the equation, we find $y = 3(1) - 2$ or $y = 1$. Therefore $x = 1$ and $y = 1$ is one solution because these values together satisfy the given equation. To obtain another solution, a different value for x can arbitrarily be selected, and then the resulting equation solved for y. For example, setting $x = 2$ and substituting it into the given equation, yields $y = 3(2) - 2$ or $y = 4$. Therefore, $x = 2$ and $y = 4$ is a second solution. Continuing in this manner, we next try $x = 0$ and find $y = -2$, and so on. Table 1.1 lists a number of these solutions, where each y value is listed immediately to the right of its corresponding x value.

TABLE 1.1 Solutions to the Equation $y = 3x - 2$

x	y
1	1
2	4
0	-2
-1	-5
3	7

The main objection to this procedure is that it provides only *some* of the solutions, not all of them. Yet, it is not likely that we can ever do better algebraically, because one equation having two unknowns generally has infinitely many solutions. If we are willing to use graphical methods, however, the prospects are brighter.

Every solution of one equation in two unknowns is a pair of numbers, such as $x = 2$ and $y = 4$, or $x = 3$ and $y = 7$ listed in Table 1.1 for the equation $y = 3x - 2$. Each solution pair then can be plotted as a single point on a Cartesian coordinate system. For Example, Figure 1.11 shows the resulting plot of the five solution pairs listed in Table 1.1.

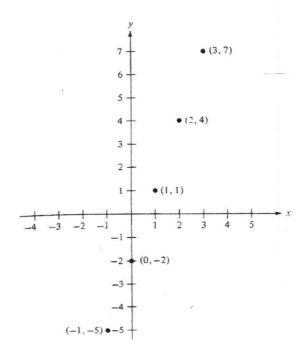

FIGURE 1.11

Graphically, the set of *all* solutions to a single equation in two unknowns becomes a curve. Typically, the exact shape of the curve often can be determined by looking at a plot of some of the solution points, and then making an educated guess. In particular, the points shown in Figure 1.11 appear to lie on a straight line; it seems likely therefore that the geometric solution of $y = 3x - 2$ is the dashed line drawn in Figure 1.12 We have drawn the line dashed to indicate that, at this stage, we cannot be certain that every point on the straight line has coordinates that are solutions to the given equation. For example, the curve illustrated in Figure 1.13 also contains the points listed in Table 1.1.

One way to be certain that Figure 1.12 is correct is to plot more points than the five listed in Table 1.1. (By using methods presented in the next chapter, it can easily be verified that Figure 1.12 is, in fact, the correct graph of the equation $y = 3x - 2$ without plotting additional points.) For now, however, we must plot as many points as necessary to gain a reasonable idea of the shape of the curve before drawing it.

Let us summarize our steps. Given an equation with two unknowns, in this case the equation $y = 3x - 2$, we want to find the set of all solutions. As a first step, some solutions are found by arbitrarily picking values for one of the unknowns, substituting these values into the given equation, and solving the resulting equation for the corresponding values of the other unknown.

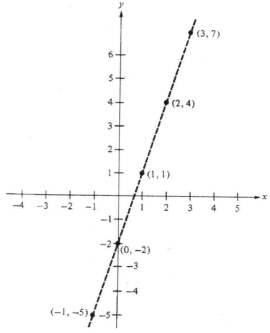

FIGURE 1.12

35

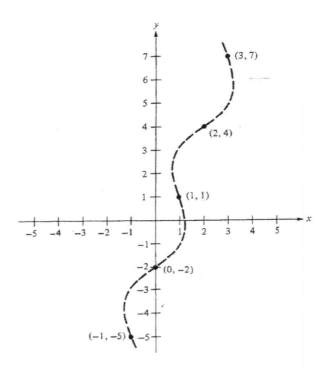

FIGURE 1.13

The second step was to plot every solution that was found, and the last step was to determine the curve that contained the plotted points. At this stage a dashed line is constructed *that appears* to fit the plotted points best. This procedure is called *graphing*, and the final curve is a *graph of the equation* under consideration. Thus, the line plotted in Figure 1.12 is the graph of the equation $y = 3x - 2$.

Example 1 Find the graph of the equation $y = 2x^2 + 1$.

Solution We begin by finding a few solutions to the equation. Table 1.2. presents a number of these. In each case the value of x listed in the first column was arbitrarily selected and the corresponding value of y determined by substituting the chosen x value directly into the equation.

TABLE 1.2 Solutions to the Equation $y = 2x^2 + 1$

x	y
0	1
1	3

-1	3
2	9
-2	9
3	19
-3	19

Having located a number of solutions, these solutions are now plotted on the Cartesian coordinate system shown in Figure 1.14. Finally, we determine the curve that contains these points. This curve appears to be the graph shown in Figure 1.15, which is the graph of $y = 2x^2 + 1$.

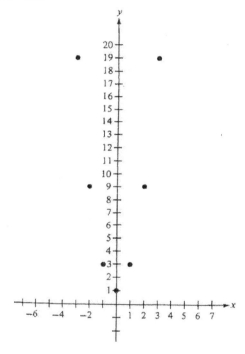

FIGURE 1.14

A few observations are now in order. First, the graph of an equation is only a geometric representation of the solutions of one equation in two unknowns. The actual solutions are the coordinates of each and every point on the graph. Thus, Figure 1.12 is the geometric representation of the solutions to $y = 3x - 2$. The solutions themselves are the coordinates of the points on this curve. In particular, the point $(\frac{1}{2}, -\frac{1}{2})$ is on the curve, so that $x = \frac{1}{2}$ and $y = -\frac{1}{2}$ is a solution to the equation $y = 3x - 2$. This can, of course, be verified by direct substitution. Additionally, we see that $(-4, -14)$ is a point on the curve, so $x = -4$ and $y = -14$ is yet another solution.

Secondly, the curves plotted in both previous examples were determined by looking at only a few points. This involves the assumption that the curve behaves nicely between the plotted points. Formal justification of this assumption, however, requires the material considered in the next chapter. For now, we will continue to assume that a curve can be drawn when a sufficient number of points has been plotted. Just how many points is sufficient depends on the curve and the foresight of the plotter. One can never plot too many points, and a good rule of thumb is, *"too many is always better than too few."*

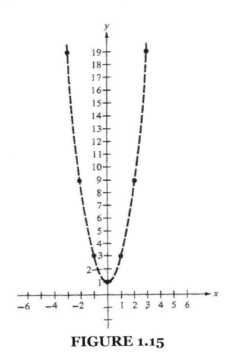

FIGURE 1.15

Finally, note that in both examples arbitrary values for x were first selected and then the equations were used to solve for the corresponding values of y. The reverse procedure is equally correct; that is, values for y could have been selected, and then the equations solved for the corresponding values of x. For example, solving $y = 3x - 2$, we could have first set $y = 2$, substituted it into the equation, and obtained $2 = 3x - 2$. It follows that $x = 4/3$ and $y = 2$ is indeed a solution.

In a similar manner, for the equation $y = 2x^2 + 1$, values for y can also be selected first, and then the equation solved for corresponding values of x. For example, setting $y = 2$, we would have to solve the equation $2 = 2x^2 + 1$ for x.

You always get the choice of which unknown is to be assigned a value initially. The selection is dictated by personal preference and the ease with which the second unknown can be determined. For example, given the equation $y^5 - 2y^2 = x + 1$, it is easier to pick values of y and then solve for x, but quite difficult to pick values of x and then solve for y.

Example 2 Graph the equation $y = x^3 - x^2 + 1$.

Solution Arbitrarily selecting values for x and solving for y, we generate Table 1.3. Plotting these points, we obtain Figure 1.16.

TABLE 1.3 Solutions to the Equation $y = x^3 - x^2 + 1$

x	y
0	1
0.5	0.875
1	1
2	5
-1	-1
-2	-11

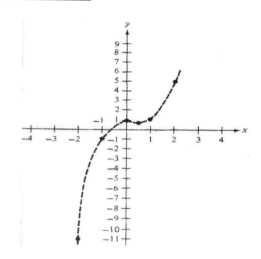

FIGURE 1.16

Example 3 Graph the equation $x^2 + y^2 = 25$.

Solution Arbitrarily selecting values for y and solving for x, we generate Table 1.4. Plotting these points, we obtain Figure 1.17.

TABLE 1.4 Solutions to the Equation $x^2 + y^2 = 25$

x	y
0	±5
5	0
-5	0
3	±4
-3	±4
4	±3
-4	±3

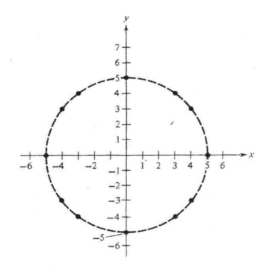

FIGURE 1.17

Section 1.6 Exercises

Plot the graphs of the equations in Exercises 1 through 10.

1. $2x - 3y = 5$

2. $y = x - 2$

3. $6x - 2y = 3$

4. $x^2 - y = 0$

5. $y = 2x^2$

6. $3y - 4x = 7$

7. $y = x^3 - 2x^2 + x$

8. $y = 3x - 4$

9. $x^2 + y^2 = 4$

10. $y = \sqrt{x}$

11. Graph $y = x$ and $y = -x$ on the same axes. How do these curves differ?

12. Graph the equation $y = 2x + 5$. Select x values of 0, 1, 3, 5, 7, -1, -3, -5, and -7. Determine from the graph the values of y when x is 2 and when x is -8.

13. Determine if the points having coordinates $(-2, 6)$, $(0, 2)$, and $(1, 9)$ lie on the graph of the equation $y = 3x^2 + 4x + 2$.

14. Graph the two equations $y = 6x + 3$ and $y = 5x - 2$ on the same coordinate system. Determine the point of intersection of these curves from the resulting graph.

15. Redo Exercise 14 for the equations $y = 5x^2 - 2$ and $y = x + 3$.

16. Graphically show that the two equations $y = x^2 + 1$ and $y = x^2$ have no points in common.

1.7 Sigma Notation

In various parts of this text, we will need the sum of large numbers of terms. Sometimes we will need the actual total, and then we will have to sum the numbers physically. Other times, however, we will only need to indicate the appropriate sum. An example is the statement, "*Yearly expenditures are the sum of weekly expenditures.*" Here we are not explicitly calculating the expenditure over the year but simply indicating that it is the sum of 52 numbers. In cases like this, there is a useful mathematical notation for indicating the appropriate sum.

Consider the case of a teacher who has a list of seven grades and wants their sum. If we denote the first grade as G_1, the second grade as G_2, and so on through the seventh grade, which we denote as G_7, the final sum can be given as

$$\text{Sum} = G_1 + G_2 + G_3 + G_4 + G_5 + G_6 + G_7 \qquad \text{(Eq. 1.8)}$$

Of course, if we had 52 items to add as opposed to only 7, writing an expression similar to Equation 1.8 would be tedious indeed. A more convenient way to represent the right side of Equation 1.8 symbolically as

$$\sum_{i=1}^{7} G_i$$

The capital Greek letter sigma (Σ) denotes a sum. The term(s) after the sigma, in this case the letter G, tells us what values are to be added, in this case we are adding G terms.

     The quantity $i = 1$ at the bottom of the sigma indicates where the sum is to start from; in this case the sum starts with G_1, that is, G_i, with i replaced with the starting value of 1. The number at the top of the sigma, indicates where the sum is to stop, which in this case is G_8. Intermediate values in the sum are obtained by replacing the subscript i on individual G terms with consecutive integers between the starting and ending numbers at the bottom and top of the sigma respectively.

     For example, the notation

$$\sum_{i=1}^{3} S_i$$

indicates a sum of S terms. The sum starts with S_3, because the starting i value is given as 3 at the bottom of the sigma sign, and ends at S_8, because the ending value of i is given as 8 above the sigma sign. Thus, the notation

$$\sum_{i=3}^{8} S_i$$

is shorthand for

$$S_3 + S_4 + S_5 + S_6 + S_7 + S_8 \ .$$

Additional examples are

$$\sum_{i=1}^{5} T_i = T_1 + T_2 + T_3 + T_4 + T_5$$

$$\sum_{i=2}^{4} x_i = x_2 + x_3 + x_4$$

and

$$\sum_{i=9}^{9} y_i = y_9$$

In general,

$$\sum_{i=m}^{n} q_i = q_m + q_{m+1} + q_{m+2} + \cdots + q_n, \quad m \le n \qquad \text{(Eq. 1.9)}$$

is the *sigma notation* for the sum of the quantities q_i ranging from q_m through q_n successively. Obviously, the left side of Equation 1.9 is more compact than the expanded form given on the right side, and is the reason for using sigma notation. When actual values are given for the terms being summed, a final value for the sum can be obtained.

Example 1 Give the expanded form of

$$\sum_{i=4}^{8} (x_i - i)$$

Solution The sigma notation indicated the sum of terms having the form $(x_i - i)$ beginning with $i = 4$ and continuing successively through $i = 8$. Therefore,

$$\sum_{i=4}^{8} (x_i - i) = (x_4 - 4) + (x_5 - 5) + (x_6 - 6) + (x_7 - 7) + (x_8 - 8)$$

Example 2 Give the expanded form of

$$\sum_{i=1}^{6} \left(\frac{i}{i+1} \right)$$

Solution

$$\sum_{i=1}^{6} \left[\frac{i}{(i+1)} \right] = \left(\frac{1}{1+1} \right) + \left(\frac{2}{2+1} \right) + \left(\frac{3}{3+1} \right) + \left(\frac{4}{4+1} \right) + \left(\frac{5}{5+1} \right) + \left(\frac{6}{6+1} \right).$$

Example 3 Determine the sigma notation for the sum

$$\left(\frac{3^2}{2} + 1\right) + \left(\frac{4^2}{2} + 1\right) + \left(\frac{5^2}{2} + 1\right) + \left(\frac{6^2}{2} + 1\right) + \cdots + \left(\frac{100^2}{2} + 1\right)$$

Solution Each term in the sum is of the form $\left(\frac{i^2}{2} + 1\right)$ where i is an integer starting at 3 and ending at 100, with all terms in between.. The sum can be given as

$$\sum_{i=3}^{100} \left(\frac{i^2}{2} + 1\right)$$

Example 4 Weekly expenditures for a given $year$ are denoted as W_1 through W_{52} successively. Develop a formula for the $yearly$ expenditure.

Solution Denote the $yearly$ expenditure as Y. Because yearly expenditure is the sum of the individual weekly expenditures,

$$Y = \sum_{i=1}^{52} W_i$$

All the examples so far have used the subscript i. Any other letter would do equally well. Thus

$$\sum_{j=2}^{4} x_j = x_2 + x_3 + x_4$$

and

$$\sum_{k=1}^{10} k^2 = 1^2 + 2^2 + 3^2 + 4^2 + 5^2 + 6^2 + 7^2 + 8^2 + 9^2 + 10^2$$

Sometimes we are given data and we would like to indicate that some portion of these data is to be summed. For example, if test scores for a particular student are 60, 70, 75, 80, 82, 83, 87, 90, and we only want to sum the 2nd through 7th scores for some reason, this is easily indicated by the notation $\sum_{i=2}^{7} G_i$. Of course this notation is good only if we understand that G_1 signifies the first score, G_2 the second score, and G_7 the next to last score. In general, we always assume that data are ordered as they appear.

Finally, when we write a 'sigma without any numbers below or above it, we mean that the sum is to include all possible terms. It should be clear from the context which terms are being considered. For example, certain data may include pairs of numbers, and we may wish to multiply the members of each pair and then sum over all the pairs. If the number of data points is not known in advance, we can still indicate the desired sum using the notation $\Sigma x_i y_i$. For the data listed in Table 1.6, this sum is (because there are only four pairs of data points)

$$\sum x_i y_i = x_1 y_1 + x_2 y_2 + x_3 y_3 + x_4 y_4$$
$$= (5)(7) + (10)(12) + (14)(8) + (20)(15) = 567$$

TABLE 1.6

x	y
5	7
10	12
14	8
20	15

Section 1.7 Exercises

1. Write the expanded form of the following expressions:

a. $\displaystyle\sum_{i=1}^{3} (x_i)^2$

b. $\displaystyle\sum_{i=3}^{11} 2x_i$

c. $\displaystyle\sum_{i=1}^{6} (x_i + y_i)$

d. $\displaystyle\sum_{j=99}^{105} (3M_j + 4)$.

2. Write the expanded form of the following expressions:

a. $\displaystyle\sum_{k=1}^{10} k$

b. $\displaystyle\sum_{m=2}^{6} \left(\frac{m+2}{m+3}\right)$

c. $\displaystyle\sum_{j=0}^{7} (j+1)$

d. $\displaystyle\sum_{i=1}^{15} 1$

e. $\displaystyle\sum_{i=0}^{6} (-1)^i$

f. $\displaystyle\sum_{p=7}^{14} (p-10)^2$.

3. Write the following expressions in sigma notation.

a. $3(2)^2 + 3(3)^2 + 3(4)^2 + 3(5)^2 + \dots + 3(29)^2$

b. $2(3)^2 + 3(3)^2 + 4(3)^2 + 5(3)^2 + \dots + 29(3)^2$

c. $2(3)^2 + 2(3)^3 + 2(3)^4 + 2(3)^5 + \dots + 2(3)^{29}$

d. $3(2)^2 - 3(3)^2 + 3(4)^2 - 3(5)^2 + \dots + 3(28)^2 - 3(29)^2$

4. Calculate the following sums for the data given in Table 1.7.

a. $\displaystyle\sum_{i=1}^{5} x_i$

b. $\displaystyle\sum_{j=1}^{5} y_j$

c. $\displaystyle\sum_{i=1}^{3} x_i$

d. $\displaystyle\sum_{k=1}^{5} (x_k + y_k)$

e. $\displaystyle\sum_{k=1}^{5} (x_k) + \sum_{k=1}^{5} (y_k)$

f. $\displaystyle\sum_{m=2}^{4} (x_m\, y_m)$.

g. What can you conclude about the sums found in parts d and e?

TABLE 1.7

i	x	y
1	0	6
2	1	7
3	2	8
4	-1	3
5	-4	-2

5. Calculate the following sums for the data given in Table 1.8.

a. $\sum x_i$

b. $\sum y_i$

c. $\sum (x_i)^2$

d. $\sum (x_i - 2)$

e. $\sum x_i y_i$

f. $\left(\sum x_i\right)\left(\sum y_i\right)$

g. What can you conclude about the sums found in parts e. and f.?

TABLE 1.8

i	x	y
1	0	3
2	8	2
3	-2	6
4	5	9
5	-3	10
6	7	1

6. Write each of the following expressions in expanded form and verify that they are equal.

a. $\sum\limits_{i=1}^{6}\left(\dfrac{1}{i}\right)$

b. $\sum\limits_{i=2}^{7}\left(\dfrac{1}{i-1}\right)$

c. $\sum\limits_{i=0}^{5}\left(\dfrac{1}{i+1}\right)$

7. Prove the following identities by converting each side to expanded form:

a. $c\left(\sum\limits_{i=1}^{n} x_i\right) = \sum\limits_{i=1}^{n} (cx_i)$

b. $\sum\limits_{i=1}^{n} (x_k + y_i) = \sum\limits_{i=1}^{n} (x_i) + \sum\limits_{i=1}^{n} (y_i)$

c. $\displaystyle\sum_{i=1}^{m} x_i + \sum_{i=m+1}^{n} x_i = \sum_{i=1}^{n} x_i$

8. Determine if the following statement is valid or not.

$$\sum_{i=1}^{n}(x_i y_i) = \left(\sum_{i=1}^{n} x_i\right)\left(\sum_{i=1}^{n} y_i\right)$$

9. Derive a formula using sigma notation for the average of a set of grades $G_1, G_2, G_3, \ldots, G_n$

1.8 Numerical Considerations

Expressing numbers in decimal form is necessary in most commercial transactions. One reason involves money. All financial figures are given in decimal form; the numbers to the left of the decimal point represent dollars, and the numbers to the right of the decimal point represent cents. Quoting the cost of an item as $1.20 is clearer than quoting six fifths of a dollar. A second reason for using decimals is mathematical. It is easier to add 0.2 and 1.5 than it is to 1/5 and 1½. In this section we present two considerations when dealing with numerical values; rounding when dealing with dollar and cents commercial transactions and scientific notation that you will sometimes encounter when using a calculator.

Rounding

Most signed numbers in decimal form are nonending. For example, $1/3 =$ 0.3333333..., $\sqrt{2} = 1.4142135...$, and $\pi = 3.1415926...$. Non-ending decimals are inconvenient arithmetically and useless financially. No one pays $0.3333333... for goods or charges $141.42135... for services. Instead one approximates these quantities by finite decimals. One–third of a dollar becomes 33¢, and the square root of $2.00 becomes $1.41. Converting non-ending decimals to finitely long decimals is called *roundoff* or *rounding*.

    The most common form of roundoff is referred to as *arithmetic rounding* or just *rounding* for short. Here one first decides how many digits are to be retained and then changes all digits to the right of those being kept to zero. Zero digits to the right of a decimal point that are not themselves followed by a nonzero number are simply disregarded. Before changing any digits to zero, however, one checks the first digit that will be discarded. If it is greater than or equal to 5, the previous digit (which is the last one being kept) is increased by 1. If the first digit being discarded is less than 5, no change is made in the previous digit.

As an example, consider the number $\pi = 3.1415926$ .... To round this number to three decimal places, first look at the digit four places to the right of the decimal point. It is 5, so we increase the previous digit by 1 and write π = 3.142 rounded to three decimal places. To round the same number to two decimal places first look at the digit three places to the right of the decimal point. It is 1, which is less than 5. Thus, π = 3.14 rounded to two decimal places.

Rounding is equally applicable to finite decimals. Anytime one uses the above procedure to reduce the number of digits in a number, one is rounding. For example, 81.314 = 81.31 rounded to two decimal places, 8595.72 = 8596 rounded to units, and 0.0051624 = 0.0052 rounded to four decimal places.

A second form of rounding is called *rounding up*. Here the last digit being kept in a number is automatically increased by 1 if *anyone* of the discarded digits is not 0. For example, 8.1403 = 8.15 rounded up to two decimal places (note that one of the discarded digits is a 3; that is, not all of the discarded digits are zero), 1.38112 = 1.382 rounded up to three decimal places, and 1.900 = 1.9 rounded to one decimal place. In the last example, we did not increase the 9, because all the discarded digits were 0.

Rounding up is used by banks for mortgage payments and merchants for determining prices. If a mortgage payment is $241.5723 exactly, a bank will charge $241.58. If the retail price of a product is $1.2905, a merchant will typically charge $1.30. Rounding up is employed when the user does not wish to absorb the losses incurred by regular arithmetic rounding.

Still a third form of rounding is *rounding down*, which is more commonly known as *truncation*. Here the lastdigit being kept is never changed, regardless of the magnitude of the numbers being discarded. Thus, 89.318 = 89.31 truncated to two decimals, and 13.75 = 13 truncated to units.

Truncation is often used in reporting the number of finished goods produced. At the end of a day, a company may have produced 82⅝ cars, but reports a production of only 82 completed cars.

Exponential Notation

Calculators that have the ability to display more decimal values than can be accommodated on their displays, typically display both very small and very large numbers using exponential notation. In this notation the letter E stands for "exponent." and the number following the E indicates the number of places the decimal point should be moved to obtain the standard decimal value. The decimal point is moved to the right if the number after E is positive, or it's moved to the left if the number after the E is negative

For example, the E10 in a display such as 1.625 E10 means move the decimal place ten places to the right, so the number becomes 16250000000. The E-8 in a display such as 7.31 E-8 means move the decimal point eight places to the left, so the number becomes .0000000731. Table 1.9 provides a number of additional examples using exponential notation.

TABLE 1.9

Exponential Notation	Decimal Notation
2.689 E5	268900.
2.689 E-5	.00002689
4.896723 E10	48967230000.
4.896723 E-10	.0000000004896723

Section 1.8 Exercises

In Exercises 1 through 5 use a calculator to find the equivalent decimal values for the given fraction, and then round (that is, use arithmetic rounding) the numbers to two decimal places.

1. 2/3.   2. 4/11   3. 4/17   4. 12/7   5. 89/31

6. Repeat Exercises 1 through 5, but round the numbers to three decimal places.

7. Round up the numbers given in Exercises 1 through 5 to three decimals.

8. Truncate the numbers given in Exercises 1 through 5 to two decimal places.

In Exercise 9 through 14 convert the numbers written in exponential notation to standard decimal numbers:

9. 3.35642 E3   10. 5.62384 E9   11. 3.356 E-3
12. 8.63 E-7   13. 3.3 E12   14. 4.3 E-12

Chapter

2

Equations and Graphs

Equations are a convenient and concise way of representing relationships between quantities, such as sales and advertising, profit and time, cost and number of units manufactured, and so on. As such, they are used to "model" or represent real-world situations.

The idea and usefulness of a model are not new; we use models every day without recognizing them as such. A Global Positioning System (GPS), for example, provides a visual model of streets and directions. It doesn't give weather, traffic conditions, or road hazards, but it is still useful in making decisions about a trip. Molecular diagrams in chemistry, organization charts in businesses, and road signs indicating a steep curve or a steep incline are other examples of useful models representing actual conditions in a simplified, compact way

In a similar manner, mathematical equations are used as models in the world of business. Although these equations, like a GPS, may not reveal all the relationships between the quantities under investigation, they often contain enough information for one to make meaningful observations and practical decisions.

2.1 Linear Equations

One of the simplest and yet most important equations in both business and mathematics is the linear equation, whose graph is a straight line. Formally, a linear equation is defined as follows.

Definition 2.1 A *linear equation* in two variables x and y is an equation of the form

$$Ax + By = C \qquad\qquad \text{(Eq. 2.1)}$$

where A, B, and C are known real umbers with A and B not both zero.

Definitions are very precise mathematical statements. Unfortunately this precision often makes a definition seem very complicated, when, in fact, it is not. Usually, a few moments of thought is all that is needed to convert the given statement to an understandable concept. As an example, let us return to the definition of a linear equation.

    Definition 2.1 simply states that any equation having the form of (that is, looks like) the equation $Ax + By = C$, where the letters A, B, and C are replaced by numbers (for example, $3x + 7y = 10$), is called a *linear* equation. Another important point is that, since by convention, an exponent of 1 is understood but not written, a necessary feature of a linear equation is that the exponent of both the x and y terms must only be 1. The definition does not give any clues as to what a linear equation means physically-that will come later. It does say that, any equation that can be written in a form that looks like Equation 2.1, it is a linear equation.

    Examples of linear equations are

$$6x + 2y = 15 \qquad\qquad \text{(Eq. 2.2)}$$

$$-x + 7y = 0 \qquad\qquad \text{(Eq. 2.3)}$$

$$0.5x - 0.75y = 1.7 \qquad\qquad \text{(Eq. 2.4)}$$

$$y = 0 \qquad\qquad \text{(Eq. 2.5)}$$

Equation 2.2 has the required form with $A = 6$, $B = 2$, and $C = 15$, while in Equation 2.3, $A = -1$, $B = 7$, and $C = 0$. For Equation 2.4 $A = 0.5$, $B = 0.75$, and $C = 1.7$. Finally, Equation 2.5 also has the form of Equation 2.1 with $A = 0$, $B = 1$, and $C = 0$.

Example 1 Determine whether or not $x^2 + y^2 = 4$ is a linear equation.

Solution For an equation to be linear it must either have the form, or be able to be put into the form of Equation 2.1. This equation cannot be put into that form, because both quantities x and y are squared, whereas Equation 2.1 requires both x and y to appear *by themselves, with an implicit exponent of one, and multiplied only by known numbers.*

Example 2 Determine whether or not $\frac{1}{x} + 2 = 0$ is a linear equation.

Solution No, it is not. Here x appears as $\frac{1}{x}$ and not as x multiplied by a known number as required in Equation 2.1.

Equation 2.1 is indeed very precise. An equation is called a linear equation *if and only if* it has the form of a constant times one quantity raised to the 1st power plus a constant times another quantity raised to the 1st power, the sum of both terms equal to a constant. No x^2 terms, no $\sqrt{y}$ terms, and no xy terms are allowed.

It should also be stressed that the letters x and y in Equation 2.1 are *not* fixed; any two letters can be used. Thus $6C + 2N = 15$ is a linear equation in the variables C and N (compare to Equation 2.2), and $0.5p - 0.75q = 1.7$ is linear equation in the 'quantities p and q [compare to Equation 2.3).

Example 3 Determine whether or not $C = 115 + 200N$ is a linear equation.

Solution If we first rewrite this equation as $C - 200N = 115$, we see that it is in the form of Equation 2.1, with $A = 1$, $B = -200$, and $C = 115$. Thus, it is a linear equation.

Example 4 A new car dealer determines that the daily cost of operating a 'showroom can be separated into a fixed cost of $115 that covers insurance, rent, lighting, and so on, and a variable salary cost. Each salesperson is paid $200 per day, but the total number of salespeople who work changes from day to day. Show that the equation relating cost to the number of salespeople at work on .any given day is a linear equation.

Solution The quantities we are trying to relate in this problem are the daily cost and the number of salespeople who work on any given day. Let C denote daily cost and N represent the number of salespeople working on any given day. Then $C = 115 + 200N$ which, from Example 3, is a linear equation.

Note in Example 4 that if we knew how many salespeople were working on a given day, we could easily determine the total cost of operating the showroom.

'We would simply substitute the number of salespeople into the equation for N, obtaining one equation in the unknown quantity C. Using the techniques of solving one equation in one unknown (see Section 1.2), we could then solve for the value of C. Similarly, knowing the cost of operating the showroom on a particular day (the value of C), we could then use the equation to find the number of employees who worked that day. We illustrate this with another example.

Example 5 The number of cans of cat food sold weekly in a particular store is related to the price charged. Let D denote the number of cans sold and P the price per can (in cents) and assume the equation relating these quantities is

$$D = 687 - 7P \tag{Eq. 2.6}$$

Using Equation 2.6, determine:

a. whether or not the equation relating D and P is a linear equation,
b. the number of cans sold when the price is 90¢ per can, and
c. the price on the day that 120 cans are sold.

Solution

a. Rewriting Equation 2.6 as $D + 7P = 687$, we see that it is a linear equation because it has the form of Equation 2.1 with $A = 1$, $B = 7$, and $C = 687$.

b. For a price of 90¢, we substitute $P = 90$ into Equation 2.6 and compute $D = 687 - 7(90) = 687 - 630 = 57$ cans sold.

c. To find the price, P, corresponding to a sale of 120 cans, we substitute 120 for D in Equation 2.6, and solve or P. Thus, we have

$$120 = 687 - 7P.$$

Subtracting 687 from both sides of the equation yields,
$$-567 = -7P$$

Dividing both sides of this equation by -7 yields $P = 81$¢.

Section 2.1 Exercises

1. Determine which of the following equations are linear:
   a. $2x = y$　　　　　b. $2x = 1/y$
   c. $xy = 4$　　　　　d. $x = 4$
   e. $2x - 3y = 0$　　　f. $y = 4x$
   g. $y = 4x^2$　　　　h. $x - 2 = 3y$
   i. $1/x + 1/y = 2$　　j. $x = y$

2. A large television manufacturer has determined that the number of television sets sold, denoted by N, is related directly to the amount of money spent on advertising. In particular, every million dollars in advertising expenditures results in an additional 50,000 television sets being sold, although 10,000 sets would be sold with no advertising. Let E denote the amount of money (in millions of dollars) committed to advertising. Determine the equation relating N to E and show that it is a linear equation.

3. After carefully studying used car price lists, Mr. Henry has determined that his particular model car, purchased yesterday for $6000, will depreciate $1,500 per year. Let V denote the value of Mr. Henry's car at any given time and let t denote time measured in years. Determine the equation relating t to V and show that it is a linear equation.

4. It has been determined by the Chubby Cat Food Corporation that the amount of cat food, denoted by A, sold on any given day in Newark, New Jersey, is given by the equation $A = 200 - p$, where p represents the price of each can in cents. Determine the number of cans of cat food the company can expect to sell if it prices each can at 50¢.

2.2 Graphing Linear Equations

Linear equations are singled out as a special class of equations because they have several useful properties. One of these properties is that the graphs of all linear equations are straight lines (we will examine the remaining properties in Section 2.3. To illustrate this straight line property, a number of linear equations will first be graphed by plotting multiple points, as was done in Section 1.6.

Example 1 Graph the equation $6x + 2y = 15$, which is Equation 2.2.

Solution We initially plot some points satisfying the equation by arbitrarily selecting values of either x or y and finding the corresponding values of the other variable in the equation. Here we will select x-values and solve for the corresponding y-values. When $x = 0$, Equation 2.2 becomes $6(0) + 2y = 15$, resulting in $y = 7.5$. When $x = 1$, Equation 2.2 becomes $6(1) + 2y = 15$ and, solving for y, we obtain $2y = 15 - 6$, *or* $2y = 9$, resulting in $y = 4.5$. Continuing in this manner, we generate Table 2.1 from which we obtain Figure 2.1.

TABLE 2.1 Solutions to the Equation $6x + 2y = 15$

x	y
0	7.5
1	4.5
2	1.5
3	-1.5
-1	10.5

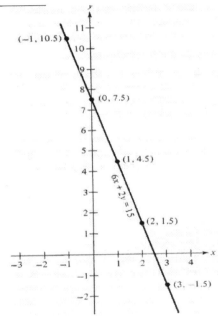

FIGURE 2.1

Example 2 Graph the equation $-x + 7y = 0$, which is Eq. 2.3.

Solution Again we first plot points on the curve by selecting arbitrary values for either x or y and then finding their corresponding y or x values. Arbitrarily selecting x-values, we compute as follows. When $x = 0$, the equation becomes -$(0) + 7y = 0$, hence $y = 0$. When $x = 1$, the equation becomes $-(1) + 7y = 0$ from which we obtain $y = 1/7 = 0.142857$, which is 0.15 rounded to two decimal places. Continuing, we generate Table 2.2 and Figure 2.2

TABLE 2.2 Solutions to the Equation -$x + 7y = 0$

x	y
0	0
1	0.15
2	0.29
3	0.43
7	1

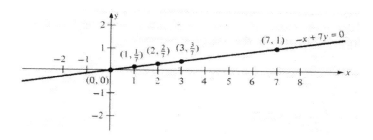

FIGURE 2.2

In Examples 1 and 2 we arbitrarily selected x-values and then solved for the corresponding y-values. We would have obtained the same graphs had we first picked y-values and then solved for the corresponding x-values.

Example 3 Redo Example 1 by selecting y-values and solving for the corresponding x-values.

Solution With $y = 0$, the equation becomes $6x + 2(0) = 15$ from which we obtain $6x = 15$, and $x = 2.5$. When $y = 3$, the equation becomes $6x + 2(3) = 15$, hence $6x + 6 = 15$, $6x = 9$, and $x = 1.5$. Continuing in this manner, we generate Table 2.3, all of whose points lie on the graph in Figure 2.1.

TABLE 2.3 Solutions to the Equation $6x + 2y = 15$

x	y
2.5	0
1.5	3
0.5	6
2.14	1.08
2.17	1

For any linear equation in two quantities, say x and y, solutions can always be found by selecting different values for one of the quantities and then using the equation to determine the corresponding values of the other quantity.[**] By choosing different values of one quantity we are obviously *varying* or changing the values of that quantity. Accordingly, the quantities themselves, say x and y, are referred to as *variables* rather than quantities. Because the term "variable" is standard mathematical terminology, we will use it interchangeably with the term unknown in the remainder of this text. Using this new terminology, Equation 2.1 can be said to be a linear equation in the variables x and y.

Graphing a linear equation is significantly simplified because, we know that the graph is straight line that is uniquely determined by two distinct points. Thus, rather than finding many points on the graph, as we did in the previous three examples, we need find only *two* points and then draw a straight line through them.

Example 4 Graph the equation $0.5x - 0.75y = 1.7$, which is Equation 2.4.

Solution We first note that Equation 2.4 is a linear equation in the variables x and y; hence its graph is a straight line, As such, it can be easily graphed by finding two points satisfying the equation and then drawing a straight line through these two points. Arbitrarily choosing two values of x, say $x = 0$ and $x = 1$, we find their associated y-values. When $x = 0$, the equation becomes

$$0.5(0) - 0.75y = 1.7$$
$$- 0.75y = 1.7$$

[**] The equation need not be linear for this approach to work; however, for non-linear equations it is frequently difficult to determine the corresponding value because simple algebraic procedures are not possible. For quadratic equations the quadratic formula can be used, if necessary, but such solutions are not available for higher-order equation.

$$y = -1.7/0.75 = -2.27$$

When $x = 1$, the equation becomes

$$0.5(1) - 0.75y = 1.7$$
$$- 0.75y = 1.7 - 0.5$$
$$- 0.75y = 1.2$$
$$y = -1.2/0.75 = -1.6$$

Plotting these two points, $x = 0$, $y = -2.27$ and $x = 1$, $y = -1.6$, we obtain Figure 2.3. Then, drawing a straight line through the points, we obtain Figure 2.4 as the graph of the equation

$$0.5x - 0.75\,y = 1.7.$$

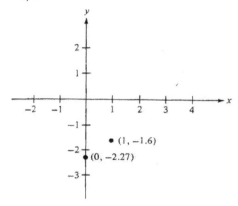

FIGURE 2.3

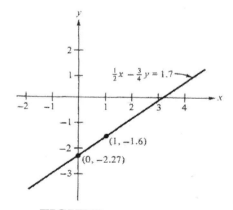

FIGURE 2.4

Example 5 Graph the equation $15p + 10q = 150$.

Solution We first note that this equation is linear in the variables p and q. Because it is a linear equation its graph is a straight line. As such, we can graph it easily by first finding two points on the line and then drawing a straight line through these points. When $p = 0$, the equation becomes $15(0) + 10q = 150$, which yields q = 15. When $p = 2$, the equation becomes $15(2) + 10q = 150$, which yields $q = 12$.

Thus, two points on this line are $p = 0$, $q = 15$ and $p = 2$, $q = 12$. Graphing these points (see Figure 2.5), we can draw the straight line given in Figure 2.6.

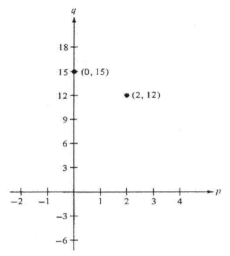

FIGURE 2.5

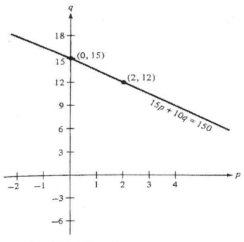

FIGURE 2.6

Warning: The method of plotting two points and then drawing a straight line through them is valid only *if* the equation is known to be a linear equation. When applied to equations that are not linear equations, for example, $x^2 + y^2 = 4$, this procedure results in erroneous graphs.

Finally, we consider the special straight lines given by Equation 2.1 when either A or B equals zero. Such lines can be simplified into the following equations:

$x = h$ (Eq. 2.7)   (the graph is a vertical line through (h, o)

$y = k$ (Eq. 2.8)   (the graph is a horizontal line through (o, k)

where $h = C/A$ when $B = o$ and $k = C/B$ when $A = o$. Equation 2.5 is an example of Equation 2.8 with $k = o$.

Example 6 Graph the equation $y = 5$.

Solution A casual approach may be to assume that x is always zero and $y = 5$, but this would be wrong and almost completely opposite the actual situation.

The equation $y = 5$ provides absolutely no constraints on x, so in fact x must be arbitrary; *that is, it can be anything.* The only way we could conclude that x is zero would be to have the equation $x = o$, which is not the case here.

From a closer look at the given equation, we see that $y = 5$ can be written as

$$0x + 1y = 5 \qquad\qquad \text{(Eq. 2.9)}$$

Thus, as long as $y = 5$, any value of x will satisfy Equation 2.9. In particular, $x = 1, y = 5$ and $x = -3, y = 5$ are two points that satisfy either Equation 2.9 or the original, given equation. Plotting these points and then drawing a straight line through them we find the graph of $y = 5$ is a straight line parallel to the x-axis having all y-coordinates equal to 5 (see Figure 2.7).

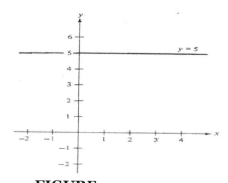

FIGURE 2.7

By generalizing Example 6, it follows that the graph of Equation 2.8, given in Figure 2.8, is a straight line parallel to the x-axis having all y-coordinates equal to

61

k, while the graph of Equation 2.7, given in Figure 2.9, is a straight line parallel to the y-axis having all x-coordinates equal to h. In particular, the line $x = 0$ is the y-axis, and the line $y = 0$ is the x-axis.

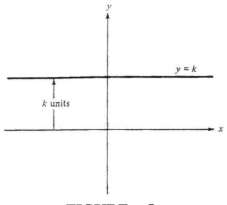

FIGURE 2.8

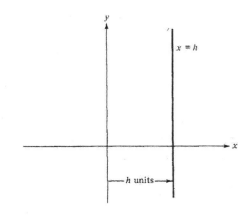

FIGURE 2.9

Section 2.2 Exercises

1. Graph the following equations:

   a. $2x + 3y = 6$ b. $-2x + 3y = 6$

   c. $2x - 3y = 6$ d. $2x + 3y = -6$

   e. $3x + 2y = 6$ f. $x = 7$

   g. $10x - 5y = 50$ h. $x = y$.

2. Graph the following equations in the given variables:

a. $2P + 3Q = 6$ b. $-N + 2M = 10$
c. $N = 1 + 2M$ d. $5r - 2s = 0$.

3. The sales (in millions of dollars) of a particular company are given by $S = 2E$ +2.14, where E represents advertising expenditures (in millions of dollars). Determine the amount of money that must be committed to advertising in order to realize gross sales of $10 million.

4. The current value V of a particular model automobile originally purchased for $6,000 is given by $V = -\$1,250t + \$6,000$, where t denotes time (in years). Determine a. the time, in years, when the car will have lost all its resale value, and b. the time, again in years, when the car will be worth exactly half its original purchase price.

5. Using the data in Exercise 4 of the previous section (Section 2.1) determine the price at which cans of cat food cease to be saleable.

2.3 Properties of Straight Lines

Straight lines and their corresponding linear equation have a number of extremely useful characteristics. These include a concept called the line's slope, the line's y-intercept, and the ease with which the linear equation can be found from its graph. This latter is the reverse process of drawing a graph given its linear equation. Each of these topics is presented in this section. We begin with the concept of a line's slope.

Definition 2.2 Let (x_1, y_1) and (x_2, y_2) be any two distinct points on the same straight line (or, alternatively, satisfying the same linear equation). The *slope* of the line, denoted as m, is

$$m = slope = \frac{y_2 - y_1}{x_2 - x_1} \qquad\qquad \text{(Eq. 2.10)}$$

Let us see what this definition says and what it does not say. The definition *does not* indicate what a slope represents; a graphical interpretation is required for this. Definition 2.2 simply tells us how to calculate something called a slope given the coordinates of any two points on a straight line. Given the two points, we first must subtract y-values, then subtract their corresponding x-values in the same order as the y-values were subtracted, and finally divide the subtracted y-values by the subtracted x-values. The number we obtain is called the slope.

To find the slope of a given equation:

- *Choose a value for x*
- *Substitute the value of x into the given equation and solve the equation for its corresponding y*
- *Repeat this process for the next x value*
- *Use the formula $m = \frac{y_2 - y_1}{x_2 - x_1}$ to find the slope of the given equation.*

Example 1 Find the slope of the line $6x + 2y = 15$.

Solution In Example 1 in Section 2.2 we found that two points on this line are $(0, 7.5)$ and $(1, 4.5)$. Therefore, letting $x_1 = 0$, $y_1 = 7.5$, and $x_2 = 1$, $y_2 = 4.5$ and substituting into Equation 2.10, we have

$$Slope = \frac{4.5 - 7.5}{1 - 0} = \frac{-3}{1} = -3.$$

Notice that the same value of the slope would be obtained if we had selected $(0, 7.5)$ as the (x_2, y_2) point and $(1, 4.5)$ as the (x_1, y_1) point, or any other two points on the line. Definition 2.2 simply requires that the x-values of the two points be subtracted in the same order as their corresponding y-values.

Example 2 Find the slope of the linear equation $y - 2x = 1$.

Solution Definition 2.2 requires that we select two points satisfying the given equation $y - 2x = 1$. Arbitrarily selecting x-values of 1 and 4 (any choice would do) we calculate the corresponding y-values as 3 and 9. Thus two points satisfying the equation are $(1, 3)$ and $(4, 9)$. Letting $(1,3)$ be the (x_1, y_1) point and $(4, 9)$ the (x_2, y_2) point, and substituting into Equation 2.10 yields:

$$Slope = \frac{9 - 3}{4 - 1} = \frac{6}{3} = 2.$$

Graphical Interpretation

For a graphical interpretation of what the slope of a straight line means, consider Figure 2.10. Here, the two points P_1 and P_2 on the line are any two randomly selected points. As indicated, the difference in the y values, $y_2 - y_1$, represents the vertical distance between the two points P_1 and P_2, while the difference in the x-

values represents the horizontal distance between the two points.

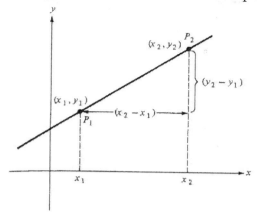

FIGURE 2.10

A specific example should clarify this point. In Example 2, we showed that the line satisfying the equation $y - 2x = 1$ had a slope of 2. This curve, along with the two points P_1 and P_2 used to calculate the slope as shown.

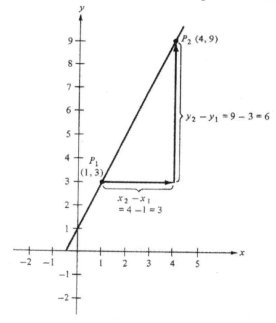

FIGURE 2.11

From the graph it is evident that, had we started at point P_1 and moved to point P_2 along the line, we would have traveled a distance of 3 units to the right and up a distance of 6 units, as indicated by the arrows. The 6 and 3 are the respective differences in y- and x-values from point P_1 to point P_2. The ratio 6/3, or simply 2, is the slope of the line.

Recall that we selected points P_1 and point P_2 in Figure 2.11 at random. Had we selected two other points on the curve and calculated the slope, we still would have found the slope to be 2. The reason for this is that any two points on the curve illustrated in Figure 2.11 are related in a particular way, as follows: by starting at one point on the curve, every other point on the line can be reached by increasing or decreasing y- and x-values in the ratio of 2 to 1. If we start at point P_1 and increase x by 1 unit, we must increase y by 2 units to land back on the line. Should we increase x by 5 units, we must increase y by 10 units to remain on the line.

The significance of the slope is that it gives us the particular ratio relating all points on a given line. As such, *the slope represents the rate of change in y associated with a change in x*, and this has both interesting and important commercial applications.

Example 3 It is known that the monthly sales of a particular model automobile S (in units) is related to the advertising expenditures E (in millions of dollars) by the equation S = 20,000 + 5,000E. Determine the rate of change in sales with respect to advertising expenditures.

Solution If we rewrite the given equation as S $-$ 5,000E = 20,000, we observe it conforms to the definition of a linear equation; as such, its graph is a straight line. The rate of change is just the slope. To find the slope, we first need two distinct points on the line. Arbitrarily choosing E_1 = 0 and E_2 = 1 (any two values could have been selected), we find the corresponding values of S as S_1 = 20,000 and S_2 = 25,000. The rate of change in sales with respect to advertising expenditures is

$$Rate\ of\ Change = Slope = \frac{25,000-20,000}{1-0} = 5,000$$

This means that whenever E is increased by 1 unit (in this case \$1 million), the monthly sales will be increased by 5,000 units (in this case cars).

Graphically, a line has a positive slope if the angle between the line and the positively directed horizontal axis is between 0 and 90 degrees. This means a line with a positive slope slants upward to the right, as shown in Figure 2.12. A line with a large positive slope, such as 100, is steeper upward than a line with a less positive slope, such as 5.

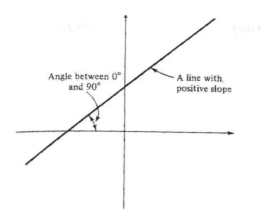

FIGURE 2.12

A line has a negative slope if the angle between the line and the positively directed horizontal axis is between 90 and 180 degrees. This means a line with a negative slope slants downward to the right, as shown in Figure 2.13. A line with a large negative slope, such as -100, is steeper downward than a line with a less negative slope, such as -5.

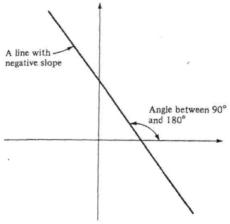

FIGURE 2.13

A line parallel to the x-axis, as previously illustrated on Figure 2.8, has a slope with a value of zero, because any two points on the line will have the same y-coordinate. A line parallel to the y-axis, as previously illustrated on Figure 2.9 does not have a slope. The reason is that any two points on such a line have the same x-coordinate and substituting this value into Equation 2.10 would result in a denominator of zero which is undefined arithmetically.

Slope-Intercept Form

Recall from Definition 2.1 that a linear equation has the form $Ax + By = C$. If B is not zero, this equation can be solved for y, which yields $y = (-A/B)x + (C/B)$. Setting $m = -A/B$ and b as C/B we obtain the equation

$$\boxed{y = mx + b}$$ (Eq. 2.11)

Equation 2.11 is an alternative representation for all straight lines not parallel to the y-axis. For lines parallel to the y-axis (see Equation 2.7), $B = o$ in Equation2.1 and the division by zero in the above manipulation is invalid. For most lines, however, Equation 2.11 is valid, and has two direct advantages over Definition 2.1.

The first advantage is that once a linear equation is in the form of Equation 2.11, the slope is given by m, the coefficient in front of the x term. To see that this is always true, let (x_1, y_1) and (x_2, y_2) be any two points on the line given by Equation 2.11. As such, the coordinates of each point are related as follows:

$y_1 = mx_1 + b$

and

$y_2 = mx_2 + b.$

Thus, Slope $= \dfrac{y_2 - y_1}{x_2 - x_1} = \dfrac{(mx_2 + b) - (mx_1 + b)}{x_2 - x_1} = \dfrac{mx_2 - mx_1}{x_2 - x_1} = \dfrac{m(x_2 - x_1)}{x_2 - x_1} = m$

The quantity b in Equation 2.11 also has geometric significance; it represents the value at which the line crosses the y-axis and is commonly referred to as the *y-intercept*.

Example 4 Determine the slope of the line 4y - 12x = 36

Solution Rewriting the equation into the form $y = mx + b$, we have

$4y = 12x + 36$
$\ \ y = 3x + 9$

Once the equation is in this form, the coefficient in front of the x term yields the slope. Thus, the slope of the line is 3.

From Points to Equation

The second advantage of Equation 2.11 over Equation 2.1 is the ease with which the equation of a line can be obtained from any two points known to be on the line. This is accomplished by first determining the slope, and then using one of the points to obtain the y-intercept.

Example 5 Find the equation of the straight line containing the two points (1, -3) and (3, 5).

Solution Because these points are on the same straight line, we can compute the slope of the line directly using Definition 2.2. Thus,

$$\text{Slope} = m = \frac{y_2 - y_1}{x_2 - x_1} = \frac{5 - (-3)}{3 - 1} = \frac{8}{2} = 4.$$

From Equation 2.11 the line will have the form $y = 4x + b$. The value of b is found by substituting the coordinates of either point into this equation. Using the point (1, -3), we obtain $-3 = 4(1) + b$, which yields $b = -7$. Notice that if we had used the other point (3,5), we would have found $5 = 4(3) + b$, which also yields $b = -7$. Having found m and b, the equation of the line containing the two points (1, -3) and (3, 5) is $y = 4x - 7$.

Example 6 At a recent sales meeting of the Lincoln Hamburger Company, Figure 2.14 was displayed to emphasize the growth in profit. Find the equation relating profit, P, to time t (in years).

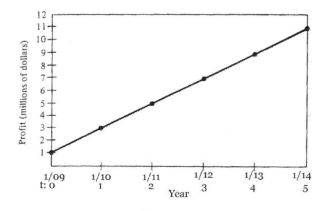

FIGURE 2.14

Solution Obviously the graph indicates a straight-line relationship between P

and t, so we seek an equation of the form

$$P = mt + b.$$ (Eq. 2.12)

Here, $t = 0$ corresponds to January 1, 2009. To find the slope, we need two points on the line. These can easily be obtained from the graph as $P = 1$ when $t = 0$ and $P = 11$ when $t = 5$. Thus,

$$m = \frac{P_2 - P_1}{t_2 - t_1} = \frac{11 - 1}{5 - 0} = \frac{10}{5} = 2$$

The y-intercept is also easily obtained from the graph as $b = 1$, where the line crosses the y-axis. Note that the y-axis here corresponding to $t = 0$ is January 1, 2009. Alternatively, we can obtain b by first substituting $m = 2$ into Equation 2.12, obtaining $P = 2t + b$, and then substituting a point on the line into this last equation to obtain b. Following this procedure and using the point $(P = 1, t = 0)$ we again find $1 = 2(0) + b$ and $b = 1$. Either way the equation of interest is $P = 2t + 1$.

Example 7 A recent survey conducted for the Chubby Cat Food Corporation resulted in Table 2.4. Assuming a linear relationship, determine the equation relating the number of cans sold daily (N) to the price of each can (P).

TABLE 2.4

Number of cans sold	18,000	17,500	17,000	16,000	14,000
Price (cents)	70	75	80	85	90

Solution Graphing these five data points, we see that the relationship appears to be a straight line, so we seek an equation of the form[§§]

$$N = mP + b,$$ (Eq. 2.13)

where N denotes the number of cans sold and P denotes the price per can (in cents). Any two of the five given data points can be used to calculate m. Taking $N_1 = 18,000$, $P_1 = 70$, $N_2 = 17,500$, and $P_2 = 75$, we compute

---

[§§] We have made the assumption here that the data conform to a straight line, and that, if we were to obtain data points between those given, they would correspond to the same line.

$$m = \frac{N_2 - N_1}{P_2 - P_1} = \frac{17{,}500 - 180{,}000}{75 - 70} = \frac{-500}{5} = -100.$$

Equation 2.13 can now be rewritten as $N = -100P + b$. To obtain b, we substitute any one of the data points, say $N_1 = 18{,}000$, $P_1 = 70$, into this last equation and find

$$18{,}000 = -100(70) + b$$
$$18{,}000 + 7{,}000 = b$$
$$b = 25{,}000.$$

Thus,

$$N = -100P + 25{,}000.$$

The last equation has interesting connotations when P equals zero. With $P = 0$. $N = -100(0) + 25{,}000 = 25{,}000$, so that, even if the Chubby Cat Food Corporation gave its product away free, only 25,000 cans would be used daily. Given that not everyone owns a cat and that each cat can eat only one can per day, this result is not unexpected.

Example 8 Table 2.5 is the result of years of data collecting by the American Citrus Corporation. Using this data, determine the equation relating the number of orange trees that bear fruit G to the number of trees planted N.

TABLE 2.5

Number of Orange trees planted (N)	120	140	160	180	190
Number that bear fruit (G)	114	133	152	171	180

Solution When these points are graphed, we see that the relationship appears to be a straight line, so we seek an equation of the form

$$G = mN + b. \qquad \text{(Eq. 2.14)}$$

Two points on the line are $N_1 = 120$, $G_1 = 114$ and $N_2 = 140$, $G_2 = 133$. Thus, the slope of Equation 2.14 is

$$m = \frac{G_2 - G_1}{N_2 - N_1} = \frac{133 - 114}{140 - 120} = \frac{19}{20} = 0.95.$$

With $m = 0.95$, Equation 2.14 becomes $G = 0.95N + b$. To obtain b, we substitute any one of the data points, say $N_1 = 120$ and $G_1 = 114$, into this last equation and find

$$114 = 0.95(120) + b$$
$$114 = 114 + b$$
$$b = 0.$$

Thus, $G = 0.95N$.

Section 2.3 Exercises

1. Find the slopes of the following straight lines:
   a. $2x + 3y = 6$ b. $-2x + 3y = 6$
   c. $2x - 3y = 6$ d. $2x + 3y = -6$
   e. $3x + 2y = 6$ f. $x = 7$
   g. $10x - 5y = 50$ h. $x = y$.

2. Find the equation of the straight line containing the given points:
   a. $(1, 2)$ and $(2, 5)$ b. $(7, -3)$ and $(-1, -8)$
   c. $(-1, 2)$ and $(4, 2)$ d. $(1, 0)$ and $(0, 1)$
   e. $(2, -1)$ and $(2, 4)$.

3. Figure 2.15 illustrates the cumulative monthly attendance at a local amusement park for the past year. Determine the equation relating attendance, A, to time t (in months), assuming t = 0 corresponds to January.

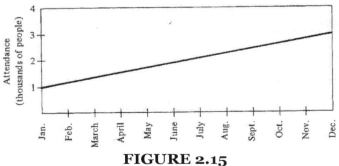

FIGURE 2.15

4. Figure2.16 illustrates the cumulative weekly sales receipts of a supermarket over the past year. a. Determine the equation relating gross

income, I, to time, *t,* for the first 20-week period. b. Determine the equation relating I to *t* for the last 32 weeks of the year.

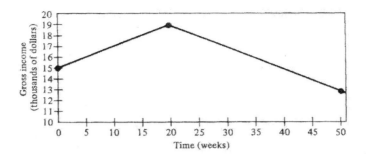

FIGURE 2.16

5. After test-marketing a new bleach, the White-All Bleach Company collected the data given in Table 2.6. Plot the points in Table 2.6 to verify that the relationship between the number of subsequent purchases *P* and the number of samples distributed S is a straight line, and then determine the equation of that line.

TABLE 2.6

Number of free samples distributed (S)	Number of subsequent purchases (P)
1000	2050
1500	2075
2000	2100
3000	2150
5000	2250

6. Quality-control tests on the manufacture of light bulbs resulted in Table 2.7. Plot the points in this table to verify that the relationship between the number of defective bulbs *D* and the number of bulbs produced *N* is a straight line, and then determine the equation of that line.

TABLE 2.7	
Number of bulbs produced (N)	Number of defective bulbs (D)
25,000	75
50,000	150
60,000	180
75,000	225
90,000	270

2.4 Break-Even Analysis

Linear equations are extremely useful in business applications for determining the relationship between short-term revenue and short-term costs. Conventionally, the term *short-term* refers to a time period in which both the price and the cost of an item remain constant. Over more extended time periods economic conditions, such as inflation, supply and demand, and other economic factors typically act to change the cost and price structures. Over the short-term, which is generally defined as a year or less, these other factors tend to have little direct influence.

The **Break-Even point** is the point at which the income from the sale of manufactured or purchased items exactly matches the cost of the items being sold. When this happens, the seller neither makes nor loses money, but simply breaks even.

The reason the break-even point is so important is that it provides a business information about the sales at which the company switches over from incurring a loss to making a profit. Should it be decided that sales can be higher than the break-even point, it means a profit can be made; otherwise, any sales less than the break-even point indicates that the venture will result in a loss. As such, it also forms as a lower bound for marketing, because if the break-even point cannot be reached, spending time and effort in marketing becomes a futile endeavor.

In determining the break-even point, both the revenue obtained by selling, and the cost involved in acquiring the items being sold must be taken into account.

The Revenue Equation

By definition, **revenue** is the income obtained from selling items. In its simplest form the revenue produced from a sale, known as the *sales revenue*, is

simply the price of each item times the number of items sold.*** Designating the sales revenue by R, the price per unit by p and the number of items sold by x, we have

$$R = px, \qquad\qquad\qquad \text{(Eq. 2.12)}$$

Because p is assumed fixed and known, Equation 2.12 is a linear equation in the variables R and x.

Example 1 A company that manufactures calculators has a contract to sell calculators for $5.00 a piece to a discount electronics outlet chain. Determine the revenue equation and the actual revenue realized if 2,000 calculators are sold.

Solution Using Equation 2.12 the revenue equation is
R = $5.00 x

If 2,000 calculators are sold, the revenue, R, realized is

R = $5.00(2,000) = $10,000.

The Cost Equation

The cost of items sold are commonly separated into two categories: fixed costs and variable costs.

    Fixed costs include rent, insurance, property taxes, and other expenses that are present regardless of the number of items produced or purchased. Over the short run these costs are fixed, because they exist and must be paid even if no items are purchased for resale, or produced and sold. We will represent the fixed cost by the variable F.

    Variable costs are those expenses that are directly attributable to the manufacture or purchase of the items themselves, such as labor and raw

---

*** Here, we are restricting ourselves to the short run (typically defined as a year or less) in which the price of each item does not change.

materials. Variable costs depend directly on the number of items manufactured or purchased - the more items manufactured or purchased, the higher the variable costs. If we restrict ourselves to short-run conditions, the cost-per-item is a fixed number, which makes the variable cost equal to this cost-per-item times the number of items purchased or manufactured. Designating the variable cost by V, the cost- per-item by a, and the number of items manufactured or purchased by x, we have

$$V = ax \qquad \text{(Eq. 2.13)}$$

Because the total cost is the sum of the variable cost plus fixed cost, the total cost equation becomes

$$C = V + F \qquad \text{(Eq. 2.14)}$$

Substituting Equation 2.13 for V into equation 2.14, the final cost equation becomes

$$C = ax + F \qquad \text{(Eq. 2.15)}$$

That is, the total cost is the sum of the variable cost and the fixed cost. The numbers a and F are assumed known and fixed, hence Equation2.15 is a linear equation in C and x.

Example 2 A company manufacturing electronic calculators has recently signed contracts with its suppliers. For the duration of these contracts, the cost of manufacturing each calculator is $1.20. The company estimates that the fixed costs for this period will be $8,000. Determine the total cost function for this process and the actual cost incurred if only 500 calculators are actually manufactured.

Solution Using Equation 2.15 with $a = 1.20$ and F = $8,000, we have

$C = \$1.20x + \$8,000.$

If 500 calculators are produced, the cost will be e $C = \$1.20(500) + \$8,000 = \$8,600$. If no calculators are produced, the total cost will be $C = \$1.20(0) + \$8,000$ or $8,000, which is the fixed cost.

From Examples 1 and 2, we note that a production run of 500 calculators will result in a total cost of $8,600 and a sales revenue of only $2,500. The company will experience a loss of $6,100. Such embarrassing situations can be avoided with a *break-even analysis*. As the name suggests, this analysis involves finding the level of sales below which it will be unprofitable to produce items and above which sales revenue exceeds costs, so that a profit is made. This level is the *break-even point*. The break-even point occurs when total cost exactly equals sales revenue.

If we restrict ourselves to the short run and assume that all items produced can be sold, the break-even point is obtained by setting the right side of Equation 2.12 equal to the right side of Equation 2.15. That is, the breakeven point occurs when $R = C$. Substituting for both the revenue, R, and cost, C, from Equations 2.12 and 2.15 yields

$$px = ax + F \qquad \text{(Eq. 2.16)}$$

Equation 2.16 is one equation in the one unknown, x. Solving for x using the algebraic methods presented in Section 1.2 yields the break-even point, *BEP*, as

$$\boxed{BEP = x = F / (p - a)} \qquad \text{(Eq. 2.17)}$$

For the electronic calculator described in Examples 1 and 2, we found $C = \$1.20x + \$8,000$ and $R = \$5.00x$. The break-even point occurs when $R = C$, or, from Equation 2.17, when $x = 8,000/(5.00 - 1.20) = 2,106$ calculators. Any production and sales below 2,106 calculators results in a loss, while any production and sales above 2,106 units produces a profit.

Example 3 A lamp component manufacturer determines that the manufacturing costs associated with each component are $5 and that the fixed costs are $7,000. Determine the break-even point if each component sells for $7. Assume that each unit made can be sold.

Solution The total cost for this process, using Equation 2.15, is $C = \$5x + \$7,000$. The sales revenue is $R = \$7x$. The break-even point is the value of x for which $R = C$. This point can be found by directly using Equation 2.17, which yields, $x = 7000/ (7 - 5) = 3,500$ components as the break-even point.

Example 4 A dress manufacturer determines that the production costs associated directly with each dress are $8 and that the fixed costs are $9,200. Determine the break-even point if each dress sells for $54. Assume that all dresses manufactured can be sold.

Solution The total cost for this process is given by Equation 2.15 as $C = \$8x + \$9{,}200$. The sales revenue is given by Equation 2.12 as $R = \$54x$. The break-even point is the solution of the equation $x = 9{,}200/(54 - 8)$, which yields $x = 200$ dresses.

Graphical Solutions

Break-even problems can be solved graphically as well as algebraically. The procedure is to plot both the revenue and cost equations on the same graph, as shown in Figure 2.17. Because both of these equations are linear, their graphs will both be straight lines.

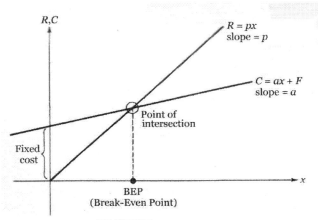

FIGURE 2.17

In reviewing Figure 2.17, note that the horizontal axis is x, the number of units produced and sold, whereas the vertical axis is R and C, depending on which equation is being considered. It follows that the unit sales price p is the slope of the revenue equation (defined by Equation 2.12), and the cost of manufacturing each unit, denoted as a, is the slope of the cost equation (defined by Equation 2.15). The y-intercept corresponding to Equation 2.15 is simply the fixed cost.

The break-even point (BEP) is the value of x for which $R = C$, which in Figure 2.17 is the value of x at the intersection point of the two lines.

Example 5 Graphically determine the break-even point for the manufacturing process described in Example 3.

Solution In Example 3, we determined the equations $C = 5x + 7{,}000$ and $R = 7x$. Using the graphing procedures given in Section 2.2, we plot each line on the same graph, as shown in Figure 2.18. The x-component of the intersection point of these two lines is read directly from the graph as $x = 3{,}500$, which is the same break-even point found algebraically in Example 3.

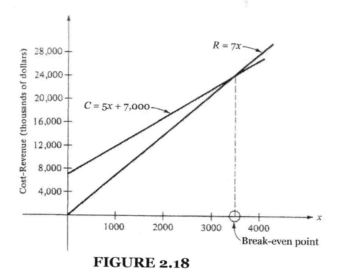

FIGURE 2.18

Section 2.4 Exercises

1. A publisher of a current economics textbook determines that the manufacturing costs directly attributable to each book are $10 and that the fixed costs are $20,000. The publisher sells each book for $12 per copy.
   a. Determine the equation relating the total cost to the number of books published.
   b. Determine the equation relating the sales revenue to the number of books published.
   c. What will the profit be if 3000 books are published?
   d. Algebraically determine the break-even point for this process.

2. Determine the break-even point in Exercise 1 graphically. Which method do you prefer?

3. A manufacturer of staplers determines that the variable costs directly attributable to each stapler are $2 and that the fixed costs are $15,000. Each stapler sells for $12.00. Determine the break-even point for this process both graphically and algebraically.

4. Using the results from Exercise 3, determine
   a. the total cost of the process at the break-even point

b. the total sales revenue of the process at the break-even point
c. the profit at the break-even point.

5. A manufacturer of light bulbs determines that each bulb costs 15¢ in direct expenses and that the process as a whole incurs fixed costs of $15,000.
   a. Determine the break-even point if each bulb sells for $1.75.
   b. Determine the break-even point jf each bulb sells for $2.50.
   c. Does it make sense that the answer in part b. is smaller than that in part a.?

6. A manufacturer of Lucite pipe holders has determined that the firm has a break-even point of 2,500 units. Determine the price of each holder if each item costs $3.00 to manufacture and the process involves fixed costs of $15,000.

7. A manufacturer of specialty bookends has determined that the break-even point for the manufacturing process is 120 units. Determine the variable cost of producing each bookend set, if the fixed costs are $1,920 and each set sells for $25.

8. A manufacturer of automatic fire alarm systems determines that its total cost is given by $C = 1,000x^2 + 5,000x + 10,000$. (Note that this equation is no longer linear.) Each system sells for $12,000. Determine the break-even point for this process a. graphically, and b. algebraically.

2.5 Quadratic Equations

By far, some of the most important business applications can be modelled using linear equation. There are, however, other applications, notably in statistics, marketing, and, finance that require slightly more complex mathematical equations. Three such equations are presented in this and the next two sections.

An equation that is more complex than a linear equation and it resulting straight line graph is one involving a quadratic (variable squared) term. Such equations are known as quadratic equations.

Definition 2.3 A *quadratic equation* in x is an equation of the form
$$y = ax^2 + bx + c \qquad\qquad \text{(Eq. 2.18)}$$

where a, b, and c are known numbers with a not equal to zero.

In Equation 2.18, the variable that is squared is referred to as the ***quadratic variable***, which in this case is x. The variable on the left side of the equal sign, in this case y, is referred to as the ***linear variable***.

Examples of quadratic equations are

$$y = 2x^2 - \tfrac{1}{2}$$ (Eq. 2.19)

$$y + x = x^2$$ (Eq. 2.20)

$$n^2 = 2p + 4$$ (Eq. 2.21)

Equation 2.19 has the required form with $a = 2$, $b = 0$, and $c = -1/2$. If we rewrite Equation 2.20 as $y = x^2 - x$, then $a = 1$, $b = -1$, and $c = 0$. Similarly, rewriting Equation 2.21, we obtain $p = 1/2\, n^2 - 2$, which has the form $p = an^2 + bn + c$ with $a = \tfrac{1}{2}$, $b = 0$, and $c = -2$.

As in the case of linear equations, the letters y and x used in Equation 2.18 are arbitrary; any other two letters [(see Equation 2.21) are equally appropriate. The essential point is the form of the relationship between the variables. That is, a quadratic equation is one in which one variable can be written as the sum of a constant times the second variable squared, plus a constant times the second variable, plus a constant.

Example 1 Determine whether or not the equation $x^2 + y^2 = 4$ is a quadratic equation.

Solution This is not a quadratic equation, because both variables appear squared, which *is not* the form of Equation 2.18.

Whereas the graphs of linear equations are straight lines, the graphs of quadratic equations are parabolas, as illustrated in the following example.

Example 2 From past experience, a small dress manufacturer knows that the profit P (in thousands of dollars) is related to number of pieces n (in thousands of units) by the equation $P = -0.05n^2 + 5n - 10$, under the assumption that all dresses produced will be sold. Graph the equation and explain the physical significance of the curve.

Solution To graph the equation, we first plot points. Arbitrarily choosing values of n, substituting these values into the given equation, and finding the corresponding values of P, we obtain Table 2.8 from which Figure 2.19 follows.

TABLE 2.8

n	P
0	-10
2	-0.2
5	13.75
25	83.75
50	115
60	110
100	-10

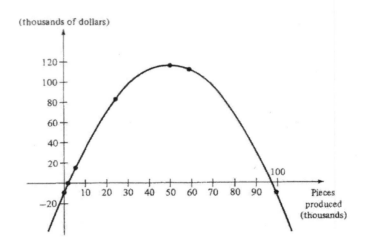

FIGURE 2.19

If no dresses are produced, $n = 0$, the manufacturer will lose \$10,000 which represents the fixed costs such as rent, insurance, and depreciation. As dresses are manufactured and sold, profits increase. Two thousand dresses, corresponding to $n = 2$, will generate almost enough capital to cover expenses. Fifty thousand dresses will result in a maximum profit of \$115,000.

The situation changes, however, with a production schedule in excess of 50,000 units. Additional dresses will require more machines, operators, internal paperwork; all resulting in increased costs that are not adequately covered by the revenue of the additional items sold.

Solving For the Quadratic Variable

In Example 2, we arbitrarily chose values of n and then solved for the corresponding P values. As in the case of linear equations, we could have chosen values of P and then solved for n. Unlike the situation encountered with linear equations, however, this second approach is more difficult. In particular, if we had substituted $P = 0$ into the equation in Example 2, we would have had to solve the resultant equation $0 = -0.05n^2 + 5n - 10$ for the variable n. The values of n can be obtained from the quadratic formula introduced in Chapter 1, but more complicated calculations are involved. Thus, it is easier to first pick n and then compute the corresponding values of P.

In general, whenever we wish to solve a quadratic equation, it is easier to select values of the variable that is squared (x in Equation 2.18) and n in Example 2, and then use the given equation to find the value of the second variable, rather than the other way around, Sometimes, however, we have no choice. As an example of this, consider the following:

Example 3 Based on observations of prices, the demand D for oranges at a local fruit stand satisfies the equation $D = -0.25P^2 + 6P + 900$, where P is the price per orange (in cents). On a given Saturday morning, the store has 100 oranges in stock. Determine the price the store should charge for oranges if it wishes to deplete its inventory by the end of the day.

Solution Here we seek the price results in zero inventory. Mathematically, this means we are asked to find the value of the quadratic term P, for a given value of 100 for the linear term, D. Substituting $D = 100$ into the demand-price equation, we find that P must satisfy the quadratic equation

$100 = -0.25P^2 + 6P + 900,$

which can be rewritten as

$0.25P^2 - 6P - 800 = 0$

Using the quadratic formula with a = 0.25 , b = -6, and c = -800, we obtain

$$P_1 = \frac{-(-6) + \sqrt{(-6)^2 - 4(.25)(-800)}}{2(0.25)} = \frac{6 + \sqrt{36 + 800}}{.5}$$

$$= \frac{6 + \sqrt{836}}{0.5} = \frac{6 + 28.91}{0.5} = \frac{34.91}{0.5} = 69.82$$

and

$$P_2 = \frac{6 - \sqrt{836}}{0.5} = \frac{6 - 28.91}{0.5} = \frac{-22.91}{0.5} = -45.82$$

As the negative solution has no practical meaning, the oranges should be priced at 69¢, which will create a demand of

$D = $ -0.25(69)² + 6(69) + 900 = 123, which will deplete the stock.

A price of 70¢ will only create a demand of

$D = $ -0.25(70)² + 6(70) + 900 = 95, which will not deplete the stock.

Example 4 A warehouse has 12,000 cans of a discontinued tennis ball which it wants to liquidate in a week. From past experience, it is known that demand D per week (in cans) is related to the price P (in dollars) by the equation

$\quad\quad$ 'D = -3,000P² - 13,500P + 27,000.

Determine the price that will result in zero inventory.

Solution We seek the price P that will yield $D = $ 12,000. Substituting this value into the given equation, we find that P must satisfy

12,0000 = -3,000P² − 13,500P + 27,000
3,000P² + 13,500P − 15,000 = 0
3P² + 13.5P − 15 = 0.

Using the quadratic formula with $a = $ 3, $b = $ 13.5, and c = -15, we obtain

$$P_1 = \frac{-13.5 + \sqrt{(13.5)^2 - 4(3)(-15)}}{2(3)} = \frac{-13.5 + \sqrt{182.25 + 180}}{6}$$

$$= \frac{-13.5 + \sqrt{362.25}}{6} = \frac{-13.5 + 19.03}{6} = \frac{5.53}{6} = 0.922$$

and

$$P_2 = \frac{-13.5 - \sqrt{362.25}}{6} = \frac{-13.5 - 19.03}{6} = -5.42$$

Again, the negative price has not practical meaning, and the tennis balls should be wholesaled at 92¢ per can.

GRAPHICAL INTERPRETATON

The graph of the quadratic equation $y = ax^2 + bx + c$ is a parabola.

If $a > 0$, then the parabola opens upward. and the minimum value of y occurs when $x = -\dfrac{b}{2a}$

If $a < 0$, then the parabola opens downward and the maximum value of y occurs of when $x = -\dfrac{b}{2a}$.

The value $x = -\dfrac{b}{2a}$ is referred to as the x-component of the parabola's *vertex*.

Section 2.5 Exercises

1. Determine which of the following equations are quadratic as defined by Equation 2.18, and for those that are quadratic, specify the quadratic variable.

   a. $x^2 - x = y$ b. $y^4 = 3$

   c. $x^2 - 2x + 2 = y$ d. $y - x^2 = 0$

   e. $y + x = 3$ f. $n^2 = 2d + 5$

   g. $R = 2S^2$ h. $\sqrt{y} = x$

2. Graph the following quadratic curves by first plotting a sufficient number of points to determine the curve's correct shape.

   a. $y = x^2$ b. $y = -x^2$

   c. $y = -x^2 - x + 4$ d. $y = x^2 + x - 4$

   e. $d = 2p^2 - 8$

3. Use the quadratic formula to find the values of x that satisfy the following equations:

   a. $x^2 - x - 6 = 0$ b. $3x^2 - 2x - 5 = 0.$

   c. $4x^2 - 7 = 0$ d. $1/3x^2 - x - 1 = 0$

   e. $x^2 - x = 4$ f. $3x^2 - 12x + 6 = 0$

4. Ogden Motors has 15 identical model automobiles which it wants to sell within a month. From past experience, it is known that the demand, d, per month is related to the price p (in dollars) by the equation $d = -0.04p^2 + 10,000$.

Determine the maximum price that will result in no inventory at the end of a month.

5. Ogden Motors uses the formula $V = (-0.005t^2 - 0.05t + 0.8)P$ to compute the book value of used cars, where V denotes the current used car price (in dollars), t denotes the age of the car (in years), and P denotes the price when the car was new (in dollars).
   a. Find the value of a $25,000 automobile after 3 years.
   b. Find the value of a $25,000 automobile immediately after it leaves the showroom.
   c. Determine the time when a $40,000 automobile will be worth $12,800.

6. A manufacturer has determined that the yearly profit P (in dollars) is directly related to the number of units sold n by the formula
$$P = n^2 - 400n - 50,000.$$
   a. Graph this equation by plotting the points corresponding to $n = 0$, 100, 200, 500, 600, 900, and 1000.
   b. Determine the loss if no units are sold.
   c. Determine the profit if 1,000 units are sold.
   d. How many units must be sold if a profit of $100,000 is desired?

2.6 Polynomial Equations

Having considered equations involving only linear terms (linear equations) and those containing squared terms (quadratic equations), we now generalize to higher-degree equations.

Definition 2.4 *An nth degree polynomial equation in x is an equation of the form*

$$y = a_nx^n + a_{n-1}x^{n-1} + \ldots + a_1x + a_0 \qquad \text{(Eq. 2.22)}$$

where n is a known nonnegative integer and $a_n, a_{n-1}, \ldots, a_1$, and a_0 are known real numbers with $a_n \neq 0$. The term $a_n x^n$ is called the **leading term** of the given polynomial and a_n is referred to as the **leading coefficient.**

Examples of polynomial curves are

$$y = 3x^4 - 2x^3 + 5x^2 - 7x + 1$$
(Eq. 2.23)

$$y = x^3 - 2x$$
(Eq. 2.24)

$$y = -x^5 + 1$$
(Eq. 2.25)

Equation 2.23 is a fourth-degree polynomial equation having the form $y = a_4x^4 + a_3x^3 + a_2x^2 + a_1x + a_0$, with $n = 4$, $a_4 = 3$, $a_3 = -2$, $a_2 = 5$, $a_1 = -7$, and $a_0 = 1$.[†††] Equation. 2.24 is a third-degree polynomial equation; it has the form of equation 2.22 with $n = 3$, $a_3 = 1$, $a_2 = 0$, $a_1 = -2$, and $a_0 = 0$. Equation 2.25 has the form of 2.22 with $n = 5$, $a_5 = -1$, $a_4 = a_3 = a_2 = a_1 = 0$, and $a_0 = 1$, and is a fifth-degree polynomial equation.

In particular, a second-degree polynomial has the form $y = a_2x^2 + a_1x + a_0$, while a first-degree polynomial equation has the form $y = a_1x + a_0$. From Equations 2.18 and 2.1, we recognize these equations as quadratic equations and linear equations, respectively.

Example 1 A large men's toiletry company plans to market a new brand of shaving cream. From past experience with other shaving creams, the company expects that the gross cumulative profit P (in millions of dollars) from this new brand will be related to time t (in years) by the equation $P = -0.014t^3 + 0.26t^2 - 0.128t - 1.5$. Graph this curve and determine the anticipated income at the end of the first year.

Solution Using the given equation with $t = 1$, we compute the anticipated income at the end of the first year as $P = -0.014(1)^3 + 0.26(1)^2 - 0.128(1) - 1.5 = -1.38$ or a loss of \$1.38 million. In order to graph the equation, we plot additional points by arbitrarily choosing different values of t and calculating corresponding values of P. In this way, we obtain Table 2.9 from which Figure 2.20 follows.

Values for t were selected and used to solve for values of P, rather than the reverse, because the resulting equation is easier to solve. The doubtful reader should try selecting a value of P and solving the equation for t.

TABLE 2.9	Solutions to the Equation $P = -0.014t^3 + 0.26t^2 - 0.128t - 1.5$													
t	-2	-1	0	0.25	0.5	1	2	3	4	8	12	13	15	17
P	-0.09	-1.10	-1.50	-1.52	-1.50	-1.38	-0.83	0.08	1.25	6.95	10.21	10.02	7.83	2.68

[†††] The degree of a polynomial equation is the highest exponential value, which in this example is 4. Hence, this is referred to as a fourth-degree polynomial equation.

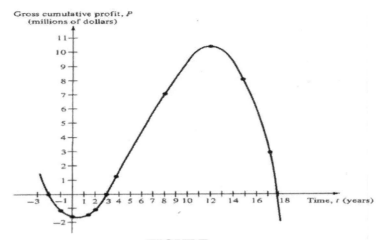

FIGURE 2.20

In Figure 2.20 the curve between $t = -2$ and $t = 17$ depicts a life cycle typical of many brands on the market. A product becomes available approximately sometime after a decision is made to produce and market it. In this case, the decision to introduce a new product triggered 2 years of research and development, with initial production expenditures resulting in a loss to the company of $1.5 million by $t = 0$, the time the product is first retailed.

An introductory period then follows, in this case 5 years, during which the product begins to establish a market. Nonetheless, even for the first years of the product's life, the company can still incur a loss, because sales are not sufficient to offset previous losses plus current advertising and production expenses. Following the introductory period, the product enjoys a rapid growth until a saturation point occurs. For the product pictured in Figure 2.20 this occurs in the twelfth year of its life-cycle, when gross profit peaks at $10.35 million. At this point, sales begin to decline, and the product, if kept on the market, will incur losses adversely affecting cumulative profits. By the eighteenth year the company will have lost all the money it had previously made.

Obviously, the product cannot generate income before it is conceived, as indicated in the graph for values of t less than -2, and it is unlikely that production will continue after the twelfth year. We discuss the more general case of restricting intervals in Chapter 6.

Polynomial curves of degree 3 or higher have limited commercial application. Nonetheless, polynomial curves can be useful on occasion, and we return to them when we discuss rates of change, in Chapter 4.

Section 2.6 Exercises

1. Determine which of the following equations represent polynomial curves and, or those that do, give the degree.

   a. $y = x^5 - 2x^2$ b. $y^2 = x^3 + 1$

   c. $y - x^2 = x^4$ d. $y^5 = 1$

   e. $y = x^2 - 2x + 5$ f. $y = \sqrt{x} + 1$.

2.7 Exponential Equations

An extremely useful curve in business problems, especially those dealing with compound interest, is one in which a variable appears as an exponent. In Chapter 3, we consider the application of compound interest and exponential equations to financial problems. Here we only define the equations.

Definition 2.5 An *exponential equation in the variable* x is an equation of the form

$$y = a(b^x) \hspace{4cm} \text{(Eq. 2.26)}$$

where a and b are known real numbers and b is positive ($b > 0$).

   Examples of exponential curves are $y = 5(3^x)$ with $a = 5$ and $b = 3$, $y = -17(\pi^x)$ with $a = -17$ and $b = \pi = 3.14159 \ldots$, and $y = 15.2(5.7^x)$ with $a = 15.2$ and $b = 5.7$. If $b = 1$, Equation 2.26 becomes $y = a(1^x) = a(1) = a$. This is a straight line having the form of Equation 2.8.

   For most commercial applications, a is also positive and Equation 2.26 has one of the two general shapes depicted in Figures 2.21 and 2.22. Note that in both cases the graph never reaches the x-axis but approaches that axis from one direction. This property is one of the primary characteristics of exponential curves.

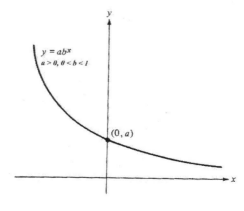

FIGURE 2.21

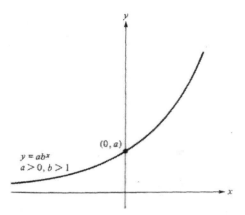

FIGURE 2.22

Many natural phenomena occur which can be accurately modeled or represented by exponential equations. Examples of such situations are pollution levels, the use of natural resources, and radioactive decay of certain materials. In practice, phenomena such as these are very misleading. Their graphs stay relatively constant or fiat for many years, very much like the graph of a linear equation. As the value of the exponent builds, however, the value of the y- variable suddenly "takes off" beyond any expectation based on a linear model of the situation. Such a situation is presented in Figure 2.23, illustrating the pollution level of nitrogen oxide versus time (in centuries).

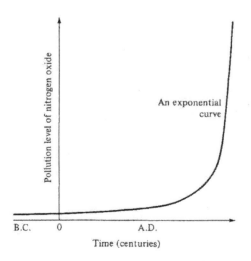

FIGURE 2.23

Note: The special base is when $b = 2.7182818284...$. This irrational number, denoted as e, is known as Euler's number (pronounced "Oiler"), and is named after the mathematician Leonhard Euler.

Section 2.7 Exercises

Determine which of the following equations are exponential equations, as defined by Definition 2.15, and for those that are, the values of a and b:

1. $y = 2(7^x)$

2. $y = (2^x)7$

3. $y = 2(x^7)$

4. $y = 2(7^{x^2})$.

5. $y = (7^x)^2$

6. $y = -2(1/2)^x$

7. $y = 2(-1/2)^x$

8. $y = \sqrt{5}\left(\sqrt{3}\right)^x$

9. $y = 9(1.1)^x$

10. A model of worldwide population growth, in billions of people, since 2010 is given by this formula, where e known as Euler's (pronounced *Oiler's*) number," is the irrational number $2.71818284...$.

$$Population = 7.5\ e^{0.02(Year - 2010)}$$

Using this formula, estimate the worldwide population in

a. 2015

b. 2020

c. 2025

11. The number of a certain type of bacteria placed in a culture dish at room temperature grows as is given by the equation:

$$Number\ of\ Bacteria = (\ Original\ Number\ of\ Bacteria)\ e^{\ 0.2t}$$

where t is the time, in hours that the culture has been in the room, and e, known as *Euler's (pronounced Oiler's) number*, is the irrational number $2.718182845...$. Using this equation determine the number of bacteria in this culture for:

a. an original number of 100 bacteria after 10 hours

b. an original number of 100 bacteria after 24 hours

c. an original number of 100 bacteria after 36 hours

d. an original number of 100 bacteria after 48 hours

12. The number of remaining bacteria that in a certain culture that is subject to refrigeration can be approximated by the equation:

Remaining Bacteria =(Original Number of Bacteria) e $^{-0.032t}$

where t is the time, in hours, that the culture has been refrigerated, and *e* known as *Euler's (pronounced Oiler's) number,"* is the irrational number 2.718182845... . Using this equation determine the number of remaining bacteria in this culture for:
   a. an original number of bacteria of 300,000 that is refrigerated for 10 hours
   b. an original number of bacteria of 300,000 that is refrigerated for 24 hours
   c. an original number of bacteria of 500,000 that is refrigerated for 48 hours
   d. an original number of bacteria of 500,000 that is refrigerated for 72 hours

13. A model to estimate the number of grams of a radioactive isotope left after t years is given by this formula:

Remaining Material = (Original Material)e$^{-0.00012t}$

where *e*, known as *Euler's (pronounced Oiler's) number,* is the irrational number 2.7182818284.... .   Using this formula determine the amount of radioactive material remaining after:
   a. 1000 years, assuming an initial amount of 100 grams
   b. 500 years, assuming an initial amount of 250 grams.

Chapter

The Mathematics of Finance

One area of business where equations are used constantly is finance. Here many questions center on the relative value of different investments that return differing amounts of money at differing future times. For example, is a $5,000 investment now, that promises a $1,500 return for the next 5 years, better than a $4,500 investment now with a guaranteed return of $2,000 every other year for the next 8 years? Or, more personally, what investment plan should be undertaken if the goal is to accumulate $50,000 after 18 years to help pay for a college education. This chapter presents the mathematical underpinnings for these types of financial decisions.

3.1 Compound Interest

Compound interest and its intimate relationship to the time value of money form the primary foundation of finance, investment analyses, and modern portfolio theory. As such, compound interest is the first topic to be considered before delving into more advanced financial topics.

The key terms used in describing compound interest are provided in Table 3.1. Initially, however, the two terms you will need a clear understanding of are the first two entries in this table, which are principal and interest.

TABLE 3.1 - BASIC FINANCIAL TERMS

Term	Meaning	Notation
Principal (also referred to as the *principal amount*)	The amount of money that is either deposited, lent, borrowed, or invested.	P
Interest	The amount of money that is earned in a conversion period (it is obtained by multiplying the interest rate per conversion period times a principal amount).	I
Conversion Period (also referred to as the *compounding interval*)	The time between successive interest rate applications.	—
Stated Annual Interest Rate (also referred to as the *annual interest rate* and the *nominal interest rate*)	The interest rate expressed on a per-year basis. It does not take into account how many times a year the interest rate is applied or compounded.	r
Effective Annual Interest Rate	The annual interest rate that does take into account how many times a year interest is applied.	E

The defining property of ***compound interest*** is that once interest is paid on an initial principal amount, the interest is immediately added to this principal amount to form a new principal amount. This new principal amount, which now consists of the original principal amount plus the interest, earns interest during the next time period. Thus, the interest earned in one time period (referred to as a conversion period) earns interest in succeeding periods; this is known as interest being paid on interest and is the defining characteristic of compound interest calculations.

As an example, consider the deposit of $1,000 in a bank paying a stated annual interest rate of 2%, with an annual conversion period (that is, interest is computed and paid once a year). In the first year the principal earns 2% of $1,000 or (0.02)($1,000) = $20. The new principal is now $1,020 (the original investment of $1,000 plus the $20 interest payment). Thus, the second year's interest payment is now based on this new amount, which becomes 2% of $1,020 or $20.40. This makes the balance at the end of the second year $1,040.40. Interest payments for the third year are now computed based on this new balance. The results of all interest computations through the fifth year have been collected into Table 3.2.

TABLE 3.1

1. Original investment	$1,000.00 = P(0)
2. Interest for the first year (2% of line 1)	20.00
3. Principal during the second year (line 1 plus line 2)	$1,020.00 = P(1)
4. Interest for the second year (2% of line 3)	20.40
5. Principal during the third year (line 3 plus line 4)	$1,040.40 = P(2)
6. Interest for the third year (2% o f line 5)	20.81
7. Principal during the fourth year (line 5 plus line 6)	$1,061.21 = P(3)
8. Interest for the fourth year (2% o f line 7)	21.22
9. Principal during the fifth year (line 7 plus line 8)	$1082.43 = P(4)
10. Interest for the fifth year (2% o f line 9)	21.65
11. Principal at the end of the fith year (line 9 plue line 10)	$1,104.08 = P(5)

Obviously we could continue Table 3.2 and find the principal at the end of any year. But this can be time consuming, especially if we are interested in the principal after 25 or 30 years. Luckily, there exists a formula that allows us to calculate such principals with very little work.

To obtain the desired formula and understand its usage, let us return to Table 3.2. For notational simplicity, as listed in the last column of the table, the original principal amount is denoted as $P(0)$. Continuing with this notation, $P(1)$ denotes the principal amount after the first year's interest has been added to $P(0)$.

As such, $P(1)$ becomes the principal on which the second year's interest calculation is based. Similarly, $P(2)$ becomes the principal amount after the second year's interest has been added to P(1), and becomes basis for the 3rd year's interest calculation, and so on. It follows then that

$$P(1) = P(0) + (0.02)P(0) = (1 + 0.02)P(0), \qquad \text{(Eq. 3.1)}$$

and

$$P(2) = P(1) + (0.02)P(1) = (1 + 0.02)P(1). \qquad \text{(Eq. 3.2)}$$

Substituting for $P(1)$ from Equation 3.1 into Equation 3.2, yields

$$P(2) = (1 + .02)(1 + 0.02)P(0) = (1 + 0.02)^2 P(0) \qquad \text{(Eq. 3.3)}$$

Similarly,

$$P(3) = (1 + 0.02)^3 P(0).$$

Figure 3.1 illustrates the compounding effect of Equations 3.1 through 3.3 .

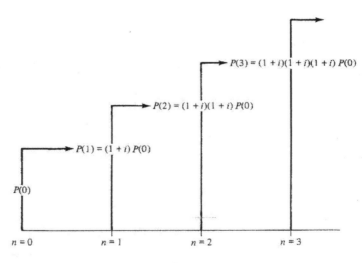

$$P(3) = (1 + i)(1 + i)(1 + i)\, P(0)$$

$$P(2) = (1 + i)(1 + i)\, P(0)$$

$$P(1) = (1 + i)\, P(0)$$

$P(0)$

$n = 0$ $n = 1$ $n = 2$ $n = 3$

FIGURE 3.1

Clearly, these interest calculations can be carried on indefinitely. For example,

$$P(4) = (1 + 0.02)^4 P(0),$$

and

$P(5) = (1 + 0.02)^5 P(0)$

This pattern can be generalized for any interest rate and time period to provide the desired final equation. Letting i denote the interest rate, n the number of interest payments that were made, and $P(n)$ the principal amount after the nth payment was made, we have,

$$P(n) = (1 + i)^n P(0) \qquad \text{(Eq. 3.4)}^{[\ddagger\ddagger\ddagger]}$$

Equation 3.4 enormously simplifies compound interest calculations. For annual interest payments, the principal amount at the end of the nth year (after which n interest payments have been made) is obtained by simply adding the interest rate to 1, raising this sum to the nth power, and multiplying this result by the original investment. To do this, a calculator that can raise a number to a power is needed to find the value of $(1 + i)^n$.

Example 1 One thousand dollars is invested in an account that pays 2% interest compounded annually. Determine the balance after 5 years and then after 25 years.

Solution Here $P(0) = \$1,000$, $i = 0.02$, and we seek the principal after 5 years. For these values, and setting $n = 5$ in Equation 3.4 we calculate

$$\begin{aligned} P(5) &= (1 + 0.02)^5 \ (\$1,000) \\ &= (1.02)^5 (\$1,000) \\ &= (1.1040808)(\$1,000) = \$1,104.08. \end{aligned}$$

Compare this value with the last dollar figure tabulated in Table 3.2.

To find the principal after 25 years, we set $n = 25$ in Equation 3.4. Again $P(0) = \$1,000$ and $i = 0.02$, hence,

$$\begin{aligned} P(25) &= (1 + 0.02)^{25}(\$1,000) \\ &= (1.02)^{25}(\$1,000) \\ &= (1.640606) \ (\$1,000) = \$1,640.61 \end{aligned}$$

[‡‡‡] It is interesting to note that equation 3.4 is an exponential equation having the form of Equation 3.18 in Chapter 2, with a = $P(0)$, b = $(1 + i)$, and the variable x replaced by n.

It is certainly easier to obtain $P(25)$ this way than to continue Table 3.2 through another 20 years.

Conversion Periods

Although interest rates are quoted on an annual basis, in practice interest is typically compounded semiannually, monthly, weekly, daily, and even continuously[§§§]. The time between successive interest computations is called the *conversion period*. Table 3.3 lists the most commonly used conversion periods and the interest rates that apply to them, where r is the stated annual interest rate.

TABLE 3.3 Calculating the interest rate per conversion period

Conversion Period	Conversion Periods per Year	Interest Rate per Conversion Period, i (r = the stated annual rate)
Annually	1	$i = r$
Semi-annually	2	$i = r/2$
Quarterly	4	$i = r/4$
Monthly	12	$i = r/12$
Daily	365	$i = r/365$

As seen in the last column of Table 3.3, the *interest rate per conversion period* is the annual rate divided by the number of compounding periods in a year. Thus, if r designates the annual interest rate, the interest rate per conversion period is $r/2$ for semiannual payments, $r/4$ for quarterly payments, $r/12$ for monthly payments, and $r/365$ for daily payments.

Equation 3.4 remains valid for all the conversion periods listed in Table 3.3, as long as we realize that i signifies the interest rate per conversion period, and $P(n)$ is the balance after n conversion periods. For example, if the interest is 2% compounded quarterly, $i = 0.02/4 = 0.005$ which is the interest rate per quarter. Also, $P(10)$, for example, denotes the principal after 10 conversion periods which, in this case, is 10 quarters, which corresponds to 2½ years.

Example 2 Ten thousand dollars is invested in an interest bearing account that pays 4% interest compounded quarterly. Determine the balance after 5 years.

[§§§] Continuous compounding is presented in Section 3.8

Solution Because interest is paid quarterly, we take one-quarter of a year as our basic time period. Then, the balance after 5 years is given by the balance after 20 quarters or $P(20)$. The rate applied each quarter is the annual rate divided by 4 or $0.04/4 = 0.01$. Using Equation 3.4 with $n = 20$, $i = 0.01$, and $P(0) = \$10,000$, we obtain[****]

$$P(20) = (1 + .01)^{20}(\$10,000)$$
$$= (1.01)^{20}(\$10,000)$$
$$= (1.220190)(\$10,000) = \$12,201.90.$$

Example 3 Ten thousand dollars is invested in a savings account that pays 4% interest compounded semiannually. Determine the balance after 5 years.

Solution Because interest is paid semiannually, we take one-half of a year as our basic time period. Accordingly, the balance after 5 years is given by the balance after 10 half-years, or $P(10)$. The applicable interest rate per conversion period is the annual rate divided by 2 or $0.04/2 = 0.02$. Using Equation 3.4 with $n = 10$, $i = 0.02$, and $P(0) = \$10,000$, we obtain

$$P(10) = (1 + .02)^{10}(\$10,000)$$
$$= (1.02)^{10}(\$10,000)$$
$$= (1.2189944)(\$10,000) = \$12,189.94.$$

Example 4 Ten thousand dollars is invested in an investment account that pays 2% interest compounded monthly, Determine the balance after 5 years.

Solution Here $i = 0.02/12$ and we seek $P(60)$, the balance after 60 months or 5 years. Using Equation 3.4, we obtain

$$P(60) = (1 + 0.02/12)^{60}(\$10,000)$$
$$= (1 + 0.001667)^{60}(\$10,000)$$

$$= (1.001667)^{60}(\$10,000)$$
$$= (1.10507895)(\$10,000) = \$11,050.79.$$

[****] Generally, 6 or more decimal places are retained in interest rate calculations for each $1,000 of principal . More complicated financial instruments typically require retaining at least 10 significant digits of accuracy in all intermediate calculations.

Section 3.1 Exercises

1. For $2,000 deposited in an account for four years that yields 2% annual interest compounded annually:
   a. Determine the values of i, n, and $P(0)$ that would be used to determine the amount in the account at the end of the fourth year.
   b. Determine the balance in the account at the end of the fourth year.

2. For $2,000 being deposited in account for 5 years that yields 3% annual interest compounded monthly:
   a. Determine the values of i, n, and $P(0)$ that would be used to determine the amount in the account at the end of the fifth year.
   b. Determine the balance in the account at the end of the fifth year.

3. Ms. Brown borrows $2,500 from a friend who charges 4% interest compounded annually. Determine her debt after 3 years.

4. Redo Exercise 3 with the interest compounded quarterly.

5. Ms. Brown invests $2,500 in a venture that pays 5% interest compounded quarterly. Determine her balance after 3 years.

6. Redo Exercise 5 with the interest compounded semiannually.

7. Mr. Johnson deposits $1,000 in an account that pays 2.5% interest compounded annually. How much will he have after 25 years?

8. Redo Exercise 7 with the interest compounded semiannually.

9. Determine the balance after 3 years resulting from $2,900 being deposited in a savings account that pays 1.5% interest compounded monthly.

10. Determine the balance after 1 year resulting from $3,500 being deposited in a savings account that yields 2.5% interest compounded daily. Set up and solve.

11. Redo Exercise 10 for the balance after 4 years.

12. Some institutions use an *approximate year* rather than a calendar year for certain interest computations. In this method, every month is assumed to have exactly 30 days, resulting in an approximate year of 360 days. Using an approximate year, set-up and determine the balance after 3 years for an initial

deposit of $2,500 if the interest rate is 3% compounded daily.

13. Redo Exercise 12 using an exact year consisting of 365 days.

3.2 Comparing Investment Alternatives

Equation 3.4 relates the principal amounts at two points in time– the present, when the principal is first deposited, and its value in the future. The reason these values differ is due to the interest that is earned.

In this section we will rewrite and use this Equation 3.4 in two different ways to emphasize this time relationship. To do this, a new notation is introduced that emphasizes the two unique usages. The first usage is to emphasize the equation's use in determining $P(n)$, the future value of the initial principal amount, given that we know $P(0)$. The second usage is to emphasize the equation's use in determining the initial amount deposited, that is $P(0)$, given that we know $P(n)$, its future value. In financial applications this second usage is typically much more important when comparing investment alternatives.

Calculating the Future Values of Investment Alternatives

For convenience we first reproduce Equation 3.4, so that we can rewrite it using a notation used almost exclusively in financial applications. The advantage of this new notation is that it clearly relates the values of the principal amounts at two differing points in time, the present and the future.

$$P(n) = (1 + i)^n P(0) \qquad\qquad\qquad \text{(Eq. 3.4)}$$

Financially, $P(0)$, the initial principal, is referred to as the *present value of the principal*, or *present value*, for short. The notation used for this quantity is *PV*. Similarly, $P(n)$, which denotes the value of this money sometime in the future, is referred to as the *future value of the principal*, or *future value*, for short. The notation used for this quantity is *FV*. Note that this notation emphasizes what these quantities actually represent in time (now and in the future), as opposed to their strictly mathematical relationship.

Using this new notation, Equation 3.4 is rewritten as:

$$FV = (1 + i)^n PV$$

(Eq. 3.5)

Figure 3.2 illustrates the relationship provided by Equation 3.5.

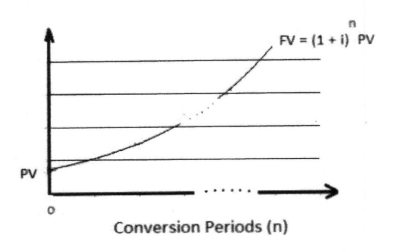

FIGURE 3.2

Realize that, mathematically, Equations 3.4 and 3.5 are identical. The notation used in Equation 3.5, however, reinforces the time dependences and is the predominate one used in almost all financial applications. Thus, given the present value of a single investment amount, denoted as PV, and the interest rate per conversion period, i, Equation 3.5 is used to calculate the future value of this investment n conversion periods later, exactly in the same manner as Equation 3.4 was used in the prior section. The relationship illustrated in Figure 3.2 is frequently referred to as **the time value of money**; that is, the value of any money received is relative to the time period in which it is received. Another way of looking at this is that a dollar received a year from now is not equivalent to a dollar received today. The reason is that a dollar received today can be placed in an interest earning account, so that it will be worth more in the future.

Equation 3.5 is particularly important when there are several different ways to invest the same amount of money and we must determine which one of the choices will be the most profitable. For example, suppose we have $10,000 in available cash and are invited to invest this money in a land venture with an expected return of $12,000 in 5 ½ years. If we decide against the land venture, we can deposit our money in an account with a guaranteed interest of 3% per year compounded quarterly. What should we do?

To answer this question based on monetary values, we must compare the amounts each investment will return at the *same point in time,* in this case after 5 ½ years. The future value of the land venture is fixed at $12,000. What is the future value of the money if it is deposited in the interest bearing account?

Because the interest is compounded quarterly, the applicable interest rate, i is $0.03/4 = 0.0075$ per quarter. Thus, the present value of our investment, PV, is $10,000, and we seek the future value, FV, after $n = 22$ quarters. Using Equation 3.5 the future value of the investment is calculated as:

$$FV = (1 + 0.0075)^{22}(\$10,000) = (1.1787667)(\$10,000) = \$11,787.67.$$

Clearly the land venture, on a purely monetary basis, is a more profitable investment by $212.33.[††††]

Example 1 Mr. James' barber would like Mr. James to lend him $6,000 for the modernization of his barber shop. The barber promises to pay Mr. James $6,500 at the end of 2 years. How does this investment compare with investing the same money in corporate bonds for 2 years at 4% compounded semiannually?

Solution At the end of 2 years, the future value of the barber shop investment is $6,500. To determine the future value of $6,000 in corporate bonds, we use Equation 3.5 with $i = 0.04/2 = 0.02$, $n = 4$, and $PV = \$6,000$. Then,

$$FV = (1 + 0.02)^{4}(\$6,000) = (1.082432)(\$6,000) = \$6,494.59.$$

Therefore, from a strictly monetary standpoint, the barber shop investment offers the greater future value at the end of 2 years by $5.41. From an investment standpoint these two returns are essentially the same, so from a strictly financial point of view, the decision, should be made on risk – that is, the investment with the least risk in terms of Mr. James actually receiving the final payment is preferable.

Example 2 Ms. Everet has $10,000 to deposit. One bank offers 1.5% interest compounded annually, while a second bank offers 1.25% interest compounded monthly. Which bank should she choose if she wants the greatest return after 4 years?

[††††] This does not consider the relative risk of each investment, which is referred to as the *credit risk.*

Solution To determine the future value of $10,000 at the first bank we use Equation 3.5 with $i = 0.015$, $n = 4$, and $PV = \$10,000$. Then

$FV = (1 + 0.015)^4(\$10,000) = (1.061364)(\$10,000) = \$10,613.64.$

To determine the future value of $1,000 at the second bank, we use Equation 3.5 with $i = 0.0125 /12$, $n = 48$, and $PV = \$10,000$. Then,

$FV = (1 + 0.0125/12)^{48}(\$10,000) = (1.051244)(\$10,000) = \$10,512.44.$

Ms. Everet will do better at the first bank.

Calculating the Present Values of Investment Alternatives

Equation 3.5 gives the future value of money in terms of the present value. In a variety of financial situations, the amount of money either needed in the future, or known to be available in the future is given, and its equivalent value today is required. For example, one might desire a specific amount of money in the future for college tuition or for a down payment on a house and want to know how much money this represents today. Or the return in the future from an investment might be known, and its equivalent value today is desired.

Solving for present values when future values are known is actually very common in financial decision making; much more common, in fact then solving for future values given present values. For these situations, Equation 3.5 is rewritten to more easily solve for the present values. Dividing both sides of Equation 3.5 by $(1 + i)^n$, we obtain

$PV = FV / (1 + i)^n$

or

(Eq. 3.6)

$$PV = (1 + i)^{-n} FV$$

Equation 3.6 gives the present value of a sum of money in terms of its future value.

Example 3 Determine the present value of $15,000 due in 5 years at 5% compounded annually.

Solution Here we have no money available in the present but we will receive $15,000 in the future. Therefore FV = $15,000. Substituting this value into Equation 3.6, with n = 5, and i = 0.05 yields

$$PV = (1 + 0.05)^{-5}(\$15,000) = 0.783526\,(\$15,000) = \$11,752.89.$$

The present value is the amount required *now* that, dollar for dollar, is equivalent to the stated future value. It follows from Example 3 that $11,752.89 now is equivalent to $15,000 in 5 years if the funds are placed in an account that pays 5% compounded annually. In other words, if $11,752,89 is invested today at 5% compounded annually, it will grow to $15,000 in 5 years.

Example 4 Mr. Kakowski's bank is offering 10-year secured certificates of deposit at 2% interest compounded quarterly. Certificates can be purchased in $100 amounts with a minimum deposit of $1,000. How much should Mr. Kakowski invest now if he wants a final return of $20,000 in ten years?

Solution We are given FV = $20,000, n = 40 and i = 0.02/4 = 0.005, and we seek the PV. Substituting these values into Equation 3.6, we obtain

$$PV = (1 + 0.005)^{-40}(\$20,000) = (0.81913886)(\$20,000) = \$16,382.77$$

Because certificates can be purchased in $100 lots only, Mr. Kakowski would need to invest $16,400 now.

Often one has to choose between several different investment opportunities each having a known future value. For example, is an investment that returns $50,000 at the end of 8 years better than one that returns $43,500 at the end of 5 years? In problems such as these the potential profits of each investment must be compared at the same point in time before an appropriate decision can be made. Because the present is a common point in time for all investments, no matter when in the future they provide a return, present values are almost always used in making such comparisons. In doing so, Equation 3.6 is used to convert all future values, no matter when they occur, to the present.

Example 5: Mr. Kingsley plans to sell his bakery and retire. Two of his employees wish to buy the bakery, but they do not have any immediate cash. They expect to make money from operating the bakery, so each makes an offer. Employee A wants the business for $50,000 payable at the end of 8 years. Employee B wants the business for $44,500 due at the end of 5 years. Which offer is better at an interest rate of 4% per year?

Solution Because each offer provides a return at a different date in the future, simply comparing the $50,000 to the $44,500 is not valid. To make a valid comparison both offers must be evaluated at the same point of time. By convention, this time is taken to be the present. Thus, we must translate each offer to its present value and then compare them.

Employee A's offer:

$$PV = (1 + 0.04)^{-8}(\$50,000)$$
$$= (0.730690)(\$50,000) = \$36,534.50$$

Employee B's offer:

$$PV = (1 + 0.04)^{-5}(\$44,500)$$
$$= (0.821927)(\$44,500) = \$36,575.75$$

Because the present value of employee B's offer is higher, it is the better offer.[‡‡‡‡] Here the present value represents the equivalent cash settlement *now*. That is, $50,000 due in 8 years is equivalent to receiving $36,534.51 today, assuming that the funds can be invested at 4%. Similarly, $44,500 due in 5 years is equivalent to $36,575.75 now; again assuming a 4% investment rate. Thus, what might appear to be the lower offer ($44,500) is actually the better offer.

Example 6: The Die-Cast Corporation has three offers for its die-casting equipment. The first buyer is willing to purchase the equipment for $50,000, payable at the end of 8 years. The second buyer is willing to spend $39,000, consisting of an immediate payment of $14,000 now and $25,000 due in 6 years. The third buyer will purchase the equipment for $35,000 payable immediately. Determine the best offer for the equipment assuming all potential purchasers can meet their obligations and the Die-Cast Corporation can deposit all money received in an interest bearing account that pays 5% interest annually.

Solution Because each offer matures at a different date, we first compute their respective monetary values at the present time (*PVs*).

First buyer:

$$PV = (1 + 0.05)^{-8}(\$50,000)$$

[‡‡‡‡] Again, this is strictly on a monetary basis, and does not taking into account any other factors, such as the relative risk between the two employees.

$$= (0.676839)(\$50,000) = \$33,841.95.$$

Second buyer:

$$PV = (1 + 0.05)^{-6}(25,000) + \$14,000$$
$$= (0.746215)(\$25,000) + \$14,000$$
$$= \$18,655.38 + \$14,000 = \$32,655.38$$

Third buyer:

$$PV = \$35,000.$$

The third offer is best, because its present value is the highest.

Section 3.2 Exercises

Future Value Problems:

1. Determine the future value of $5,000 after 10 years if it is deposited in an account that pays 4%
   a. annually
   b. semi-annually
   c. quarterly
   d. daily (assume each year consists of 365 days)

2. Determine the future value of $12,000 after 5 years at 2% interest compounded
   a. annually
   b. semi-annually

3. Determine the future value of $12,000 after 7 years at 5% interest compounded quarterly.

4. Determine the future value of $8,000 after 10 years at 1.5% interest compounded semiannually.

5. A man has $1,000 to deposit. Should he put it in a bank offering 2% interest compounded quarterly or one offering 4% interest compounded annually?

6. Ms. Field's financial advisor has recommended that she invest $20,000 in a new housing development with an anticipated return of $28,000 in 6 years. The advisor claims that this is a better investment than investing her money in an account that pays 6% interest compounded annually. Is the advisor correct?

7. Ms. Wilson has $2,000 to invest. Either she can deposit this money in a time savings plan that will pay 1.5% annual interest or she can lend the money to a friend who will repay her $750 at the end of each year for the next 3 years. Which opportunity is more profitable assuming that interest rates remain at their current level?

8. For Exercise 7, determine the more profitable opportunity if the interest rate is 8% annually.

Present Value Problems:

9. Determine the present value of $15,000 due in 8 years at
   a. 2% interest compounded annually.
   b. 4% interest compounded annually
   c. 8% interest compounded annually.
   d. Based on the present values determined in parts a. through c. what can you say is the relationship between present values and the interest rate?

10. With the birth of their son, the Boswells decide to deposit a sum of money in government bonds paying 3% annual interest compounded annually. Their objective is to accumulate enough money to provide the son with $20,000 at his 18th birthday. Determine the amount that they should invest now in order to meet their objective.

11. How much money should be deposited in a Certificate of Deposit that pays 4% compounded semi-annually if the desired objective is $10,000 after 4½ years?

12. With the birth of their daughter, the Tucks decides to place a sum of money in an account which yields 3.5% compounded semiannually. If the objective is to accumulate $30,000 for their daughter's twenty-first birthday, determine the amount of the deposit. How much money will be available if the Tuck's give the money to their daughter on her twenty-fifth birthday?

13. Dr. Baxter has $10,000 for investment purposes. She can put it into a friend's business with an expected return of $12,000 in 3 years, or she can invest it in an account that pays 4% interest compounded quarterly. Which opportunity is the most profitable?

14. Mr. Jones has two buyers for his business. Buyer A will pay $10,000 immediately and another $25,000 in 7 years. Buyer B will pay $8,000 immediately and another $27,000 in 5 years. Which is the better offer if the interest rates are 3% compounded annually?

15. A small business owner has three buyers for his business. Buyer A will pay $20,000 now and another $5,000 at the end of 4 years. Buyer B will pay $15,000 now and another $10,000 at the end of 3 years. Buyer C will pay $10,000 now and another $18,000 at the end of 6 years. Which is the best offer if the interest rate is 4% compounded annually?

16. An individual has three possible opportunities for investing the same amount of money. The first will return $8,000 in 4 years, the second will return $7,000 in 2 years, and the third will return $10,000 in 7 years. Which opportunity is the most attractive if the interest rate is 2% compounded annually?

17. Redo Exercise 16 with an interest rate of 6% compounded annually.

Interest Rate Problems

18. Solve Equation 3.5 for i and show that
$$i = \left(\frac{FV}{PV}\right)^{1/n} - 1.$$

19. Using the results from Exercise 18, determine the annual interest rate required to convert $1,000 to $1,350 in 3 years.

20. Using the results from Exercise 18, determine the annual interest rate required to convert $10,000 to $15,000 in 10 years.

21. Using the results from Exercise 18, determine the annual interest rate required to double an investment after 10 years.

3.3 Net Present Values of Cash Flows

In both Sections 3.1 and 3.2 we concerned ourselves with single sum payments, which are frequently referred to as **lump sum** investments. Thus, we either calculated the future value of a lump sum invested now, or we calculated the present value of a lump sum payment to be made in the future. In this section we consider investments consisting of a *set* of payments due at *different* times, a situation known as a **cash flow**.

As an example of a cash flow problem, consider an investment that will return $500 in 1 year, another $300 in 3 years, and a final $400 in 4 years, with interest rates of 5% compounded annually. What is the present value of such an opportunity? That is, what is the cash equivalent now of the entire transaction?

A simple approach is to compute the present value of each of the individual payments using Equation 3.6, repeated below for convenience, and then sum the individual present values to obtain the present value of the entire cash flow.

$$PV = (1 + i)^{-n}\, FV \qquad\qquad\qquad \text{(Eq. 3.6)}$$

Example 1 Compute the present value of the cash flow that return $500 in 1 year, another $300 in 3 years, and a final $400 in 4 years, with interest rates of 5% compounded annually.

Solution The first payment of $500 is due in 1 year. The present value of this amount, computed using Equation 3.6 is

$$PV_1 = (1 + 0.05)^{-1}(\$500) = \$476.19.$$

The second payment of $300 is due in 3 years. Again using Equation 3.6, we find its present value as

$$PV_2 = (1 + 0.05)^{-3}(\$300) = \$259.15.$$

Similarly, the present value of the last payment is

$$PV_3 = (1 + 0.05)^{-4}(400) = \$329.08.$$

Summing these three present values, we obtain the present value of the entire investment as

$PV = PV_1 + PV_2 + PV_3 = \$476.19 + \$259.15 + \$329.08 = \$1{,}064.42.$

In most present-value problems, a *time diagram* illustrating the contributions to the total present value from the individual payments is helpful. The time diagram for the cash flow given in Example 1 is shown as Figure 3.3.

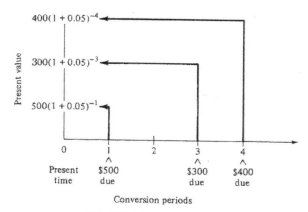

FIGURE 3.3

This approach of summing individual present values is the general procedure for calculating present values of all cash flows. Simply use Equation 3.6 to find the present values of each payment and then sum the results. One modification, however, is usual. Rather than finding the present value, it is more common to find the **net present value** which is the present value *minus* the cost of the investment. The net present value measures the additional money over and above the cost of the investment, which would have to be deposited in a bank to equal the returns guaranteed by the investment. The net present value, which is also referred to as the *discounted cash flow* (this is an older term) is obtained as:

$Net\ PV = \sum PV\ of\ all\ cash\ inflows - \sum PV\ of\ all\ cash\ outflows$ (Eq. 3.7)

Example 2 Ms. Tilson invests \$1,000 in a friend's business. In return, her friend promises to pay Ms. Tilson \$500 in a year, another \$300 in 3 years, and an additional \$400 in 4 years. Determine the net present value of this investment if the current interest rate is 5% compounded annually.

Solution We previously calculated the present value of this investment as \$1,064.42. Because the investment costs \$1,000, the net present value is

Net PV = \$1,064.42 - \$1,000.00 = \$64.42.

Example 3 Determine the net present values of the following two investments using an interest rate of 2% per annum compounded quarterly. The first is a $5,000 investment which returns $1,500 every year for the next 5 years while the second is a $4,500 investment which returns $2,000 every other year for the next 8 years.

Solution First, because the interest is compounded quarterly, we take one-quarter of a year as our basic time unit and $i = 0.02/4 = 0.005$. Time diagrams for both investments are given in Figures 3.4 and 3.5, respectively.

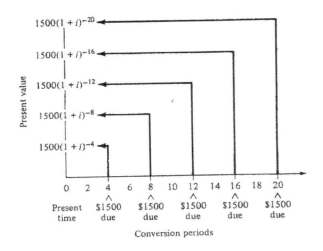

FIGURE 3.4

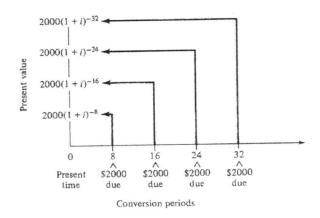

FIGURE 3.5

The individual present values for the first investment are:

$(1 + 0.005)^{-4}$ ($1,500$) = $1,470.37
$(1 + 0.005)^{-8}$ ($1,500$) = 1,441.33
$(1 + 0.005)^{-12}$ ($1,500$) = 1,412.86
$(1 + 0.005)^{-16}$ ($1,500$) = 1,384.95
$(1 + 0.005)^{-20}$ ($1,500$) = 1,357.59
$$\text{Total} = \$7,067.10$$

Because the cost of participating in this investment is $5,000, the net present value is:

Net PV = $7,067.10 - $5,000 = $2,067.10.

The individual present values for the second investment are:

$(1 + 0.005)^{-8}$ ($2,000$) = $1,921.77
$(1 + 0.005)^{-16}$ ($2,000$) = 1,846.60
$(1 + 0.005)^{-24}$ ($2,000$) = 1,774.37
$(1 + 0.005)^{-32}$ ($2,000$) = 1,704.97
$$\text{Total} = \$7,247.71$$

Because the cost of participating in the second investment is $4,500, the net present value is:

Net PV = $7,247.71 - $4,500 = $2,747.71.

As the second investment has the higher net present value, it is the more attractive investment. Again, this is based strictly on a monetary analysis and assumes the credit risk of both investments are equal.

The type of cash flow illustrated in Figures 3.4 and 3.5, where the same monetary amount is received at equal periods of time, occur quite frequently in a number of practical investment situations. For a specific type of cash flow, where the conversion periods and payment dates coincide, single formulas exist for directly computing both the cash flows' present and future values. We turn to these cash flows in the next section.

Section 3.3 Exercises

1. Mr. Samuels is invited to invest $2,500 in a venture that will return $750 in 1 year, another $1,100 in 2 years, and a final $2000 in 4 years. Determine whether or not this is a profitable investment if current interest rates are 2% per annum compounded annually.

2. The guaranteed returns of three different investment opportunities are listed in Table 3.4. Which one is the most desirable at an annual interest rate of 3% compounded quarterly if each investment requires an initial cash outlay of $2,400?

TABLE 3.4

	Guaranteed Returns				
	In 1 year	In 2 years	In 3 years	In 4 years	In 5 years
Investment A	$1,000	$1,000	$1,000	$1,000	$1,000
Investment B	0	$2,500	0	0	$2,500
Investment C	$600	$800	$2,200	$800	$600

3. Determine the net present value of an opportunity that costs $2,900 and will return $500 in half a year, $1,000 in a year and a quarter, and $2,000 in 3 years if the current interest rate is 2.5% per annum compounded monthly.

4. A man can invest $50,000 now and receive $12,000 at the end of each six-months for the next 2 years plus an additional $12,000 at the end of the second year, or he can invest $70,000 now and receive $21,000 at the end of each six months for the next 2 years. Which opportunity is the most attractive at 4% interest per annum compounded semi-annually?

3.4 Ordinary Annuities

The present and future values of a cash flow can always be determined by calculating the present or future values, respectively, of each individual payment using the appropriate equation – either Equation 3.8 or 3.9 – and then summing the results.

$$PV = (1 + i)^{-n}\, FV$$

(Eq. 3.8)

or

$$FV = (1 + i)^n\, PV$$

(Eq. 3.9)

For a specific type of investment, however, known as an *annuity*, the final sum can be calculated using a single formula.

Definition 3.1 An *annuity* is a set of equal payments made at equal intervals of time.

Car loans, mortgages, life insurance premiums, social security payments, and bond coupon payments are all examples of annuities. In each, one party, be it an individual, company, or government, pays to another party a set of equal payments, called *periodic installments* or *rents*, denoted as R, at equal periods of time, called *rent period, payment intervals, or conversion periods*. Each of these terms can be used interchangeably.

Annuities are classified as either *ordinary* or *due*. With an ordinary annuity, payments are made at the end of each payment period, whereas with an annuity due, payments are made at the beginning of each period. Examples of ordinary annuities are car loan payments, mortgages, and bond coupon payments. Examples of annuities due are typically savings plans, pension plans, and lottery winnings that are paid over time.

An annuity is *simple* if the conversion period at which interest is paid coincides with the payment dates. In this section we consider simple ordinary annuities; simple annuities due are presented in Section 3.5.

Present Value of an Ordinary Annuity

Figure 3.6 illustrates a typical ordinary annuity, with R dollars due each conversion period for the next n periods, and where the present value of the complete cash flow is desired.

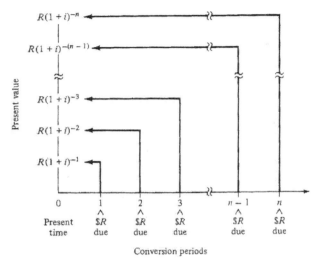

FIGURE 3.6

As shown in Figure 3.6, the present value of the ordinary annuity illustrated is given by:

$$PV = R(1 + i)^{-1} + R(1 + i)^{-2} + R(1 + i)^{-3} + \ldots + R(1 + i)^{-(n-1)} + R(1 + i)^{-n} \qquad \text{(Eq . 3.10)}$$

Note that each term containing R represents the present value of *one* of the future payments. In particular, $R(1 + i)^{-1}$ is the present value of the first payment, $R(1 + i)^{-2}$ is the present value of the second payment, and $R(1 + i)^{-n}$ is the present value of the last payment. Factoring R from these terms, we have

$$PV = R[(1 + i)^{-1} + (1 + i)^{-2} + (1+ i)^{-3} + \ldots + (1 + i)^{-(n-1)} + (1 + i)^{-n}] \qquad \text{(Eq. 3.11)}$$

The terms in brackets are a geometric series, whose sum can be written as:

$$\left[\frac{1 - (1 + i)^{-n}}{i} \right]$$

Thus, the Present Value becomes

116

$$PV = R \left[\frac{1-(1+i)^{-n}}{i} \right]$$ (Eq. 3.12)

If the net present value is required, which takes into account the amount paid to receive the stream of income shown in Figure 3.4, all that is required is to subtract out this initial payment, denoted as C_0. That is,

$$NPV = R \left[\frac{1-(1+i)^{-n}}{i} \right] - C_0$$ (Eq. 3.13)

Example 1 Determine the value of

$$\left[\frac{1-(1+0.07)^{-15}}{0.07} \right]$$

Solution Using a calculator, the value of this term is determined as

$$\left[\frac{1-(1+0.07)^{-15}}{0.07} \right] = \left[\frac{1-0.36244602}{.07} \right] = \frac{.63755398}{.07} = 9.107914$$

Example 2 Determine the value of

$$\left[\frac{1-(1+0.005)^{-120}}{0.005} \right]$$

Solution

$$\left[\frac{1-(1+0.005)^{-120}}{0.005} \right] = \left[\frac{1-.54963273}{0.005} \right] = \left[\frac{.45036727}{0.005} \right] = 90.073453$$

Example 3 Determine the present value of an investment that returns $25 every month for the next 4 years at 2% compounded monthly.

Solution Using Equation 3.12 with $i = 0.02/12$, $n = 48$, and $R = \$25$ we have

$$PV = \$25 \left[\frac{1 - \left(1 + \frac{0.02}{12}\right)^{-48}}{\frac{0.02}{12}} \right] = \$25 \left[\frac{1 - 0.92317782}{\frac{0.02}{12}} \right]$$

$$= \$25 \left[\frac{0.07682218}{0.02/12} \right] = \$25[46.093308] = \$1,152.33$$

Example 4 Determine the net present value of an investment costing $900 that will return $45 every quarter for the next 5 and ½ years if current interest rates are 4% per annum compounded quarterly.

Solution Because interest rates are compounded quarterly, we take one-quarter of a year as our basic time period. Then $i = 0.04/4 = 0.01$ Here R = $45, n = 22, and C_o = $900. Using Equation 3.14, we calculate

$$Net\ PV = \$45 \left[\frac{1 - \left(1 + \frac{0.04}{4}\right)^{-22}}{\frac{0.04}{4}} \right] - \$900$$

$$= \$45 \left[\frac{1 - 0.80339621}{\frac{0.04}{4}} \right] - \$900$$

$$= \$45 \left[\frac{0.19660379}{0.01} \right] - \$900$$

$$= \$45[19.660379] - \$900$$

$$= \$884.72 - \$900 = -\$15.28,$$

which is negative. A negative NPV indicates the investment results in a loss. Here, putting the $900 in a bank at 4% compounded quarterly for 5 ½ years yields $900 (1 + .04/4)^{22} = \$900 (1.244716) = \$1,120.24$. Obviously, it is more profitable *not to* partake in the investment and simply deposit the available cash in an account paying the stated rate of 4%.

Equations 3.12 and 3.13 are relatively easy to use when they apply, however, one must be careful to apply them correctly. **First**, *these equations are valid only if the payment dates and the conversion dates coincide.* This is not the case, for example, in Example 2 of the prior section, where the first investment has four conversion dates between successive payment dates, and the second investment has eight conversion dates between successive payment dates. **Second**, *the payments must all be equal.* **Third**, *one must remember that i denotes the rate per conversion period*, which generally is not the annual rate, and that n denotes the number of conversion periods in the investment, which usually differs from the number of years of the investment. Nonetheless, when Equations 3.12 and 3.13 are applicable, they save a good deal of work. It even can be combined with Equation 3.7 to determine net present values of investments involving both time and single lump sum payments.

Example 5: Dr. Ericson plans to invest in a corporate bond that returns $20 in dividends every half-year for the next 20 years plus an additional $1,000 at the end of the twentieth year. Determine the total present value of this investment if interest rates are 3% per annum compounded semiannually?

Solution We separate the problem into two parts: one involving the $20 payments, and the other involving the $1,000 final payment. We find the total present value by first calculating the present value of each part of the investment, and then summing to obtain the total present value.

The dividend payments represent an ordinary annuity.[§§§§] Thus, the present value of the dividend cash flow is obtained from Equation 3.12. Here $R = 20$, $n = 40$, and $i = 0.03/2 = 0.015$. Therefore,

$$PV = \$20 \left[\frac{1 - \left(1 + \frac{0.03}{2}\right)^{-40}}{\frac{0.03}{2}} \right] = \$20 \left[\frac{1 - 0.55126232}{0.015} \right]$$

$$= \$20 \left[\frac{0.44873768}{0.015} \right] = \$20[29.91584533] = \$598.32$$

The present value of the $1,000 lump sum payment due in 20 years or 40 half-years can be obtained directly from Equation 3.6.

$$PV = (1 + 0.015)^{-40}(\$1,000) = (0.55126232)(\$1,000) = \$551.26.$$

Therefore, the total present value of the entire transaction is

---

[§§§§] This is true for the majority of all corporate and government issued bonds.

$PV = \$598.32 + \$551.26 = \$1,149.58$

Example 6: Redo Example 5 if the interest rate is 6%

Solution Applying the same calculations as in Example 5, the total present value of the entire cash flow (\$20 annuity payments plus the final \$1,000 payment is:

$PV = \$462.30 + \$306.56 = \$768.86$

Note that at the higher interest rate, the present value is less than it is at the lower interest rate.

Commentary: Financially, the present value of a bond represents its price, and what is being paid for is a stream of income from the coupons and the return of the initial principal. Examples 5 and 6 illustrate the fundamental inverse relationship between bond prices and interest rates; that is, *if interest rates rise the price of a bond falls, and if interest rates fall the price of the bond rises*. The reason is that the coupon payment is fixed when the bond is issued. Because the coupon payment amounts are fixed, the interest rate an investor receives when the bond is subsequently traded, is adjusted by paying more or less for the fixed income stream, depending on the current interest rate.

A second adjustment made to a bond's price occurs when the bond is purchased on a non-coupon payment date. In these cases, which form the majority of bond trading, the price of the bond (its present value) is determined at the next closest coupon payment date, and the buyer pays the seller the portion of the coupon payment for the time the seller owned the bond. This prorated portion of the coupon payment is referred to as *accrued interest*.

Future Value of an Ordinary Annuity

Figure 3.7 illustrates the calculations required for calculating the future value of an ordinary annuity. Because it is an ordinary annuity, the equal payments, R, are due at the end of every conversion period for the next n periods Notice that the payment schedule shown on the x-axis is the same payment schedule as previously shown in Figure 3.6, except that now we are determining the future value, rather than the present value of the payments. Investment plans to which equal contributions are made at the end of each period, and for which a future amount is desired, are typical of this type of time diagram.

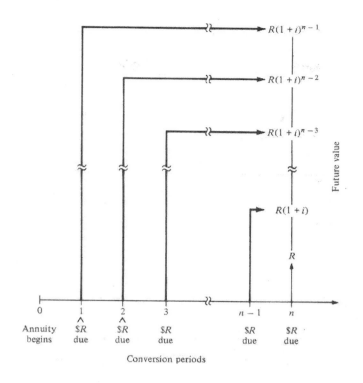

FIGURE 3.7

As shown in Figure 3.7, the future value of the payments at the end of the nth period is obtained by finding the future value of each individual payment and then summing the results. Thus,

$$FV = R + R(1 + i) + R(1 + i)^2 + \ldots + R(1 + i)^{n-3} + R(1 + i)^{n-2} + R(1 + i)^{n-1}$$

Factoring R from this equation, we have

$$FV = R\,[\,1 + (1 + i) + (1 + i)^2 + \ldots + (1 + i)^{n-3} + (1 + i)^{n-2} + (1 + i)^{n-1}\,] \qquad \text{(Eq. 3.14)}$$

The terms in brackets are a geometric series, whose sum can be written as:

$$\left[\frac{(1 + i)^n - 1}{i}\right]$$

Thus, the Future Value becomes

$$FV = R\left[\frac{(1+i)^n - 1}{i}\right]$$ (Eq. 3.15)

Example 7: Isabel Johnson decides to save for a new computer tablet by depositing $30 at the end of each month in an account that pays 1.2% interest compounded monthly. How much will she have at the end of six months?

Solution A time diagram for this situation is given in Figure 3.8.
The payments are due at the end of each period, hence, this is an example of an ordinary annuity. Observe that because the first payment is not made until the end of the first month, it will draw interest for only 5 months. Similarly, the last payment, made at the end of the 6-month interval of interest, will draw no interest, but will, of course, contribute to the final sum. Using Equation 3.15 with $i = 0.012/12 = 0.01$, $R = \$30$, and $n = 6$, we compute

$$FV = \$30\left[\frac{(1 + 0.01)^6 - 1}{0.01}\right]$$

$$= \$30\left[\frac{(1.06152015) - 1}{0.01}\right]$$

$$= \$30\,[6.152015]$$

$$= \$184.56$$

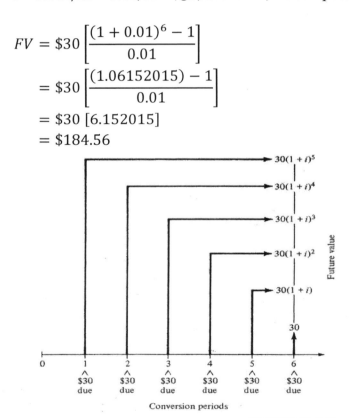

FIGURE 3.8

Section 3.4 Exercises

Present and Net Present Value Exercises

1. Determine the present value of a $50 return every quarter for the next 10 years at 4% annual interest compounded quarterly.

2. Mrs. Wilson has $1,500 to invest. Determine the NPV of her investment if she lends the money to a friend who repays her $750 at the end of each year for the next 3 years. Use an annual interest rate of 3.5%.

3. Determine the NPV of the investment described in Exercise 2 if the annual interest rate is 8%.

4. Ms. Johnson is offered two investment opportunities. The first will return $500 at the end of the year for the next 20 years, while the second will return $1,000 at the end of the year for the next 7 years. Which is more profitable at an annual interest rate of 6%?

5. A woman can invest $70,000 now and receive $2,000 at the end of each month for the next 2 years plus an additional $38,000 at the end of the second year, or she can invest the $70,000 now and receive $3,500 at the end of each month for the next 2 years. Which opportunity is the most profitable at 4% annual interest per annum compounded monthly?

6. Determine the present value of an investment that will return $500 at the end of each year for the next 15 years at an annual interest rate of 3%.

7. A man can initially invest $20,000 and receive $2,300 at the end of each quarter for the next 3 years, or he can invest $18,000 now and receive $1,500 at the end of each quarter for the next 4 years. Which opportunity is more profitable at an annual interest rate of 4% compounded quarterly?

8. A bond pays $50 every six months. How much should you pay for the bond (that is, what is its present value) if you want a 4% return on your money and the bond has ten payments left. Additionally, on the tenth payment you will also receive $1,000, which is the original price of the bond.

9. A bond pays $80 every six months. How much should you pay for the bond (that is, what is its present value) if you want a 6% return on your money and

the bond has twenty payments left. Additionally, on the twentieth payment you will also receive $1,000, which is the original price of the bond.

Future Value Exercises

10. Determine the future value of an ordinary annuity in which $1,000 is deposited at the end of each year for 10 years at 4% annual interest compounded annually.

11. Determine the future value of an ordinary annuity in which $400 is deposited at the end of each quarter for 3 years at 4% annual interest compounded quarterly.

12. Determine the future value of an ordinary annuity in which $100 is deposited at the end of each month for three years at 2% interest compounded monthly.

13. Mr. Hamedi deposits $20 at the end of each week in an account at 5% annual interest compounded weekly. How much money will he have to spend on holiday gifts when he takes the money out at the end of 48 weeks.

14. To provide for her child's education, a mother deposits $1,000 every June 30 and December 31 for 17 years. Determine the value of the annuity just after her last payment, which occurs on December 31, if her investment plan pays 4% annual interest compounded semiannually.

3.5 Mortgages and Amortization

A mortgage on a house or land is one of the most common types of ordinary annuities. The mortgage is a loan used to pay for the property, with the property serving as collateral for the loan. This gives the lender, known as the *mortgagor*, a claim on the property should the borrower, known as the *mortgagee*, default on paying the mortgage. Full title to the property is only transferred to the mortgagee when the loan is fully paid.

In a traditional fixed-rate mortgage the monthly payment and interest rate are fixed for the life of the mortgage. Each payment is used to pay both the interest and principal for the loan. First, the monthly interest charge on the loan is determined and paid, with the remaining portion of the monthly payment applied to paying off the loan.*****

Although the monthly payment is fixed, the interest due changes each month, decreasing with every payment. This occurs because the interest due is computed anew each month on the unpaid balance of the loan. As the loan gets paid off, the unpaid balance decreases, which means that the interest due each month also decreases. Thus, each month more and more of the payment gets applied to paying off the loan. This method of payment is commonly referred to as the United States Rule.

The main consideration with mortgages is to determine the amount of the monthly payment, which depends on the original amount of the loan, the interest rate, and the length of the loan. For all mortgages that adhere to the United States Rule, the payment, R, is determined as

$$R = \frac{PV}{\left[\dfrac{1 - (1 + i)^{-n}}{i}\right]} \qquad\qquad \text{(Eq. 3.16)}$$

where:
R = the monthly payment
PV = the original amount of the loan
i = the monthly interest rate = (the annual interest rate) / 12
n = the length of the loan, in months, = 12 * (the number of years of the loan)

Notice that Equation 3.16 is the same as Equation 3.12, except that it is used to solve for the value of R given PV, rather than solving for PV given the value of R.

Example 1 Mr. Johnson receives a $100,000 mortgage for 30 years at 4% annual interest. Determine his monthly payment.

Solution Twenty years corresponds to n = (12)(30) = 360 months, and the monthly interest rate is i = 0.04/12. Substituting these values into Equation 3.16, with the initial amount of the loan, PV = $100,000, we find

---

***** With adjustable-rate mortgages, known as ARMs, the interest rate is only fixed for an initial term, but then fluctuates with market interest rates. This provides an initially lower monthly payment than that of a traditional fixed-rate mortgage, but makes the monthly payments unpredictable after the initial term.

$$R = \frac{\$100,000.}{\left[\frac{1-\left(1+\frac{0.04}{12}\right)^{-360}}{\left(\frac{0.04}{12}\right)}\right]} = \frac{\$100,000.}{\left[\frac{1-0.3017959}{\left(\frac{0.04}{12}\right)}\right]}$$

$$= \frac{\$100,000.}{\left[\frac{.6982041}{\left(\frac{0.04}{12}\right)}\right]} = \frac{\$100,000.}{209.46123} = \$477.42$$

Example 2 Mr. Kokowski has agreed to sell a small piece of his property to his neighbor Mr. Brown for $50,000. They agree that Mr. Brown will pay this amount in monthly payments over the next 5 years at 6% interest. How much will each payment be?

Solution Here PV = $50,000, i = 0.06/12 = 0.005, and n = (5)(12) = 60. Using Equation 3.16, we calculate the monthly payment, R, to be

$$R = \frac{\$50,000.}{\left[\frac{1-(1+0.005)^{-60}}{(0.005)}\right]} = \frac{\$50,000.}{\left[\frac{1-0.74137220}{(0.005)}\right]}$$

$$= \frac{\$50,000.}{\left[\frac{0.25862780}{0.005}\right]} = \frac{\$50,000.}{51.72556} = \$966.64$$

Determining Total Interest Paid

Once the monthly payment has been determined using Equation 3.16, the total interest paid on the mortgage is easily determined as follows:

Total Interest Paid $= (R * n) - PV$ (Eq. 3.17)

Example 3 Determine the total interest paid on a 30 year, 4% mortgage for a loan of $100,000.

Solution The monthly payment for this mortgage was determined to be $477.42 in Example 1. Therefore, using Equation 3.17, the total interest paid when the mortgage is completed is

Total Interest Paid = ($477.42 * 360) - $100,000.
                    = $171,871.20 - $100,000
                    = $71,871.20

Example 4 Determine the total interest paid on the mortgage described in Example 2.

Solution The monthly payment for this mortgage was determined to be $966.64. Here n = 60 and the PV = $50,000. Using Equation 3.17, the total interest paid for this mortgage is

Total Interest Paid = ($966.64 * 60) - $50,000.
                    = $57,998.40 - $50,000
                    = $7,998.40

Amortization Schedules

Amortization refers to the repayment of a loan using regular installments over a period of time. Because this is the type of payment used to repay mortgages, mortgage loans are said to *amortized*.

An *amortization schedule* is a table that shows the amount of each payment, and lists the portion of each payment that goes toward paying the interest, the portion of the payment credited against the principal and, finally, the outstanding loan balance after the payment has been made.

Table 3.5 provides an amortization schedule for a loan of $1,000 made at 5% annual interest under the United States Rule. The monthly payments for this loan, which can be verified using Equation 3.17, is $85.61.

In reviewing Table 3.5, first notice that the final outstanding balance at the end of last column is zero, which means the loan has been fully repaid. Next, notice that each payment in the second column is the same monthly payment of $85.61. This is always true, except possibly for the last payment. In general, the last payment is adjusted, if necessary, so that the balance of the loan is zero when the last payment is made. This can occur because of rounding to the nearest cent in the calculations of the monthly payment and interim balances.

Table 3.5

Amortization Scheduled for a $1,000 Loan over 12 Months at 5% Interest

Payment Number	Payment Amount	Interest Paid	Principal Paid	Outstanding Balance
0	-	-	-	$1,000.00
1	$85.61	$4.17	$81.44	$918.56
2	$85.61	$3.83	$81.78	$836.78
3	$85.61	$3.49	$82.12	$754.66
4	$85.61	$3.14	$82.46	$672.20
5	$85.61	$2.80	$82.81	$589.39
6	$85.61	$2.46	$83.15	$506.24
7	$85.61	$2.11	$83.50	$422.74
8	$85.61	$1.76	$83.85	$338.89
9	$85.61	$1.41	$84.20	$254.70
10	$85.61	$1.06	$84.55	$170.15
11	$85.61	$0.71	$84.90	$85.25
12	$85.61	$0.36	$85.25	$0.00

Now notice that the interest paid each month (the third column), decreases with each payment, while the principal paid (fourth column) increases with each payment. The values in these two columns are constructed as follows:

The interest due each month is the monthly interest rate times the outstanding balance. Because this is a 5% annual loan, the monthly interest rate, i, is $0.05/12$, and the initial outstanding balance is $1,000.

Thus, the interest for the first month is

$$I_1 = (0.05/12) \$1,000 = \$4.17$$

Because part of the monthly payment must be used to cover this interest, we are left with $85.61 - $4.17 = $81.44 as the payment applied to the loan itself. Thus, the outstanding balance at the end of the first month is

$$P_1 = \$1,000 - \$81.44 = \$918.56$$

For the second month the interest is again calculated as the monthly interest rate times the outstanding balance. Now, however, the outstanding balance is $918.56. Thus,

$$I_2 = (0.05/12) \$918.56 = \$3.83$$

and the amount of the payment that is left to be applied to paying the loan balance is $85.61 - $3.83 = $81.78. With this amount applied to the loan, the new outstanding balance at the end of the second month is

P_2 = $918.56 - $81.78 = $836.78

Continuing in this manner, the complete amortization schedule listed in Table 3.5 was generated.

Because the outstanding balance is reduced with each payment, the interest owed also declines from payment to payment, and a larger portion of each monthly payment is credited against the loan balance. For larger mortgages having a longer life than the one in this example, the size of the interest portion of each payment, especially in the first few years of the mortgage, is much more dramatic. This is illustrated in the next example.

Example 4 Calculate the first two lines of an amortization schedule for a 30 year, $100,000 loan, at an annual interest rate of 4%.

 Solution The monthly payment for this mortgage is $477.22 (see Example 1). Thus, the first month's interest is

I_1 = (0.04/12) $100,000 = $333.33.

That is, $333.33 out of the first monthly payment of $477.42 is paid as interest to the institution making the loan (this is 69.82% of the payment). This leaves ($477.42 - $333.33) = $144.09 of the payment to be applied directly to paying off the loan. Thus, the outstanding balance at the end of the first month is

P_1 = $100,000 - $144.09 = $99,855.91

The interest charge for the second month is again calculated as the monthly interest rate times the outstanding balance. Thus,

I_2 = (0.04/12) $99,855.91 = $332.85
and the amount of the payment that is applied to paying the loan balance is $477.42 - $332.85 = $144.57. When this amount applied to the loan, the new outstanding balance at the end of the second month is

P_2 = $99,855.91 - $144.57 = $99,711.34

Creating Amortization Schedules using Excel®[†††††]

Amortization schedules are extremely easy to create using Excel. One additional advantage in using this program is that it provides a payment function for directly calculating the monthly payment. Figure 3.9 shows an Excel spreadsheet for the mortgage described in Example 3.

	A	B	C	D	E	F
1	Amount of Loan:	1000				
2	Length of Loan (in years):	1				
3	Annual Interest Rate:	5%				
4	Monthly Payment:	$85.61				
5						
6			Payment Number	Payment Amount	Interest Paid	Principal Paid	Outstanding Balance
7			0				$1,000.00
8			1	$85.61	$4.17	$81.44	$918.56
9			2	$85.61	$3.83	$81.78	$836.78
10			3	$85.61	$3.49	$82.12	$754.66
11			4	$85.61	$3.14	$82.46	$672.20
12			5	$85.61	$2.80	$82.81	$589.39
13			6	$85.61	$2.46	$83.15	$506.24
14			7	$85.61	$2.11	$83.50	$422.74
15			8	$85.61	$1.76	$83.85	$338.89
16			9	$85.61	$1.41	$84.20	$254.70
17			10	$85.61	$1.06	$84.55	$170.15
18			11	$85.61	$0.71	$84.90	$85.25
19			12	$85.61	$0.36	$85.25	$0.00

FIGURE 3.9

The relevant formulas used to create the spreadsheet shown in Figure 3.9 are shown in Figure 3.10. In particular, look at the formula entered into cell B4, which uses the PMT() function. This function computes the mortgage payment that we have been calculating by hand using Equation 3.16.

The PMT() function requires three parameters; the monthly interest rate, the length of the loan, in months, and the amount of the loan. For the spreadsheet shown in Figure 3.10 the PMT( ) entry in cell B4 is

=-PMT(B3/12, B2*12, B1)

[†††††] Excel is a registered trademark of Microsoft Corporation

The reason for the negative sign in front of the PMT() function has to do with the convention of money flows. Positive values, such as the amount of the loan, are considered funds that flow *to the* borrower. Negative values indicate funds that the borrower pays; as such, they are considered funds that *flow away* from the borrower. Thus, the PMT() function will report a negative amount as the monthly payment, because this is an amount that effectively "flows away" from the borrower. To counteract this, the negative sign in front of the PMT() function forces the calculated payment to appear as a positive value.

Note also that once the formulas have been placed in Row 8, they can be copied down to the end of the spread sheet, as shown by the arrowed lines in Figure 3.10.

	A	B	C	D	E	F
1	Amount of Loan:	1000				
2	Length of Loan (in years):	1				
3	Annual Interest Rate:	0.05				
4	Monthly Payment:	=-PMT(B3/12,B2*12,B1)				
5						
6		Payment Number	Payment Amount	Interest Paid	Principal Paid	Outstanding Balance
7		0				=B1
8		1	=$B$4	=$B$3/12*F7	=C8-D8	=F7-E8
9		2	=$B$4	=$B$3/12*F8	=C9-D9	=F8-E9
10		3	=$B$4	=$B$3/12*F9	=C10-D10	=F9-E10
11		4	=$B$4	=$B$3/12*F10	=C11-D11	=F10-E11
12		5	=$B$4	=$B$3/12*F11	=C12-D12	=F11-E12
13		6	=$B$4	=$B$3/12*F12	=C13-D13	=F12-E13
14		7	=$B$4	=$B$3/12*F13	=C14-D14	=F13-E14
15		8	=$B$4	=$B$3/12*F14	=C15-D15	=F14-E15
16		9	=$B$4	=$B$3/12*F15	=C16-D16	=F15-E16
17		10	=$B$4	=$B$3/12*F16	=C17-D17	=F16-E17
18		11	=$B$4	=$B$3/12*F17	=C18-D18	=F17-E18
19		12	=$B$4	=$B$3/12*F18	=C19-D19	=F18-E19

FIGURE 3.10

Section 3.5 Exercises

1. Determine the monthly payment for a 30 year, $36,000 mortgage, having a 4% interest rate.

2. Determine the monthly payment for a 25 year, $30,000 mortgage, having an 8% interest rate.

3. Determine the total interest paid for the mortgage in Exercise 1.

4. Determine the total interest paid for the mortgage in Exercise 2.

5. Either using a calculator or Excel, determine the sum of the individual interest payments in column D of Figure 3.9 and then verify that this same sum is obtained using Equation 3.17 for this loan.

6. Mr. O'Toole agrees to sell his business to Mr. Johnson. The mortgage obtained by Mr. Johnson for this business is for $20,000 over 5 years at 5%.
   a. Determine the monthly payments.
   b. Determine the total interest paid for this mortgage
   c. Complete the first three lines of an amortization schedule for this mortgage.

7. Ms. Tilson agrees to sell some property to a friend. The mortgage obtained by the friend for this property is for $45,000 over 4 years at 4%.
   a. Determine the monthly installment.
   b. Determine the total interest paid for this mortgage
   c. Complete the first three lines of an amortization schedule for this mortgage.

8. Either by hand, or using an Excel spreadsheet, complete an amortization schedule for an $800 loan to be amortized over 1 year with monthly payments at 4% interest under the United States Rule.

9. Create an Excel spreadsheet that calculates the payment and produces the amortization schedule for the mortgage in Exercise 8.

10.Create an Excel spreadsheet that calculates the payment and produces the amortization schedule for the mortgage in Exercise 1.

3.6 Installment Loans and Interest Charges

Unlike mortgages that calculate monthly interest based on the unpaid balance of the loan, some commercial loans, such as, vacation loans, home improvement loans, and a host of other cash advances for specific purposes, can use two related but different interest determination methods. These are known as the *add-on method* and *discount method*, respectively.

Add-On Installment Loans

In the add-on method of interest and payment calculations, the total finance charge for a loan is determined as

Total Finance Charge
    = (Annual Rate) (Amount of Loan) (Length of the loan, in years)   (Eq. 3.18)

The monthly installment payment, R, is then obtained by adding the total finance charge to the amount of the loan and then dividing this result by the total number of months, n, in the life of the loan.

$$R = \frac{(Total\ finance\ charge) + (Amount\ of\ the\ loan)}{(Length\ of\ the\ loan, in\ months)} \quad\quad (Eq.\ 3.19)$$

Example 1 A $1,000 loan is negotiated for 2 years at 8% interest under the add-on method. Determine the monthly installments.

Solution Using Equation 3.18, the total finance charge is

Total Finance Charge = (.08)($1,000)(2) = $160.

Because it is a 2 year loan, the length of the loan, in months, is 24. Therefore, the monthly installment payment, R, is obtained using Equation 3.19, as

$R = ($160 + $1,000) / 24 = $1,160 / 24 = 48.33

If the borrower in this example thinks he is paying 8% interest for his loan, he is badly mistaken. In fact, he is paying a good deal more. To determine the actual interest, we can use Equation 3.12., which is repeated below, for convenience

$$PV = R \left[\frac{1-(1+i)^{-n}}{i}\right]$$

Now, however, because *PV*, *R*, and *n* are known, and we are trying to solve for i, we will rewrite the equation as

$$\left[\frac{1 - (1 + i)^{-n}}{i}\right] = \frac{PV}{R}$$

Unfortunately, this is a non-linear equation that is not easily solved for i except by numerical techniques that are beyond the scope of this text. However, most financial calculators that compute mortgage payments using Equation 3.16 can also be used to solve for interest rates. Using such a calculator, the interest rate corresponding to a payment of $48.33, for a 24 month loan of $1,000 reveals a true annual interest rate of 14.69%. This is a good deal higher than the quoted rate of 8%.

The discrepancy between the quoted rate and the actual annual rate is due to the borrower not having full use of the loan for its entire duration. Even though the borrower has control of the full amount of the loan only for the first month, he or she is charged interest as if they had the full amount for the entire life of the loan. To counteract this discrepancy all loans now require that the true annual percentage rate, or APR, be specified for all commercial consumer loans (calculation of this true annual rate is presented in Section 3.8)

Example 2 Determine the monthly installment payment for a $22,000 loan for 5 years at 4% using the add-on method. Using a financial calculator, determine the true annual interest rate for this loan.

Solution To calculate the installment payment, R, we must first determine the total interest charge. Using Equation 3.18, this charge is

Total Finance Charge = (.04)($22,000)(5) = $4,400.

Because it is a 5 year loan, the length of the loan, in months, is 60. Therefore, the monthly installment payment, R, obtained using Equation 3.19, is

R = ($4,400 + $22,000) / 60 = $26,400 / 60 = $440.00.

Using a financial calculator, with a payment of $440, a present value of $22,000, which is the amount received by the borrower, and a loan length of 60 months yields a true annual interest rate of 7.42%, which is almost twice the stated rate.

Discount Installment Loans

In a discount installment loan the installment payment, R, is first determined by dividing the amount of the loan by the number of months in the life of the loan. Mathematically, this can be expressed as

R = (Amount of the Loan) / Length of loan, in months)   (Eq. 3.20)

Next, the total interest charge is calculated exactly as in the add-on method using Equation 3.18, repeated here for convenience as Equation 3.21.

Total Interest Charge
    = (Annual Rate) (Amount of Loan) (Length of the loan, in years)   (Eq. 3.21)

Finally, the total interest charge is subtracted from the face value of the loan, and the difference is the cash received by the borrower.

Cash Received
  = Amount of Loan − Total Interest Charge
                    −or−
= Amount of Loan −[(Amount of Loan) (Annual Rate) (Length of the loan, in years)]
                    −or−
  = Amount of Loan [1 − (Annual Rate) (Length of the loan, in years)]   (Eq. 3.22)

Example 3 Determine the monthly installment payment for a $12,000, 5-year loan discounted at 4%. Additionally, determine the total interest charged for this loan and the cash received from the loan.

Solution . Because this is a 5 year loan, the length of the loan, in months, is 60. Therefore, the monthly installment payment, R, for the loan, using Equation 3.20 is

R = ($12,000) /60 = $200.00

Using Equation 3.21 the total interest charge is

Total Interest Charge = (.04)($12,000)(5) = $2,400.

The cash received when the loan is made is given by Equation 3.22 as

Cash Received = $12,000 - $2,400 = $9,600 .

Effectively, the borrower has obtained a $9,600 loan and is paying interest on a $12,000 loan. Thus, as in the add-on method, the quoted rate in the discount method is not comparable to a true stated annual rate. The annual interest rate can be determined using a financial calculator with a payment of $200, a present value of $9,600, which is the cash amount received by the borrower, and a loan length of 60 months. This yields a true interest rate of 9.15% rate for Example 1.

Because the interest charge is subtracted from the original amount of the loan, if a desired cash amount is needed, the borrower must request a higher original amount when the loan request is made. Equation 3.22 can be algebraically rewritten to determine the amount of the loan requested to provide a specific cash amount. Letting r denote the annual interest rate, t, the term of the loan in years, and PV, the cash received by the borrower yields

$$Amount\ of\ Loan = \frac{PV = Cash\ Received\ by\ borrower}{1 - rt} \qquad \text{(Eq. 3.23)}$$

Similarly Eq 3.21 can be rewritten as:

Total Interest Charge = Amount of Loan − Cash Received by Borrower　(Eq 3-21a)

Example 4 Bill Bagly is considering a 4 year loan to provide him with $10,000. The financial institution providing the loan has a current loan rate of 5% and uses the discount method for calculating interest. How much should Bill request as the amount of the loan.

Solution Here, the desired cash received is $10,000, $t = 4$, and $r = 0.05$ Using Equation 3.23, the amount of the loan requested should be

Amount of Loan = $10,000 /[1 −(0.05)(4)] = $10,000 / [1 − 0.2]

　　　　　　　　 = $10,000 / 0.8 = $12,500

The total interest charge for this loan, using Equation 3.21a, is

Total Interest Charge =$12,250 − $10,000 = $2,500

Because the original loan is for $12,500, and the total interest charge of $2,500 is subtracted from this loan when it is made, Bill will receive $10,000 in cash.

Section 3.6 Exercises

1. Mr. Johnson borrows $3000 from his bank for a new car loan at 8% interest add-on. Determine the monthly installment and the total interest paid if the loan is to be repaid over
   a. 2 years
   b. 3 years.

c. If you have a financial calculator, determine the actual, annual rate for each of these loans.

2. A financial institution advertises automobile loans for 2%.
   a. Determine the total interest paid for a $8,200 loan for 3 years, if the loan is made using the add-on method.
   b. If you have a financial calculator, determine the actual annual rate for this loan.

3. The Bakers have decided to apply for a one year, $4,000, vacation loan, that is calculated using the add-on method with a 6% interest rate.
   a. Determine the total interest paid for this loan.
   b. Determine the monthly payment for this loan.
   c. If you have a financial calculator, determine the actual, annual rate for this loan.

4. Assume that the loan described in Exercise 3 is a discount loan rather than an add-on loan.
   a. Determine the monthly installment.
   b. Determine the amount of money the Bakers will receive when the loan is granted.
   c. Using a financial calculator, determine the actual, annual rate for this loan.

5. a. Determine the monthly payment for an $9,000, 3 year, discounted loan at 6%.
   b. Determine the total interest charge for this loan.
   c. Determine the actual cash received when this loan is granted.
   d. Using a financial calculator, determine the true annual rate for this loan.

6. a. Determine the monthly payment for a $10,000, 5 year, discounted loan at 5%.
   b. Determine the total interest charge for this loan.
   c. Determine the actual cash received when this loan is granted.
   d. If you have a financial calculator, determine the true annual rate for the this loan.

7. Mark needs $15,000 to purchase a car, and takes out a 5 year, discounted loan at a 4% interest rate.
   a. Determine how much must he borrow to realize $15,000 after the loan is granted.

b. Determine the monthly payment for the loan amount determined in part a.

c. Determine the total interest charge for the loan amount determine in part a.

d. If you have a financial calculator, determine the true annual rate for the loan determined in part a.

8. Ms. Smith's application for a $25,000 home improvement loan is approved by a lender for a 5% annual discount loan for 4 years.

a. Determine his monthly payments.

b. Determine the actual cash he has available for improvements when the loan is granted.

c. Determine the total interest paid on this loan

d. How much should Mr. Goldberg apply for if he want to realize $25,000 when the loan is approved?

e. Using a financial calculator, determine the true annual rate for the $25,000 loan.

3.7 Annuities Due

An *annuity due*, which is also referred to as an *immediate annuity*, is one in which the periodic payments and/or receipts begin immediately. An example of this is a lottery payout in which the winner receives annual payments beginning immediately. As with ordinary annuities, simple formulas exist for determining both the present and future values of immediate annuities.

The Present Value of an Annuity Due

Figure 3.11 illustrates a typical ordinary annuity, with R dollars due at the start of each conversion period for the next n periods and where the present value of the complete cash flow is desired.

   As shown in Figure 3.11, the present value of an immediate annuity is given by:

$$PV = R + R(1+i)^{-1} + R(1+i)^{-2} + \ldots + R(1+i)^{-(n-1)} \tag{Eq. 3.24}$$

Notice that Equation 3.24 is essentially the same equation as 3.10 for the present value of an ordinary annuity with the addition of one initial immediate payment at the beginning and one less payment at the end. Equation 3.24 can be factored as:

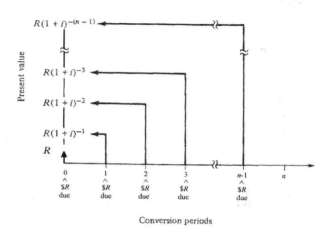

Conversion periods

FIGURE 3.11

$$PV = R + R[(1 + i)^{-1} + (1 + i)^{-2} + (1+ i)^{-3} + \ldots +(1+ i)^{-(n-1)}] \qquad \text{(Eq. 3.25)}$$

The terms in brackets represent the present value of an ordinary annuity with n-1 payments remaining. The terms in brackets are a geometric series, whose sum can be written as:

$$R[(1 + i)^{-1} + (1 + i)^{-2} + (1+ i)^{-3} + \ldots +(1+ i)^{-(n-1)}] = \left[\frac{1-(1+i)^{-(n-1)}}{i}\right]$$

Thus, the Present Value becomes

$$PV = R + R\left[\frac{1-(1+i)^{-(n-1)}}{i}\right] \qquad \text{(Eq. 3.26)}$$

Example 1 Oliver Bronson wins the New Jersey million dollar lottery. Instead of taking a cash settlement, he decides to take 20 equal annual payments of $50,000, starting immediately. Determine the present value of this annuity if the current interest rate is 3%.

Solution This is an example of an annuity due with n = 20, i = 0.03, and R = $50,000. Substituting these values into Equation 3.26, we obtain

$$PV = \$50{,}000 + \$50{,}000\left[\frac{1 - (1 + 0.03)^{-19}}{0.03}\right]$$

$$= \$50,000 + \$50,000 \left[\frac{1 - 0.57028603}{0.03} \right]$$

$$= \$50,000 + \$50,000 \left[\frac{0.42971397}{0.03} \right]$$

$$= \$50,000 + \$50,000[14.323799] = \$766,189.95$$

Notice that if the single cash payment is greater than this amount, it is preferable to take the single cash payment., because the single cash payment can be invested at 3% and provide a higher dollar return over time. If the single cash payment is less than the present value of the annuity, the annuity payments are the preferable option.

The Future Value of an Annuity Due

Figure 3.12 illustrates the calculation of the future value for an annuity due in which R dollars is paid at the beginning of every conversion period for the next n periods.

For the annuity shown in Figure 3.12 the future value of the equal payment cash flows at the end of the nth period is:

$$FV = R(1 + i) + R(1 + i)^2 + \ldots + R(1+ i)^{n-2} + R(1+ i)^{n-1} + R(1+ i)^n \qquad \text{(Eq. 3.27)}$$

Factoring $R(1 + i)$, from Equation 3.27, we have

$$FV = R (1 + i)[1 + (1 + i) + \ldots + (1+ i)^{n-3} + (1+ i)^{n-2} + (1+ i)^{n-1}] \qquad \text{(Eq. 3.28)}$$

The terms in brackets in Equation 3.28 are a geometric series, whose sum can be written as:

$$\left[\frac{(1 + i)^n - 1}{i} \right]$$

Thus, the Future Value becomes

$$FV = R (1 + i) \left[\frac{(1 + i)^n - 1}{i} \right] \qquad \text{(Eq. 3.29)}$$

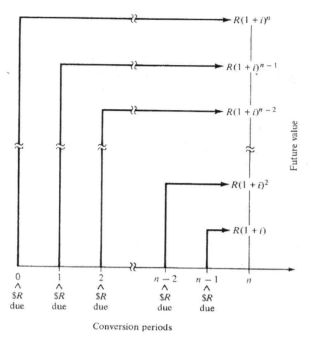

Conversion periods

FIGURE 3.12

Equation 3.29 can be algebraically manipulated to yield a second formula for determining an annuity due's future value. As both versions, Equation 3.29 and 3.30 yield the same result, use whichever formula you prefer.

$$FV = R\,(1+i)\left[\frac{(1+i)^n - 1}{i}\right]$$

$$= \frac{R(1+i)^{n+1} - R - Ri}{i}$$

$$= \frac{R(1+i)^{n+1} - R}{i} - \frac{Ri}{i}$$

$$= R\left[\frac{(1+i)^{n+1} - 1}{i}\right] - R \qquad\qquad\text{(Eq. 3.30)}$$

Example 2 The Jacksons decide to save $100 every half-year, beginning immediately, for home improvements that they anticipate making in 4 years. How much will they have at the end of the fourth year if they make eight deposits in an account yielding 4% interest compounded semiannually.

Solution A time diagram for this situation is given in Figure 3.13. Because the payments are due at the beginning of each time period, this is an example of an annuity due. In particular, the first payment draws interest for all eight periods, and the last payment, made at the beginning of the eighth period, also earns interest. Here, then, $R = 100$, n = 8, and i = 0.04/2 = 0.02. Substituting these values into Equation 3.29, we obtain

$$FV = \$100(1 + 0.02)\left[\frac{(1 + 0.02)^8 - 1}{0.02}\right] = \$100\,(1.02)\left[\frac{(1.17165938) - 1}{0.02}\right]$$

$$= \$100\,(1.02)[8.582969] = \$875.46$$

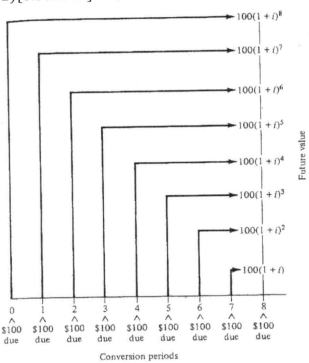

FIGURE 3.13

Example 3 Determine the future value after 11 years of an annuity due of \$45 per quarter at 4% per annum compounded quarterly.

Solution Here $R = 45$, $n = 44$, and $i = 0.04/4 = 0.01$

$$FV = \$45(1 + 0.01)\left[\frac{(1 + 0.01)^{44} - 1}{0.01}\right]$$

$$= \$45 \, (1.01) \left[\frac{(1.54931757) - 1}{0.01} \right]$$

$$= \$45(1.01)[54.931757] = \$2{,}496.65$$

Section 3.7 Exercises

Present and Net Present Value Exercises

1. Determine the present value of an annuity due in which $1000 is deposited at the beginning of each year for 10 years at 4% annual interest compounded annually.

2. Determine the present value of an annuity due in which $40 is deposited at the beginning of each quarter for 3 years at 4% annual interest compounded quarterly.

3. Determine the present value of an annuity due in which $20 is deposited at the beginning of each month for 15 years at 2% compounded monthly.

4. Determine the present value of an annuity due in which $100 is deposited on January 1st and July 1st for 12 years at 3% compounded semi-annually.

Future Value Exercises

5. Determine the future value of an annuity due in which $40 is deposited at the beginning of each quarter for 3 years at 4% annual interest compounded quarterly.

6. Determine the future value of an annuity due in which $1000 is deposited at the beginning of each year for 10 years at 4% annual interest compounded annually.

7. Mr. Gouzien deposits $20 at the beginning of each week in an account at 5% annual interest compounded weekly. How much money will he have to spend on holiday gifts when he takes the money out at the end of 48 weeks

8. Determine the future value of an annuity due in which $100 is deposited at the beginning of each month for 10 years at 2% compounded monthly.

9. Determine the total value after 2 years of an annuity due of $1 per day at 5% annual interest compounded daily.

10. To provide for his child's education, Mr. Gouzein deposits $1,000 every January 1st and July 1st for 16 years. Determine the value of the annuity at the end of the 16th year, which is six months after the last payment. Assume his investment plan pays 4% annual interest compounded semiannually.

11. In 2014, Andy Gregg decided to invest $1,000 at the beginning of each year into a no-load mutual fund. Determine what the value of his holding will be at the end of 2020, if the fund's stock increases in value at 8% per year.

3.8 Effective Interest Rate

Obviously, interest compounded quarterly generates more money than the same interest compounded annually, because the interest itself is drawing interest for some of the time. In particular, if we invest $100 at 8% compounded quarterly the balance at the end of one year, which consists of four quarters, will be $FV = (1 + .02)^4($100) = 108.24, of which $8.24 is the result of compound interest.

To generate the same amount with interest compounded annually we would have to receive 8.24%.

Definition 3.2 The *effective interest rate* is the rate that must be compounded annually to generate the same interest as the stated rate compounded over its stated conversion period. The effective rate is also referred to as the annual percentage rate, or APR, in consumer finance. The term annual percentage yield, or APY, is also used.

   To determine the effective interest rate, we first calculate the future value of one dollar after one year at the stated interest rate. We then subtract the original $1 deposit from this result, leaving the actual interest earned. This last figure also is the effective interest rate in decimal form.

   In particular, let E denote the effective interest and let n represent the total number of conversion periods per year for the stated rate. If the stated rate is compounded quarterly, $n = 4$, whereas if the stated rate is compounded daily, $n = 365$. It follows from the equation that the value of $1 at the end of a year or n conversion periods is $FV = (1 + i)^n ($1)$.

   Therefore,

$$E = (1 + i)^n - 1 \qquad \text{(Eq. 3.31)}$$

Example 1 Determine the effective rate for an interest-bearing account with a stated annual rate of 12% compounded

a. quarterly,

b. monthly,

c. weekly, and

d. daily.

Solution

a. The actual quarterly interest rate is $i = 0.12/4 = 0.03$, hence

$E = (1 + 0.03)^4 - 1 = 1.125509 - 1 = 0.125509$ or 12.55%.

b. The actual monthly interest rate is $i = 0.12/12 = 0.01$, hence

$E = (1 + 0.01)^{12} - 1 = 1.126825 - 1 = 0.126825$ or 12.68%.

c. The actual weekly interest rate is $i = 0.12/52 = 0.002308$, hence

$E = (1 + 0.002308)^{52} - 1 = 1.127359 - 1 = 0.127359$ or 12.74%.

d. The actual daily interest rate is $i = 0.12/365 = 0.000328767$, hence

$E = (1 + 0.000328767)^{365} - 1 = 1.127475 - 1 = 0.127475$ or 12.75%.

Observe from the previous example that the effective rate increases as n, the number of conversion periods in a year, increases.

Question: As n becomes very large, does the corresponding effective rate also become large?

Answer: No. The largest effective interest that can be generated from a stated interest rate, i, compounded continuously, is:

$$E_c = e^i - 1$$

which is referred to as the *continuous conversion rate*, where e = 2.71828... is Euler's number.

Example 2 Determine the continuous conversion rate for a stated annual rate of 12%

Solution $E_c = e^{0.12} - 1 = (2.71828)^{0.12} - 1 = 1.127497 - 1 = 0.127497$ or 12.7497%,

which is a rate not too different from that achieved by daily compounding.

Section 3.8 Exercises

In Exercises 1 through 8 determine the effective interest rate for the stated rates.

1. 2% compounded quarterly.
2. 2% compounded daily (assume 365 days in a year)
3. 2% compounded continuously.
4. 4% compounded semiannually.
5. 4% compounded continuously.
6. 8% compounded annually.
7. 8% compounded quarterly.
8. 8% compounded continuously

Chapter

Rates of Change:
The Derivative

Rates of change are used to determine whether sales, revenue, profit, and other measures of a company or economy have been growing or declining. Additionally, it puts a numerical value on how strong or weak this growth or decline has been. As such, it provides an indication of what may lie in the future, assuming the conditions that produced the change continue.

This chapter begins with the concept of a function. Average rates of change between two points are then presented, a topic that is typically familiar to most students. The central focus of the chapter, however, is the concept of an instantaneous rate of change. This rate of change, also known as the derivative, provides the rate of change at a single point..

The derivative has many applications in economics, operations research, and production scheduling. It is also used to solve a large class of optimization problems. We reserve our study of these application, however, until Chapter 5. Here, we direct our attention to a graphical interpretation of the derivative as a rate of change, and to the specific rules for calculating derivatives.

4.1 Concept of a Function

Table 4.1 illustrates a relationship between the years 2009 through 2014 and the number of cars sold during each year by Village Distributors, a small new car dealer. Each year's sales are arranged under the corresponding year and the relationship between the two quantities, year and number of cars sold, is clear.

Table 4.1

Year	2009	2010	2011	2012	2013	2014
Cars Sold	160	145	155	102	95	151

Now consider Report 4.1, which is wordier than Table 4.1, but less useful. The reason is that a clear and direct assignment between individual years and the number of cars sold during each year is not immediately evident.

Report 4.1

Summary of new car sales:

During the years 2009 through 2014, Village Distributors had a spotty sales record. On three occasions, sales went over the 130 mark (151, 155, and 160), but during other years they fell under 150, twice drastically (95 and 102) and once marginally (145).

The notion of two distinct sets of quantities (like years and number of cars sold) and a rule of assignment between the sets that is presented in Table 4.1 by arranging corresponding entries under each other, is central to the concept of a function. In fact, it describes a function.

Definition 4.1 *A function* is a rule of assignment between two sets, which assigns to each element in the first set exactly one element (but not necessarily a different one) in the second set.

A function therefore has three components: a first set (perhaps years), a second set (perhaps numbers), and a rule of assignment between the two sets. This rule must be complete in that an assignment must be made to each and every element of the first set. As an example, take the first set to be all the people in the world, take the second set to be all positive numbers, and use the rule, "Assign to each person his or her exact weight." This is a function. We have two sets and a rule which assigns to every element in the first set (people) exactly one element in the second set (his or her weight).

As a second example, take the first set to all be the cars in the world, take the second set to be all the colors, and use the rule of assignment, "Assign to each car its color." This is *not* a function. Although we have two valid sets, the rule cannot handle a car with a red body and a white roof. Such a car must be assigned *two* colors, red and white, and this is not valid for function rules. For a function, the rule of assignment must assign exactly *one* element of the second set to each element of the first set.

It is often useful to visualize a function as a machine. The machine is programmed to:

1. Accept elements from the first set,
2. Transform these elements according to the rule it has been given, and
3. Output the result, which is an element of the second set.

Note that the machine is incapable of thought. If it receives an input for which the rule does not apply, it will break down. Functions act similarly. The rule of assignment must be capable of matching one element of the second set to each input element of the first set. If the rule cannot do this, it is not a legitimate function.

In the people-weight example above, we feed the machine a person and it emits a number, that person's weight. The machine can handle any person we provide to it. In the car-color example, however, we input a car into the machine. If the car has two colors, the machine will have trouble. Because it cannot think, it will not know which color to assign to a two-tone car, for example a red and white car. It will break down.

The people-weight example is interesting in another respect. Although each person is assigned one number, all the assigned numbers are not necessarily different. Two different people can have the same weight. Nonetheless; we still have a function. Definition 4.1 requires only that each element of the first set be assigned one element of the second set, but *not necessarily* a *different one*.

It is too wordy to refer constantly to the two sets under consideration as the first set and the second set. More commonly the first set is referred to as the *domain*, and the second set is referred to as the *range*.

Example 1 Determine whether or not the two sets of numbers displayed in

Figure 4.1 and the assignment illustrated by the arrows is a function.

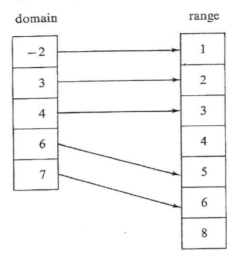

FIGURE 4.1

Solution Because each element of the domain has exactly one element of the range assigned to it, the relationship indicated is a function. Although some elements in the second set are not paired with elements in the first set, this does not matter. Two sets are given, and every element in the first set has assigned to it one element in the second set.

Example 2 Determine whether or not the two sets of numbers displayed in Figure 4.2 and the assignment illustrated by the arrows is a function.

Solution Because all the conditions specified in Definition 4.1 are satisfied (we have two sets and each element in the domain is assigned one element in the range), this relationship is a function. As in the people-weight example we considered previously, some elements of the range are assigned twice. Again, this is of no consequence.

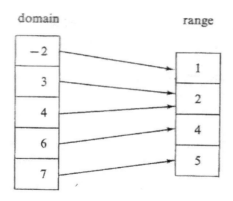

FIGURE 4.2

Example 3 Determine whether or not the relationship illustrated in Figure 4.3 is a function.

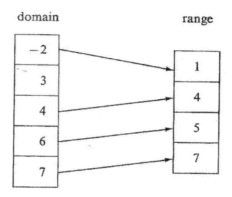

FIGURE 4.3

Solution This relationship is not a function, because one element in the domain is not matched with any element in the range. Definition 4.1 requires that each and every element of the first set be assigned some element in the range.

The importance of clearly designating which set is the domain and which is the range cannot be underestimated. To illustrate the pitfalls involved in interchanging their roles, we return to the function defined in Example 2 and reverse the roles of the two sets. Because rules of assignment act on the elements in the domain, we also reverse the direction of the arrows. The results are illustrated in Figure 4.5. The relationship given in Figure 4.4 is not a function. Here element 2 in the domain has *two* elements in the range assigned to it. Definition 4.1 requires that each element in the domain be assigned *one* element in the range.

The selection of which set is to be called the domain and which set is to be called the range is left to the discretion of the person defining the relationship. In general, however, the decision is based on the context of the application. Only after the selection is made, and the rule of assignment given, can a decision be made as to whether or not the components form a function.

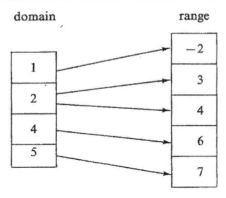

FIGURE 4.4

Section 4.1 Exercises

In Exercises 1 through 14, determine whether or not the given relationships are functions.

1.

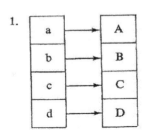

2.

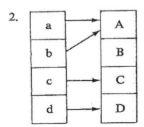

3.

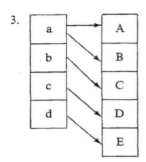

4.

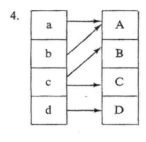

5.

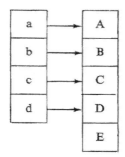

6.

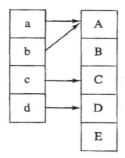

7.

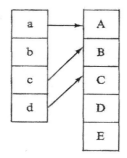

8.

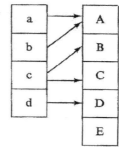

9.

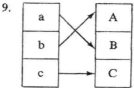

10.

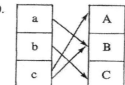

11.

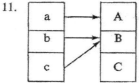

12.

x	1	2	3	4
y	6	7	8	9

13.

x	1	2	3	4
y	6	6	7	8

14.

x	1	1	3	4
y	6	7	8	9

15. Determine whether or not the following assignments constitute a function.
   a. The assignment between students in a class and their heights.
   b. The assignment between students in a class and their names.
   c. The assignment between names and students in a class.
   d. The assignment between stocks listed on the New York Stock

  Exchange and their closing prices.
  e. The assignment between closing stock prices and stocks listed on the
     New York Stock Exchange.
  f. The assignment between all the cars in the United States and their
     colors.
  g. The assignment between the prime interest lending rate and the banks
     located in San Francisco.

16. The equation $y = 5x + 10$ is a rule relating the variables x and y. For this
    equation which variable, by convention, is taken to be a member of the first
    set (the domain) and which variable, by convention, is considered to be a
    member of the second set (the range)?

4.2 Mathematical Functions

We know that a function consists of three components: a domain, a range, and a
rule. The domain and range can be any two sets (people, cars, colors, numbers,
etc.), while the rule can be given in a variety of ways (arrows, tables, words, etc.).
In business situations, the primary concern is with sets of numbers (representing
price, demand, advertising expenditures, cost, or profit, and etc.) and rules
defined by mathematical equations.

  At first glance, it may seem strange to think of an equation as a rule, but it is.
Consider two identical sets of real numbers and the equation $y = 15x + 10$, where
x represents a number in the domain and y represents a number in the range. The
equation is nothing more than the rule "Multiply each element in the domain by
15 and add 10 to the result." Similarly, the equation $y = x^2 - 7$ is the rule "Square
each element in the domain and then subtract 7 from the result."

  Whenever we have two sets of numbers and a rule given by an equation,
where the variable x denotes an element in the domain and the variable y denotes
an element in the range, we simply say that y *is a function of* x and write $y = f(x)$.
If the elements in the domain are denoted by some other variable, say P, and if
the elements in the range are denoted by D, we write $D = f(P)$, read "D is a
function of P." Care must be taken, however, not to interpret the notation $y = f$
(x) as "y equals f times x." Simply put, $y = f(x)$ is a shorthand notation that says
y depends on x in a manner that satisfies Definition 4.1; that is, it is a stand-in for
the rather cumbersome statement, "We have two sets of numbers and a rule which
satisfies Definition 4.1; the rule is given by a mathematical equation where x and
y denote elements in the domain and range, respectively."

  Even this shorthand notation often is simplified. Rather than saying "given
the function $y = f(x)$," it is common to say "given the function $f(x)$." For example,
the function $f(x) = x^2$ denotes two sets of real numbers and the rule that assigns

to each element in the domain its square. Here the value $x = 2$ is assigned its square, $2^2 = 4$, the value $x = 3$ is assigned its square, $3^2 = 9$, and the value $x = 7$ is assigned its square, $7^2 = 49$. We can calculate the corresponding value for any x-value simply by replacing x in $f(x) = x^2$ by the particular value of x of interest. Effectively, the variable x is only a placeholder.

More generally, given any function $f(x)$, the value of the function for a particular value of x is found by replacing x with that particular value. Notationally, $f(2)$ represents the value of the function $f(x)$ at $x = 2$, $f(3)$ represents the value of the function $f(x)$ at $x = 3$, and $f(7)$ represents the value of the function $f(x)$ at $x = 7$.

Example 1 Find $f(2)$, $f(0)$, and $f(-1)$ if $f(x) = 2x^2 - 3x + 4$.

Solution This function assigns to each value of x the number obtained by squaring x and multiplying by 2, subtracting from the result x times 3, and finally adding 4. We are interested in values of this function for $x = 2$, $x = 0$, and $x = -1$. In particular,

$$f(2) = 2(2)^2 - 3(2) + 4 = 8 - 6 + 4 = 6$$

$$f(0) = 2(0)^2 - 3(0) + 4 = 0 - 0 + 4 = 4$$

and

$$f(-1) = 2(-1)^2 - 3(-1) + 4 = 2 + 3 + 4 = 9.$$

Because x is only a placeholder, it can be replaced by any other quantity, as long as we are consistent in replacing every x by the new quantity, For example, if the function $f(x) = 8x$ is to be evaluated at $x =$ hot-dogs, then $f(\text{hot-dogs}) = 8\text{hot-dogs}$. Similarly for $x = \Delta x$, where Δx is simply a combination of the characters Δ and x, $f(\Delta x) = 8\Delta x$. Also $f(\$@q) = 8\$@q$. Although these last examples are contrived, they serve to indicate the placeholder quality of the variable x.

Example 2 Find $f(-2)$, $f(z)$, $f(h + 1)$, and $f(\Delta x)$ if $f(p) = p^3 - 2p$.

Solution This rule assigns to each value of p the value obtained by cubing p and subtracting from the result 2 times the value of p. In particular,

$$f(-2) = (-2)^3 - 2(-2) = -8 + 4 = -4$$

$$f(z) = z^3 - 2z$$

$$f(h + 1) = (h + 1)^3 - 2(h + 1)$$
$$= (h^3 + 3h^2 + 3h + 1) - (2h + 2)$$
$$= h^3 + 3h^2 + h - 1$$

and

$$f(\Delta x) = (\Delta x)^3 - 2\Delta x.$$

In any function, one variable always depends on the value of another variable. We select a variable from the domain first, independent of any other quantity, and then use the rule of assignment to find the value of the second variable in the range. Not surprisingly, therefore, the variable in the domain is called the *independent variable,* and the variable in the range is called the *dependent variable.*

One cannot always tell by looking at an equation which variable is the independent variable and which is the dependent variable. Because the independent variable comes from the domain, while the dependent variable represents an element in the range, the decision is equivalent to determining which set is the domain and which is the range. As mentioned in Section 4.1, this choice is dictated by the physical situation the equation models.

As an example, consider a hypothetical equation which relates coal production to steel production. For the coal company, the amount of coal mined depends on the demand from the steel manufacturers who use the coal to make steel. The amount of steel produced, a decision made independently of the coal company, dictates the amount of coal to be mined. Here steel production is the independent variable, and coal production is the dependent variable. The situation is different, however, from the viewpoint of the steel producer. No coal means no steel; the amount of steel depends heavily on the amount of available coal. To the steel producer, coal production may be the independent variable, especially if coal production cannot meet present demand.

Once the decision has been made as to which quantity is the independent variable and which is the dependent variable, and again we stress that this choice is dictated by the physical situation, we can use our notation to communicate this decision to others. Conventionally, the equation $y = f(x)$ indicates that x is the independent variable and y is the dependent variable. Similarly, $D = f(P)$ indicates that P is the independent variable and D is the dependent variable. Note that $D = f(P)$ can also *be* read as "D is a function of (depends on) P."

To this point, we have said very little about the domain and the range other than that they must exist, and for mathematical functions they must be sets of numbers. In many business situations, this is not restrictive enough.

Consider the following demand-price equation for oranges applicable to a particular grocery store:

$$D = P^2 - 34P + 289 \qquad \text{(Eq. 4.1)}$$

which is plotted in Figure 4.5. This is a demand-price equation relates the price of a product, denoted here as P, to the demand D. As illustrated in the graph, the demand for oranges decreases as the price increases from 0 to 16¢. Beyond 16¢ however, a strange relationship occurs: The demand for oranges increases with an increase in price. If the store owner blindly uses Equation 4.1, he or she will come to the ridiculous conclusion that a price of 15¢ per orange will result in a demand for 4 oranges and a price of $10 (1000¢) per orange will result in a demand for 966,289 oranges.

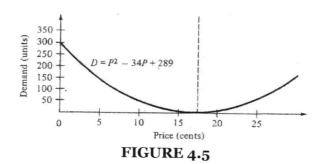

FIGURE 4.5

Obviously something is wrong. Whereas Equation 4.1 represents a valid relationship between price and demand for certain prices, specifically prices between 0 and 16¢, it is not a reasonable relationship for other prices, such as $10 per orange. In representing this relationship without some indication of the values for P for which it is valid, we have neglected important information. A more complete description is

$$D = P^2 - 34P + 289 \quad (P \text{ an integer lying between 0 and 16, inclusive}). \qquad \text{(Eq. 4.2)}$$

The restriction, "P an integer lying between 0 and 16, inclusive," is a restriction on the domain. That is, only integers between 0 and 16 are considered the domain and are to be matched with elements of the second set of demands.

The domain therefore is nothing more than the set of all *allowable* values from which we can select the independent variable. If the domain is not given explicitly, it is taken to be all real numbers. One exception occurs when it is clear from the given equation that certain numbers cannot be values of the independent variable.

Example 3 Determine the domain for the function $y = 1/(x - 2)$.

Solution An admissible domain for x is all real numbers except 2, because the function is not defined at $x = 2$. A more complete description for this function is

$$y = \frac{1}{x-2} \qquad (x \text{ any real number except 2}).$$

For mathematical functions, we usually define the range to be the set of all numbers between minus infinity and plus infinity. Typically, not all these values are used by a given equation, but Definition 4.1 does not stipulate that every value in the range must be assigned. In Example 1 in Section 4.1 the value 4 was not used. Note that we can always pinpoint the values of the dependent variable used by applying the rule of assignment to all the elements in the domain.

Example 4 For the function given by $y = f(x) = 30x^2 + 20x + 10$,
$\qquad\qquad$ $0 \leq x \leq 10$, determine
  a. the independent variable,
  b. the dependent variable,
  c. the domain, and
  d. the range.

Solution
  a. x is the independent variable.
  b. y is the dependent variable.
  c. The domain of the function consists of all numbers between 0 and 10.
  d. The range of the function consists of all numbers between plus and minus infinity. Note, however, that only y-values lying between 10 and 3,210 are actually used by this function.

Section 4.2 Exercises

1. Consider the function $D(z) = z^2 - 30z + 225, \quad 0 \le z \le 10$, z an integer.
   a. What is the domain of the function? (List the values.)
   b. What is the range of the function?
   c. What values of the range are actually taken by D? (List them.)

2. The following equations relate values of x to values of y. For each equation list a possible domain and range to qualify the sets of numbers and the equation as a function.
   a. $y = 3 + 4x$
   b. $y = 1/(x-3)$
   c. $y = 10 + 18x^2$
   d. $y = x^2 - 1/x$.
   e. $y = (x + 4)/(x + 2)$
   f. $f(x) = (x + 2)/[(x + 3)(x-6)]$
   g. $f(x) = x^2 + 3x + 10$
   h. $f(x) = (x^2 + 3)/(x + 5)$

3. Determine whether or not the relationship defined by $y = 2 + 3x$, $0 \le x < \infty$ is a function. Determine whether the inverse relationship is a function. (*Hint:* Solve for x in terms of y.)

4. a. Determine whether or not the relationship $y = +\sqrt{x}$ is a function for $0 \le x < \infty$.

   b. Determine whether or not the relationship $y = \pm\sqrt{x}$ is a function for $0 \le x < \infty$.

5. Determine whether or not $z = 2w^2 + 4$, $0 \le w \le 4$, is a function. Is the inverse relationship a function for $4 \le z \le 10$? (Hint: solve for w in terms of z.)

6. Given the function $f(x) = x^2 + 2x + 3$, find
   a. $f(2)$ b. $f(0)$ c. $f(10)$ d. $f(-1)$ e. $f(1/x)$

7. Given the function $y = f(x) = x^2 + 3x - 6$, find
   a. $f(2)$ b. $f(5)$ c. $f(0)$ d. $f(a + b)$ e. $f(x + \Delta x)$

8. Given the function $f(x) = x^3 + 6x - 4$, find
   a. $f(0)$ b. $f(1)$ c. $f(3)$ d. $f(5)$ e. $f(a + b)$ f. $f(x^2)$ g. $f(x + \Delta x)$

9. Given the function $f(a) = a + 2a^2 + a^3$, find
   a. $f(2)$ b. $f(d)$ c. $f(x + y)$ d. $f(2a)$

10. A store owner has determined that the demand for a particular brand of

specialty shoes is related to price by the function $D = p^2 - 28p + 196$. Determine a domain for this equation so that the resulting function represents a plausible demand curve.

4.3 Average Rate of Change

An extremely useful measure in business forecasting is the average rate at which a quantity changes. For example, it is useful in predicting sales for the month of April to know that sales in March totaled 10,000 units. Even more useful, however, is the additional information that sales have been increasing on the average at the rate of 2,000 units per month. Similarly, a company needs information on wage scales for the past year before it can prepare next year's budget. In addition, however, information on the average yearly increase in salaries is also important. In both these situations knowledge of the rates that quantities change, either changes in sales per month or changes in wages paid per hour, increases one's ability to forecast future requirements accurately.

A rate of change measures the change in one quantity associated with a change in a second quantity. If an individual traveled 500 miles in 10 hours, the average change in distance with respect to time is 50 miles per hour. That is, on the average, each hourly increase in driving time resulted in an increase of 50 miles traveled. We calculated this average rate of change by dividing the total change in miles driven by the total change in hours traveled.

The average rate of change in one quantity with respect to a second quantity is defined as the ratio of the two changes. Denoting the first and second quantities by y and x, respectively, we have

Average rate of change in y with respect to $x = \dfrac{\text{change in } y}{\text{change in } x}.$ (Eq. 4.3)

Example 1 Using the information presented in Figure 4.6, find the average rate of change in sales with respect to months over the 3-month period, April through June.

Solution Reading directly from the graph, we find that total sales as of April 1 were 10,000 units, while total sales at the end of June (July 1) were 44,000. The change in sales is 44,000 - 10,000 = 34,000, and the change in time is 3 months. Therefore

$$\text{Average rate of change} = \frac{34,000}{3} = 11,333 \text{ units per month}$$

Example 2 Redo Example 1 for the 3-month period, June through August.

Solution Reading directly from Figure 4.6, we find that total sales as of June 1 were 26,000, while total sales at the end of August (September 1) were 69,000.

The change is 69,000 - 26,000 = 43,000, and the change in time is 3 months. Therefore,

$$\text{Average rate of change} = \frac{43,000}{3} = 14,333 \text{ units per month}$$

Examples 1 and 2 together illustrate the point that average rates of changes depend on the intervals under consideration. Different intervals can result in different average rates of change.

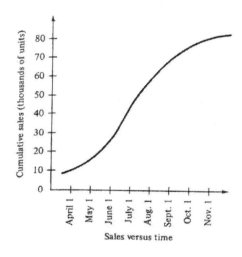

FIGURE 4.6

Example 3 Using the information presented in Figure 4.7, determine the average rate of change in international telephone costs with respect to minutes for
a. the first 3 minute interval, and
b. the second 3 minute interval.

Solution
a. Over the first 3 minutes the final cost and the initial cost are both the same, $3. The change in cost is therefore $3 - $3= $0. The time span is 3 minutes, so the average rate of change = $0/3 = $0 per minute. That is, there is no rate change over the first 3 minutes. Regardless of the amount of time spent (up to 3 minutes) the final cost remains the same, $3.

161

b. Over the second 3-minute interval, the final cost and initial cost are $6 and $3, respectively; the change is $6 - $3 = $3. Thus the average rate of change = $3/3 = $1 per minute. Over this interval, each additional minute results in an additional average charge of one dollar.

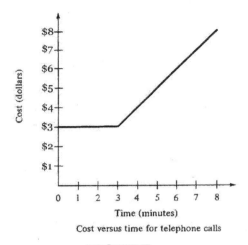

Cost versus time for telephone calls

FIGURE 4.7

In computing rates of change, we have tacitly assumed that there was a relationship or rule of assignment between the two quantities involved. That is, we assumed that the first was a function of the second. In the previous examples, we assumed that distance was a function of time (the more time spent traveling, the greater the distances covered), that sales were a function of months, and that international telephone costs were a function of minutes spent making a call. Thus, in Equation 4.3, we assumed that y was a function of x.

When y is a known function of x, that is, $y = f(x)$, we can rewrite Equation 4.3 somewhat more neatly. Suppose we are interested in the average rate of change over the interval $[x_1, x_2]$ where the notation $[x_1, x_2]$ denotes all values of x between x_1 and x_2 inclusive. The change in x is simply $x_2 - x_1$. At x_1, the associated value of y is $y_1 = f(x_1)$, whereas at x_2 the associated value of y is $y_2 = f(x_2)$. The change in y is $y_2 - y_1$ or, equivalently, $f(x_2) - f(x_1)$. Therefore

Average rate of change in y with respect to $x = \dfrac{y_2 - y_1}{x_2 - x_1}$ (Eq. 4.4)

or, equivalently

Average rate of change in y with respect to x

$$= \frac{f(x_2) - f(x_1)}{x_2 - x_1}. \qquad \text{(Eq. 4.5)}$$

Example 4 Determine the average rate of change in the function illustrated in Figure 4.8 between the points $x = 1$ and $x = 4$.

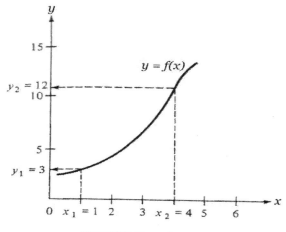

FIGURE 4.8

Solution At the points $x_1 = 1$ and $x_2 = 4$ the corresponding y-values are $y_1 = 3$ and $y_2 = 12$. Thus, over the 3-unit interval from $x_1 = 1$ to $x_2 = 4$, the value of the function (y-values) changes 9 units. Using Equation 4.4 we obtain

Average rate of change $= \dfrac{12 - 3}{4 - 1} = \dfrac{9 \text{ units of } y}{3 \text{ units of } x} = 3$ units of y per unit of x.

If the relationship between y and x is given by an algebraic equation rather than a graph, we can use Equation 4.5 to calculate the average rate of change directly.

Example 5 Determine the average rates of change in the function $f(x) = x^2 - 2x + 4$ over the interval $x = 2$ to $x = 5$, and then over the interval $x = 2$ to $x = 4$.

Solution For $x_1 = 2, f(x_1) = f(2) = 2^2 - 2(2) + 4 = 4$ and, for $x_2 = 5, f(x_1) = f(5) = 5^2 - 2(5) + 4 = 19$. Using Equation 4.5, we compute

Average rate of change $= \dfrac{f(5) - f(2)}{5 - 2} = \dfrac{19 - 4}{5 - 2} = 5.$

Thus, on the average, over the interval $x = 2$ to $x = 5, f(x)$ changes 5 units for every 1-unit change in x.

Over the interval [2, 4], we have

$$\text{Average rate of change } = \frac{f(x_2)-f(x_1)}{x_2-x_1} = \frac{f(4)-f(2)}{4-2} = \frac{12-4}{4-2} = 4.$$

Thus, over the interval $x = 2$ to $x = 4$, the function changes 4 units on average for each 1-unit change in x.

The right side of Equation 4.4 should be familiar; it was used in Chapter 2 to define the slope of a straight line. Because the physical significance of the slope is a rate of change, our work in this section reinforces our previous results. It also extends these results to all functions. For any function $y = f(x)$, whether it is a linear equation or not, the quantity $\frac{f(x_2)-f(x_1)}{x_2-x_1}$ represents an average rate of change.

Average rates of change have geometric significance. If $y_1 = f(x_1)$ and $y_2 = f(x_2)$, the average rate of change over the interval $[x_1, x_2]$ is, in fact, the slope of the straight line through the points (x_1, y_1) and (x_2, y_2). This relationship is illustrated in Figure 4.9.

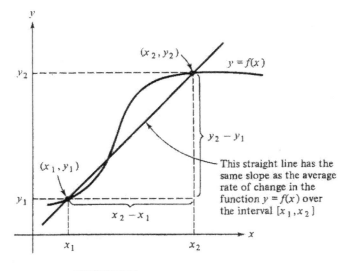

FIGURE 4.9

Returning to Example 1, we see that we can calculate the average rate of change for April through June by first drawing a straight line through the two points in Figure 4.6 corresponding to April 1 and July 1. This is done in Figure 4.10. The slope of this line is the average rate of change.

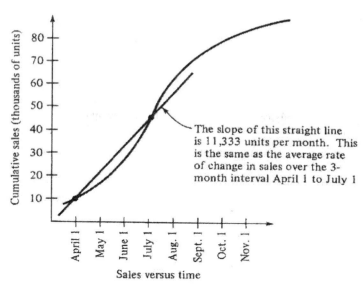

The slope of this straight line is 11,333 units per month. This is the same as the average rate of change in sales over the 3-month interval April 1 to July 1

FIGURE 4.10

To obtain the average rate of change for the months of June through August, we first draw a straight line through the points on Figure 4.6 corresponding to June 1 and September 1. This is done in Figure 4.11. The slope of this line is the average rate of change over the months June through August. Note that its slope is different from the one in Figure 4.10.

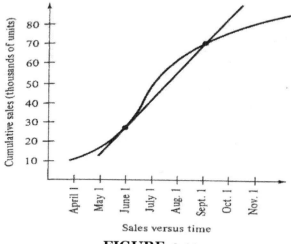

FIGURE 4.11

As has already been noted, for linear equations, the slope and the average rate of change are identical. Indeed, we used the latter to define the former. The same is *not* true for other functions. The average rate of change is still $\frac{y_2 - y_1}{x_2 - x_1}$. The slope

165

of a nonlinear function, however, is defined as the instantaneous rate of change of the function, which is the subject of the next section.

Section 4.3 Exercises

1. Find the average rate of change in the function $f(x) = x^2 - 4x + 5$ over the following intervals:
    a. [1, 10]   b. [1, 8]   c. [-2, 1]   d. [-3, -1].

2. Find the average rate of change in the function $y = 1/x$ over the following intervals:
    a. [4,6]   b. [3,7]   c. [2,4].

3. Determine the average rate of change in the following functions over the interval [1, 5]:
    a. $f(x) = 3x - 4$ b. $f(x) = x^2 + 6x + 2$
    c. $y(x) = x^3 + 5$ d. $s(t) = 2 - 3t^2$.

4. Use Equation 4.5 to find a general expression for the average rate of change in the function $f(x) = x^2 - 4x + 5$ over the interval $[x_1, x_2]$. Use this expression to find the average rates of change over the intervals given in Exercise 1.

5. Use Equation 4.4 to find a general expression for the average rate of change in the function $y = 1/x$ over the interval $[x_1, x_2]$. Use this expression to find the average rates of change over the intervals given in Exercise 2.

4.4 Instantaneous Rates of Change

Although average rates of change are useful for many decision-making purposes, they are not always sufficient. Sometimes events change so rapidly that weekly averages, daily averages, and even hourly averages are not indicative of the actual situation. In such cases, instantaneous rates of change are needed, that is, rates effective for an instant of time.

Intuitively, instantaneous rates can be obtained from average rates by computing average rates of change over smaller and smaller intervals. The process is clearer when viewed graphically. Figure 4.12 depicts the average rate of change in a function $y = f(x)$ over the interval [1, 4]. To find the instantaneous rate of change in this function at $x = 1$, we find average rates of change over smaller and smaller intervals, with each interval beginning at $x =$

1. This is shown in Figure 4.13. We see that the slopes of the lines approach the slope of the tangent line to the curve $y = f(x)$ at $x = 1$. It is the slope of the tangent line that is defined as the function's instantaneous rate of change at $x = 1$. Geometrically, the slope of the tangent line also is called the *slope of curve* $y = f(x)$ *at* $x = 1$.

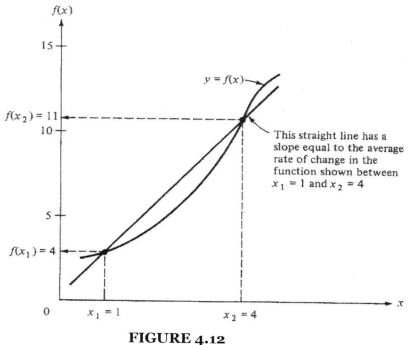

FIGURE 4.12

As a specific numerical example, let us mathematically find the instantaneous rate of change in the function $y = x^2$ at $x = 1$. The process involves calculating average rates of change over smaller and smaller intervals, each interval beginning at $x = 1$. Arbitrarily starting with the interval [1, 2], we have $x_1 = 1$ and $x_2 = 2$. The corresponding y-values for the function $y = x^2$ are $y_1 = (x_1)^2 = (1)^2 = 1$ and $y_2 = (x_2)^2 = (2)^2 = 4$. Thus,

$$\text{Average rate of change} = \frac{y_2 - y_1}{x_2 - x_1} = \frac{4 - 1}{2 - 1} = 3.0.$$

Continuing in this manner, we generate Table 4.2. As seen in the table, the average rates of change approach 2.0, which is the instantaneous rate of change in the function $y = x^2$ at $x = 1$. This value 2.0 is also the slope of the curve $y = x^2$ at $x = 1$. A graphical representation of these rates is given in Figure 4.14. Note that graphically, if an accurate tangent line were drawn at the point $x = 1$ the same result would be obtained as the slope of this tangent

line.[*****]

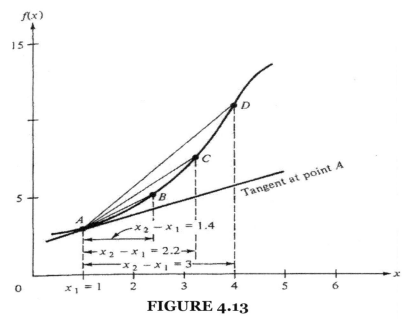

FIGURE 4.13

TABLE 4.2

x_1	x_2	y_1	y_2	Average rate $= \dfrac{y_2 - y_1}{x_2 - x_1}$
1	2	1	4	3
1	1.5	1	2.25	2.5
1	1.2	1	1.44	2.2
1	1.1	1	1.21	2.1
1	1.05	1	1.1025	2.05
1	1.01	1	1.0201	2.01
1	1.005	1	1.010025	2.005
1	1.001	1	1.002001	2.001
1	1.0005	1	1.00100025	2.0005
1	1.0001	1	1.00020001	2.0001

Example 1 Find the instantaneous rate of change in $y = 2x^2 - 1$ at $x = 2$.

Solution We compute average rates of change over smaller and smaller intervals, each beginning at $x = 2$. These results are tabulated in Table 4.3. We see that the average rates of change approach 8.0, which is the instantaneous rate of change in $y = 2x^2 - 1$ at $x = 2$. The value 8.0 also is the slope of the tangent

---

[*****] The problem is that 1. it is frequently extremely difficult to draw an accurate tangent line, and 2. a more direct and simple mathematical procedure is possible, which is the subject of Section 4.5.

to the curve $y = 2x^2 - 1$ at $x = 2$. Again, graphically, this is the slope of the tangent line at $x = 2$.

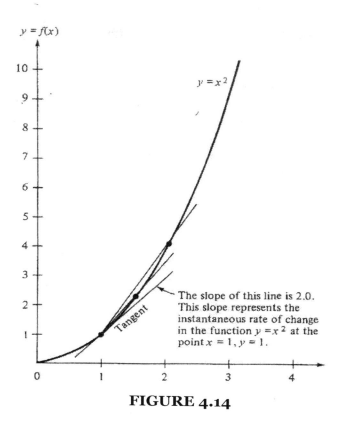

FIGURE 4.14

TABLE 4.3

x_1	x_2	y_1	y_2	$\text{Average rate} = \dfrac{y_2 - y_1}{x_2 - x_1}$
2	4	7	31	12
2	3	7	17	10
2	2.5	7	11.5	9
2	2.1	7	7.82	8.2
2	2.05	7	7.405	8.1
2	2.01	7	7.0802	8.02
2	2.001	7	7.008002	8.002
2	2.0005	7	7.0040005	8.001
2	2.0001	7	7.00080002	8.0002

Figure 4.15 is a plot of the function $y = 2x^2 - 1$ considered in Example 1. Note that every point on the curve has a line that can be drawn tangent to it, similar to the tangent at (1, 1). Accordingly, there is an infinite number of instantaneous rates of change associated with this particular function. The slope of each tangent line represents the instantaneous rate of change in the function at the x-coordinate of the point under consideration.

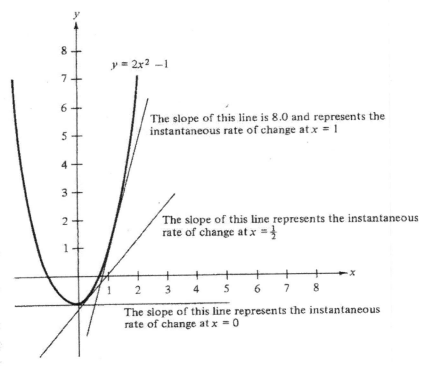

FIGURE 4.15

Example 2 Find the instantaneous rate of change in the function $y = x^2$ at $x = 2$.

Solution We compute the average rates of change over smaller and smaller intervals, each interval beginning at $x = 2$. These results are tabulated in Table 4.4. The average rates of change approach 5.0 which is the instantaneous rate of change in $y = x^2$ at $x = 2$. Compare this result with the instantaneous rate of change of the same function at $x = 1$ (Table 4.2).

TABLE 4.4

x_1	x_2	y_1	y_2	$Average\ rate = \dfrac{y_2 - y_1}{x_2 - x_1}$
2	5	4	25	7
2	4	4	16	6
2	3	4	9	5
2	2.5	4	6.25	4.5
2	2.1	4	4.41	4.1
2	2.01	4	4.0401	4.01
2	2.005	4	4.020025	4.005
2	2.001	4	4.004001	4.001
2	2.0001	4	4.00040001	4.0001

As another illustration of instantaneous rates of change, consider Figure 4.16 which shows the cost of producing a particular textbook as a function of the number of copies ·produced. Three tangents are drawn at points A, B, and C, corresponding to production runs of 10,000, 20,000, and 30,000 respectively. The slope of each tangent line represents the instantaneous rate of change (here cost per book) for the associated production run.

The slope of the tangent line at A is greater than the slope of the tangent line at B, which in turn is greater than the slope of the tangent line at C. Accordingly, the instantaneous rate of change, cost per book, is greater at A than at B, and the instantaneous rate of change at B is still greater than at C

That is, the additional cost of producing book 10,001 is greater than the additional cost of producing book 20,001, which in turn is greater than the additional cost of producing book 30,001. As more books are produced, it becomes cheaper per book to produce additional books.

We devote all of Chapter 5 to discussing other important commercial applications of instantaneous rates of change. For the remainder of this chapter, we confine ourselves to developing simple methods for computing these rates. Finding instantaneous rates of change by calculating average rates of change over smaller and smaller intervals, as in Examples 1 and 2, is tedious and time-consuming. The work usually can be simplified with an algebraic procedure.

In the previous two examples, we calculated $(y_2 - y_1)/(x_2 - x_1)$ or, equivalently $[f(x_2) - f(x_1)]/(x_2 - x_1)$ over the interval $[x_1, x_2]$ as x_2 approached x_1. This concept of having one point approach another point, here x_2 approaching x_1 is fundamental to all of calculus. We are interested in knowing what happens as x_2 gets arbitrarily close to x_1; the words *arbitrarily* and *close* are both important.

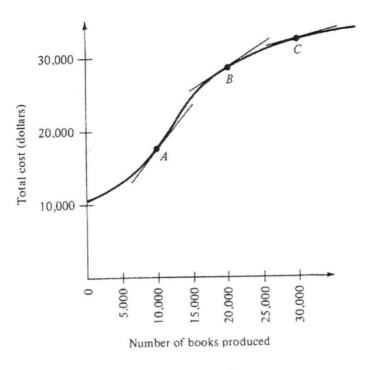

Number of books produced

FIGURE 4.16

First, we are not interested in what happens when x_2 equals x_1 but only in the result as x_2 gets close to x_1 Just how close is another matter, and we use the word *arbitrarily* to signify as close as the mind can conceive. The mathematical notation for this concept is $\lim_{x_2 \to x_1}$, read "the limit as x_2 approaches x_1."

An example may clarify the concept. Imagine a talented bug placed on one end of a yardstick and instructed to move one-half the distance remaining to the other end of the yardstick every second. During the first second, the bug moves 1/2 yard. There is still 1/2 yard to go and, since it must move half the remaining distance each second, the bug moves 1/4 yard during the next second and still has 1/4 yard to go. During the third second, the bug moves one-half of this distance or 1/8 yard. It continues this process forever. Does the bug ever reach the other end of the yardstick? Obviously not, since it still has some distance left after each move. But it does get close to the end— arbitrarily close.

Leaving the bug, we consider the mathematical problem of calculating $\lim_{x_2 \to 5} (2x_2 - 1)$, that is, finding the value of the quantity $(2x_2 - 1)$ as x_2 approaches 5.

As x_2 gets arbitrarily close to 5, $2x_2$ approaches 10 and $2x_2 - 1$ approaches 9. We write this as

$$\lim_{x_2 \to 5} (2x_2 - 1) = 9.$$

The same answer could have been obtained by simply substituting $x_2 = 5$ into $2x_2 - 1$, *but such a substitution is procedurally wrong. First, $\lim_{x_2 \to 5}$ is shorthand notation for x_2 approaching 5, not x_2 equaling 5.* More importantly, however, direct substitution does not always work, as Example 3 illustrates.

Example 3   Evaluate $\lim_{x_2 \to 3} \dfrac{(x_2)^2 - 9}{x_2 - 3}$.

Solution Simply substituting the value 3 for x_2 in the given expression yields 0/0 which is arithmetically meaningless. However, an algebraic approach is often successful in finding the limit rather than using the tabular approach used in Examples 1 and 2.

    Note that the numerator $(x_2{}^2 - 9)$ can be factored into $(x_2 - 3)(x_2 + 3)$, and we can then cancel the common factor, $(x_2 - 3)$, from both the numerator, resulting in

$$\lim_{x_2 \to 3} \frac{(x_2)^2 - 9}{x_2 - 3} = \lim_{x_2 \to 3} \frac{(x_2 - 3)(x_2 + 3)}{(x_2 - 3)} \quad , x_2 \neq 3$$
$$= \lim_{x_2 \to 3} (x_2 + 3) = 6$$

Example 3 is a prototype for many problems involving instantaneous rates of change, in which we must calculate

Instantaneous Rate of change in $f(x)$ at $x_1 = \lim\limits_{x_2 \to x_1} \dfrac{f(x_2) - f(x_1)}{x_2 - x_1}$ (Eq. 4.6)

If we simply substitute $x_2 = x_1$ into Equation 4.6 we will always obtain 0/0, which is meaningless. The algebraic approach used in Example 3, however, is often successful. That is, we first factor $(x_2 - x_1)$ from the numerator, when possible, and then cancel a common factor from both the numerator and the denominator before letting x_2 approach x_1,

Example 4 Find the instantaneous rate of change $f(x) = x^2$ at $x = 1$ using Equation 4.6.

Solution Here $x = 1$ (the point at which we want information about the function) and $f(x) = x^2$, hence $f(x_1) = (x_1)^2 = (1)^2 = 1$ and $f(x_2) = (x_2)^2.$ Note that we do not substitute a numerical value for x_2, because it represents a moving point which will later approach $x_1 = 1$. Using Equation 4.6, we obtain

$$\lim_{x_2 \to 1} \frac{f(x_2) - f(x_1)}{x_2 - x_1} = \lim_{x_2 \to 1} \frac{(x_2)^2 - 1}{x_2 - 1}$$

$$= \lim_{x_2 \to 1} \frac{(x_2 - 1)(x_2 + 1)}{(x_2 - 1)} \quad , x_2 \neq 1$$

$$= \lim_{x_2 \to 1} (x_2 + 1) = 2$$

Compare this approach to the one used in Table 4.2.

Rather than working with Equation 4.6 directly, it is sometimes easier first to change notation by setting $h = x_2 - x_1$. Here h represents the distance between x_2 and x_1. On solving, $h = x_2 - x_1$ for x_2, we also have $x_2 = x_1 + h$, and can replace the requirement "x_2 approaches x_1" with the requirement "h approaches 0." That is, because $x_2 = x_1 + h$, the condition that h approaches 0 is equivalent to the condition that x_2 approaches x_1. Substituting the quantities $h = x_2 - x_1$, $x_2 = x_1 + h$, and $\lim_{x_2 \to x_1} = \lim_{h \to 0}$ into Equation 4.6, we obtain

Instantaneous Rate of change in $f(x)$ at $x_1 = \lim_{h \to 0} \dfrac{f(x_1 + h) - f(x_1)}{h}$ (Eq. 4.7)

The last expression gives the instantaneous rate of change in a given function $y =$ $f(x)$ at a specific point x_1. Generally, one needs the instantaneous rate of change for a given function at many points. For example, in the textbook case illustrated in Figure 4.16, we found the instantaneous rate of change at three points. To find instantaneous rates at several points, we can proceed in one of two ways. First, we can evaluate Equation 4.7 separately at all the points x_1 that we need. A more efficient procedure is first to evaluate Equation 4.7 at the arbitrary point $x_1 = x$ and then substitute the required values of x into the result.

Replacing x_1 by x in Equation 4.7, we conclude that the

Instantaneous Rate of change in $f(x)$ at any point $x = \lim_{h \to 0} \dfrac{f(x + h) - f(x)}{h}$ (Eq. 4.8)

We can use Equation 4.8 to calculate the instantaneous rate of change in a given function $f(x)$ at any point x. Should we require the instantaneous rate of change at a particular point, we simply evaluate the resulting expression at the required point.

The following four-step process is recommended for evaluating Equation 4.8

Step 1   Find $f(x + h)$ by replacing x with the quantity $x + h$ in the given function $f(x)$.

Step 2   Calculate $f(x + h) - f(x)$ by subtracting $f(x)$ from the expression for $f(x + h)$ found in Step 1. Simplify the resulting difference.

Step 3   Divide by h.

Step 4   Let h approach zero.

Example 5 Determine a general expression for the instantaneous rate of change in the function $f(x) = x^2$ using Equation 4.8. Evaluate this expression at the points $x = 1, x = 3$, and $x = 5$.

Solution Using the recommended four-step procedure for evaluating Equation 4.8 .with $f(x) = x^2$, we find

Step 1: $f(x + h) = (x + h)^2,$

Step 2: $f(x + h) - f(x) = (x + h)^2 - x^2$
$$= (x^2 + 2xh + h^2) - x^2$$
$$= 2xh + h^2$$

Step 3: $\dfrac{f(x+h)-f(x)}{h} = \dfrac{2xh + h^2}{h} = \dfrac{h(2x+h)}{h} = 2x + h \quad , h \neq 0$

Step 4: As h approaches zero, the expression $2x + h$ approaches $2x$. Therefore,

$$\lim_{h \to 0} \frac{f(x + h) - f(x)}{h} = \lim_{h \to 0}(2x + h) = 2x.$$

What this means is that the instantaneous rate of change in the function $f(x) = x^2$ at any point x is $2x$. In particular, the instantaneous rate of change at $x = 1$ is $2(1)$ $= 2$. The instantaneous rate of change at $x = 3$ is $2(3) = 6$, whereas the instantaneous rate of change at $x = 5$ is $2(5) = 10$.

Example 6 Determine a general expression for the' instantaneous rate of change in the function $f(x) = 2x^2 + 3x - 2$.

Solution Following the recommended four-step procedure, we have

Step 1: $f(x + h) = 2(x + h)^2 + 3(x + h) - 2$

Step 2: $f(x + h) - f(x) = [2(x + h)^2 + 3(x + h) - 2] - [2x^2 + 3x - 2]$
$$= [2x^2 + 4xh + 2h^2 + 3x + 3h - 2] - [2x^2 + 3x - 2]$$
$$= 4xh + 2h^2 + 3h$$

Step 3: $\dfrac{f(x+h)-f(x)}{h} = \dfrac{4xh + 2h^2 + 3h}{h} = \dfrac{h(4x+2h+3)}{h} = 4x + 2h + 3, h \neq 0.$

Step 4: As h approaches zero, the expression $4x + 2h + 3$ approaches $4x + 3$. Therefore,

$$\lim_{h\to 0}\frac{f(x + h) - f(x)}{h} = \lim_{h\to 0}(4x + 2h + 3) = 4x + 3.$$

which is a general expression for the instantaneous rate of change in $f(x) = 2x^2 + 3x - 2$ at any point x

We conclude this section with a few observations. First, the general expression for the instantaneous rate of change in a given function at an arbitrary point x is itself a function of x. In Example 5 we found the instantaneous rate of change in $f(x) = x^2$ to be $2x$, while in Example 6 we found the instantaneous rate of change in $f(x) = 2x^2 + 3x - 2$ to be $4x + 3$. This is not at all surprising. Because most functions are not linear equations, it follows that the graphs of such functions are not straight lines. Therefore most curves have different tangents at different points on the curve, and these different tangents have different slopes (for examples, see Figures 4.15 and 4.16.) Because the slopes of the tangent lines are the instantaneous rates of change, these rates depend on (are functions of) the particular point under consideration.

Throughout this section we have assumed that x_2 was always greater than x_1 or, equivalently, that h was always positive. This need not be the case. As we take smaller and smaller intervals, we require only that x always be in each interval. It need not be the left-hand end point. In actuality, one should show that the answer obtained for the instantaneous rate of change using x_1 as the left end point of each interval is the same answer obtained using intervals with x_1 as the right-hand end point. Only if both approaches yield the same answer can we mathematically say that an instantaneous rate of change exists. Exercise 14 is an example in which both approaches are not the same. For most functions encountered in commercial applications, however, both approaches yield the same result.

Even though the algebraic procedure given by Equation 4.8 is often quicker than the tabular approach used in Examples 1 and 2, it too is formidable. The real value of Equation 4.8 is that it can be used to develop other rules which are simpler and quicker for calculating instantaneous rates of change. These rules are the subject of Sections 4.5 and 4.6.

Section 4.4 Exercises

1. Sketch the function $f(x) = x^2 - 6x + 10$ and graphically determine the slope of the tangent lines at the points:
   a. $(1, 5)$ b. $(3, 1)$ c. $(5, 5)$.

2. a. Sketch the function $f(x) = x^2 - 4x + 5$ and graphically determine the slope of the tangent line at $(3, 2)$.
   b. Complete Table 4.5. Do the values in the last column approach the slope determined in part a.?

TABLE 4.5

x_1	x_2	y_1	y_2	$Average\ rate = \dfrac{y_2 - y_1}{x_2 - x_1}$
3	5.0	2		
3	3.5	2		
3	3.2	2		
3	3.1	2		

3. a. Sketch the function $f(x) = x^2 + x$ and graphically determine the slope at $x=2$.
   b. Complete Table 4.6 for this function. Do the values in the last column approach the slope determined in part a.?
   c. Use Equation 4.8 to find the exact answer.

TABLE 4.6

x_1	x_2	y_1	y_2	$Average\ rate = \dfrac{y_2 - y_1}{x_2 - x_1}$
2	5.0	6		
2	3.0	6		
2	2.5	6		
2	2.2	6		
2	2.1	6		

In Exercises 4 through 13, use Equation 4.8 to find a general expression for the instantaneous rate of change in the given function. Use this result to find the instantaneous rate of change at $x = 1$ and $x = $ -5.

4. $f(x) = 3x - 2.$ 5. $f(x) = 2 - 3x.$

6. $f(x) = \frac{1}{2}x^2 - 7.$ 7. $f(x) = x^2 - 2x + 10.$

8. $f(x) = x^3.$ 9. $f(x) = 2x^3 - 2x^2 + 3x - 1.$

10. $f(x) = \frac{1}{x}.$ 11. $f(x) = \frac{x}{x+2}.$

12. $f(x) = \frac{1}{x} + x.$ 13. $f(x) = \frac{1}{x^2}.$

14. Consider the function

$$y = \begin{cases} 2 + 5x & (x \le 3) \\ 23 - 2x & (x > 3) \end{cases}$$

which is sketched in Figure 4.16.

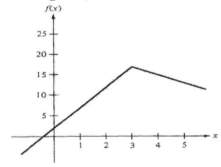

FIGURE 4.16

a. Determine graphically whether this curve has a tangent at $x = 3$.
b. Compute average rates of change for this function over the intervals having $x = 3$ as one end point and the second end point given successively by 3.2, 2.8, 3.1, 2.9, 3.05, 2.95, 3.01, 2.99, 3.005, and 2.995. Do these rates approach a fixed value? What can you conclude about the instantaneous rate of change at $x = 3$?

15. Consider the function

$$y = \begin{cases} 7 & (x \le 5) \\ 12 & (x > 5) \end{cases}$$

which is sketched in Figure 4.18. Calculate average rates of change for this function over the intervals having $x = 5$ as one end point and the second end point given successively by 3, 7, 4,6, 5.3, 5.3, 5.7, 5.3, 5.9, 5.1, 5.95, 5.05 ,5.99, and 5.01. What is the instantaneous rate of change in this function at $x = 5$?

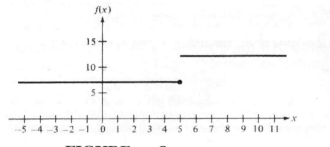

FIGURE 4.18

16. A company's sales are known to be related to advertising expenditures by the equation $S(x) = 150,000 + 6000x - 50x^2$, where x denotes the monthly advertising expenditures in thousands of dollars.
    a. Find the instantaneous rate of change in sales with respect to advertising expenditures.
    b. Using your answer to part a, determine whether an increase in advertising would increase sales if the present advertising budget is $45,000. Would the situation be different with a$60,000 advertising budget?

17. A firm's total sales, in millions of dollars, are given by the function $R(x) = 3x + \frac{1}{2} x^2,$ where x denotes the number of years the firm has been in operation.
    a. Determine the firm's average growth rate in sales for its first 7 years in business.
    b. Determine the firm's instantaneous rate of growth after its seventh year in business.
    c. What will the firm's total sales be at the end of the tenth year if sales continue to follow the given equation?
    d. What will the firm's total sales be at the end of the tenth year if the growth in sales after the seventh year always equals the growth achieved at the end of the seventh year?

18. Determine the values of x for the function illustrated in Figure 4.19 between or at which the instantaneous rate of change in y with respect to x is:

a. positive,
b. negative,
c. zero.

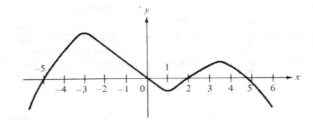

FIGURE 4.19

4.5 The Derivative

The instantaneous rate of change in a function is referred to as the derivative of the function. The following definition is an immediate consequence of Equation 4.8.

Definition 4.2 The *derivative* of the function $y = f(x)$ at the point x is

$$\lim_{h \to 0} \frac{f(x + h) - f(x)}{h}$$

Two different but equally common notations are used for the derivative of $y = f(x)$, namely, dy/dx, read "dee y dee x" and $f'(x)$, read " f prime of x." The choice of notation is strictly one of personal preference; we use both interchangeably in this text. In Example 5 in Section 4.4, we found that the instantaneous rate of change, and therefore the derivative, of $y = f(x) = x^2$ is $2x$. Notationally, we write either $dy/dx = 2x$ or $f'(x) = 2x$. Note, however, that dy/dx does *not* mean dy divided by dx, and $f'(x)$ does *not* mean f' times x. Both symbols are only notations for "the derivative of $y = f(x)$ with respect to the independent variable x" or, equivalently, "the instantaneous rate of change in $y = f(x)$ with respect to x."

Because the derivative is nothing more than an instantaneous rate of change, we can use the four-step procedure described on page 163 to calculate it. As we noted in Section 4.4, however, this procedure is both time-consuming and tedious. More efficiently, Definition 4.2 is used to generate simple general rules for calculating derivatives. These rules are then used to find specific function derivatives as needed (the interested reader can refer to almost any calculus text for a derivation of the rules that follow from this definition). The rules themselves are as follows.

Rule 1: The derivative of a constant is zero. That is, if $f(x) = c$, where c is a given fixed real number, $f'(x) = 0$.

Interpretation: This rule is straightforward and with some thought obvious. The graph of the equation $y = f(x) = c$ is a straight line parallel to the x-axis. The rate of change of y as x changes, that is, the derivative, of a line parallel to the x-axis is zero. This is because the y value is the same for all values of x, *as* the y value never changes.

Example 1 Determine the derivative of the function $f(x) = 10$.

Solution Using Rule 1 with $c = 10$, we obtain $f'(x) = 0$.

Example 2 Determine the derivative of the function $f(x) = 255$.

Solution Using Rule 1, $f'(x) = 0$.

Rule 2: The derivative of the function $f(x) = x^n$, where n is an real number, is $f'(x) = nx^{n-1}$.

Interpretation: Rule 2 provides the derivative of a class of functions having the form x^n. Examples of such functions are x^2, x^{10}, x^{-8}, $x^{-1/2}$, and $x^{3.1}$. The rule states that if we are given this type of function, which is x raised to a power, the derivative of this function is the power times x raised to one less power.

Example 3 Determine the derivative of $f(x) = x^2$.

Solution $f(x) = x^2$ is of the form x raised to a power. Using Rule 2 with $n = 2$, we obtain $f'(x) = 2x$. (Compare this result to that obtained in Example 5, using algebraic methods, in the previous section)

Example 4 Determine the derivative of $f(x) = x^{10}$.

Solution As this function has the form x^n, Rule 2 applies. Here, n = 10, and using

Rule 2, with n $=$ 10, we obtain $f'(x) = 10x^9$.

Example 5 Determine the derivative of $f(x) = x^8$.

Solution Again, this function had the form x^n, so Rule 2 applies, where n = -8. Using Rule 2, with n $=$ -8, we obtain $f'(x) = -8x^{-9}$.

Example 6 Determine the derivative of $f(x) = x^{-1/2}$

Solution Using Rule 2, with n $=$ - ½, we obtain $f'(x) = -\frac{1}{2}x^{-3/2}$

Example 7 Determine the derivative of $f(x) = x^{3.1}$

Solution Using Rule 2, $f'(x) = 3.1\,x^{2.1}$.

Having given rules for finding the derivative of two specific types of functions, namely,

1. a function consisting of a single constant, and
2. a function consisting of a single function having the form x^n,

we now present three rules that deal with combinations of functions, such as $f(x)$ = $10x^8$ and $f(x) = x^{-4} + x^7 + 20$.

Rule 3: If $f(x) = cg(x)$, where c is a fixed real number and $g(x)$ is a function of x whose derivative is known, then $f'(x) = cg'(x)$.

Interpretation: This rule states that the instantaneous rate of change (that is, the derivative) of a number times a function is simply the number itself times the derivative of the function. Note that this is a general rule that applies to many function, not just functions of the form x^n.

Example 8 Find $f'(x)$ if $f(x) = 20x^5$.

Solution The function $f(x) = 20x^5$ has the form $cg(x)$, where c is the number 20 and $g(x)$ is the function x^5. Thus, we can use Rule 3 to find its derivative. The derivative of x^5 is $5x^4$ (Why?) Then, using Rule 3, $f'(x) = 20(5x^4) = 100\,x^4$.

Example 9 Find $f'(x)$ if $f(x) = 6x^9$.

Solution Using Rule 3, $f'(x) = 6(9x^8) = 54x^8$.

A question that frequently arises is, Why is $g(x)$ used in Rule 3, rather than the statement, "The derivative of cx^n is c times nx^{n-1}"? The reason is that Rule 3 applies to many other functions besides cx^n, as we will see later in Example 12.

Rule 4a (Addition Rule): If the functions $g_1(x)$ and $g_2(x)$ both have derivatives, then the derivative of the function
$f(x) = g_1(x) + g_2(x)$ is $f'(x) = g_1'(x) + g_2'(x)$.

Interpretation: This rule, like Rule 3 is a general rule that applies to many functions. It states that the derivative of a sum of two functions is simply the sum of the derivatives of each function by itself.

Example 10 Determine the derivative of the function $f(x) = 3x^6 + 5$.

Solution The given function is the sum of the two functions $3x^6$ and 5. Here $g_1(x) = 3x^6$, so $g_1'(x) = 18x^5$ (Rule 3), and $g_2(x) = 5$, so $g_2'(x) = 0$ (Rule 1). It now follows from Rule 4 that $f'(x) = 18x^5 + 0 = 18x^5$.

Rule 4 can be extended in the obvious fashion to include the sum of any number of terms. Furthermore, if we replace the plus signs in Rule 4 with minus signs, we obtain:

Rule 4b (Subtraction Rule): If the functions $g_1(x)$ and $g_2(x)$ both have derivatives, then the derivative of the function
$f(x) = g_1(x) - g_2(x)$ is $f'(x) = g_1'(x) - g_2'(x)$.

As with the addition rule (Rule 4), the subtraction rule also can be extended to include the difference of any number of terms.

Example 11 Find $f'(x)$ for $f(x) = 2x^2 - 3x - 5$.

Solution The derivative of $f(x)$ is the difference of the derivatives of the three terms x^2, $3x$, and 5. Here,

1. $g_1(x) = 2x^2$, hence $g_1'(x) = 4x$ (Rule 3),
2. $g_2(x) = 3x$, hence $g_2'(x) = 3$ (Rule 3), and
3. $g_3(x) = 6$, hence $g_3'(x) = 0$ (Rule 1).

Therefore $f'(x) = g_1'(x) - g_2'(x) - g_2'(x) = 4x - 3 - 0 = 4x - 3$.

If all functions were polynomials, then Rules 1 through 4 would be sufficient to handle most cases. Most functions are not polynomials, however, and they cannot be differentiated using any of the previous rules. If you blindly apply Rule 2, for instance, to any function, you invariably will obtain the wrong derivative. A case in point is the exponential function $f(x) = e^x$, introduced in Section 1.5.

Rule 5: The derivative of the function $f(x) = e^x$ is $f'(x) = e^x$.

Interpretation: The function e^x is indeed a remarkable function. The derivative of the function equals the function itself; it is impervious to change by differentiation. Geometrically, this signifies that the slope of the tangent line to e^x at any point x is numerically equals the value of e^x at that point.

Example 12 Determine the derivative of the function $f(x) = 10e^x$.

Solution Using Rules 3 and 5, we have $f'(x) = 10e^x$.

Example 13 Determine the derivative of the function

$$f(x) = 5x^5 + 6x^3 - 3x + 5 - 8e^x$$

Solution Differentiating $f(x)$ term by term, we obtain

$$f'(x) = 25x^4 + 18x^2 - 3 - 8e^x.$$

When the derivative of a function is needed at a particular point, it is obtained by first finding the derivative and then evaluating it at the point of interest. The notation for the derivative of $y = f(x)$ evaluated at $x = x_0$ is either

$$f'(x_0)$$

or

$$\frac{dy}{dx}\bigg|_{x_0}$$

Both symbols are read "the derivative of $y = f(x)$ evaluated at the point $x = x_0$."

Example 14 Find the derivative of $f(x) = 2x^2 - 3x - 6$ at both $x = 5$ and

$x = -2$.

Solution First, we determine the derivative of f(x), which is (see Example 11)

$$f'(x) = 4x - 3 - 0 = 4x - 3.$$

Evaluating this derivative at the required points, we obtain

$$f'(5) = \left.\frac{dy}{dx}\right|_5 = 4(5) - 3 = 17$$

and

$$f'(-2) = \left.\frac{dy}{dx}\right|_{-2} = 4(-2) - 3 = -11.$$

Warning: $f'(5)$ denotes the "derivative of $f(x)$ evaluated at $x = 5$" and *not* the "derivative $f(5)$", which is zero. That is, the value $x = 5$ is substituted into the expression for the derivative $f'(x)$ and not the function $f(x)$. The derivative is taken first and then evaluated; the function is *not* evaluated first and then differentiated.

Section 4.5 Exercises

In Exercises 1 through 16, find $f'(x)$.

1. $f(x) = x^5 - 7x^3 + 4x + 2$

2. $f(x) = x^5 - 7x^2$

3. $f(x) = x^7 + 6x^3 - 4x^2$

4. $f(x) = 9x^2 + 3x + 5$

5. $f(x) = \frac{x^5}{5} - \frac{x^3}{3} - \frac{x^2}{2} + 10$

6. $f(x) = (x^2 + 3) x^5$

7. $f(x) = (x^2 + 4)(x^5 + 3)$

8. $f(x) = (x + 3)(x - 9)$

9. $f(x) = 10e^x$

10. $f(x) = x^3 + 6e^x$

11. $f(x) = x^4 - 7x^2 + 7e^x$

12. $f(x) = (x + 3)(x - 9) + 10e^x$

13. $f(x) = x^2(x + 2) + 8e^x$

14. $f(x) = (x^2 + 4)(x + 7) + e^x$

15. $f(x) = \frac{x^2 + 12x + 20}{x + 2}$ (*Hint:* First factor the numerator.)

16. $f(x) = \frac{x^2 - 4x - 21}{x + 3}$

In Exercises 17 through 24, find dy/dx.

17. $y = x^7 + 6x^5 + 3x + 5$

18. $y = x^3 - 3x + 5$

19. $y = x^5 - \frac{x^4}{4} + 7e^x$

20. $y = \frac{x^4}{4} + 4e^x$

185

21. $y = \dfrac{x^4}{4} - \dfrac{x^3}{3} - \dfrac{x^2}{2}$

22. $y = (x + 4)(x - 7)$

23. $y = (x^2 + 2)(x - 3)$

24. $y = \dfrac{x^3 - 4x^2 + 5x - 20}{x - 4}$

25. A company's sales are known to be related to advertising expenditures by the equation $S(x) = 150{,}000 + 6000x - 50x^2$, where x denotes the monthly advertising expenditures in thousands of dollars.
    a. Find the instantaneous rate of change in sales with respect to advertising expenditures.
    b. Using your answer to part a, determine whether an increase in advertising would increase sales   if the present advertising budget is \$45,000. Would the situation be different with a \$60,000 advertising budget?

26. A firm's total sales, in millions of dollars, is given by the equation $R(x) = 3x + 1/2\, x^2$, where x denotes the number of years the firm has been in operation.
    a. Determine the firm's average rate of growth in sales for its first 7 years in business.
    b. Determine the firm's instantaneous rate of growth after its seventh year of business.
    c. What will the firm's total sales be at the end of the tenth year if sales continue to grow *at the same rate of growth* achieved after the seventh year?
    d. What total sales has the firm actually reached after its tenth year of business? Compare your answer to the answer for part c. and explain the discrepancy.

27. Figure 4.20 illustrates the distance traveled as a function of time for Mr. Williams' 2-mile trip through the Holland Tunnel. The equation of the curve illustrated is $D = -0.05t^3 + 0.25t^2 + 0.3t$, where D is the distance traveled in miles and t is measured in minutes from the start of the trip.

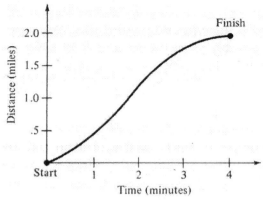

FIGURE 4.20

a. Determine the average rate of change in distance with respect to time for the complete 2-mile trip. Physically, what does your answer represent?

b. Redraw Figure 4.20 on a separate sheet of graph paper. Draw a line on the graph whose slope represents the average speed determined in part a.

c. Determine the speed of Mr. Williams' car at exactly 1 minute after the start his trip. (*Hint:* Speed is the instantaneous rate of change in distance traveled with respect to time.)

d. Draw a line on the graph constructed for part b, whose slope represents the instantaneous speed determined in part c.

e. Determine the exact speed that would be indicated on Mr. Williams' speedometer as he emerges from the tunnel ($t = 4$).

28. Determine the values of x for the function illustrated in Figure 4.21 between or at which

a. the derivative is positive,

b. the derivative is negative, and

c. the derivative is zero.

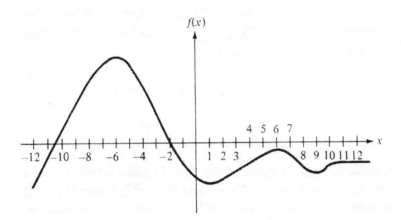

FIGURE 4.21

29. From past experience it is known that an increase in the price of wheat leads to a decrease in the demand for wheat. Based on this information, determine which of the following equations may possibly relate the demand, D, for wheat to its price, p.

a. $D = 30p^2 + 5p + 2000$
b. $D = 3000/p$
c. $D = 5p^2 - 2000$
d. $D = 5p^2 - 2000p$.

30. From past experience it is known that an increase in the price of silver leads to an increase in the demand for this commodity. Based on this information, determine which of the following equations may possibly relate the demand D for silver to its price p.

a. $D = \dfrac{200}{p}$ b. $D = 300p^2 + 5p + 200$

c. $D = 2000 - 2p^3$ d. $D = \dfrac{150}{p^2}$.

4.6 Additional Rules

Rules 1, 2 and 5 in the previous section provided the derivatives of the three specific function types listed in Table 4.7.

Table 4.7

Derivatives of Three Specific Types of Functions

If $f(x)$ is	Its Derivative is	Examples	Comments
c	0	If $f(x) = 10$ $f'(x) = 0$	Rule 1: The derivative of a constant is 0
x^n	nx^{n-1}	If $f(x) = x^6$ $f'(x) = 6x^5$	Rule 2, with n = 6 and n-1 = 5
e^x	e^x	If $f(x) = e^x$ $f'(x) = e^x$	Rule 5:

Also given were rules for finding the derivatives of combinations of functions (rules, 3, 4, and 4a) which are summarized in Table 4.8. In this section additional rules are provided that will complete Table 4.8 by providing rules for finding the derivatives of functions that are multiplied, divided, and raised to a power.

Table 4.8

Rules for Finding the Derivatives of Combinations of Functions

Combination Type	General Format	Derivative	Comment
A Constant times a function	$f(x) = cg(x)$	$f'(x) = c\,g'(x)$	Rule 3
Addition	$f(x) = g_1(x) + g_2(x)$	$f'(x) = g_1'(x) + g_2'(x)$	Rule 4
Subtraction	$f(x) = g_1(x) - g_2(x)$	$f'(x) = g_1'(x) - g_2'(x)$	Rule 4a

Having general rules for finding the derivatives of functions that are added and/or subtracted, our next rule shows how to find the derivative of two functions that are multiplied together

> **Rule 6 (Product Rule):** If the functions $g_1(x)$ and $g_2(x)$ both have derivatives, then the derivative of the function $f(x) = g_1(x)\,g_2(x)$ is
> $$f'(x) = g_1(x)\,g_2'(x) + g_2(x)g_1'(x)$$

Interpretation: This rule states how to take the derivative of two functions that are multiplied together. It says *that the derivative of a product of two functions is the first function times the derivative of the second function plus the second function times the derivative of the first function* (note that the derivative of a product is *not* equal to the product of the individual derivatives).

Example 1 Find $f'(x)$ if $f(x) = x^2 e^x$.

Solution We first note that the function whose derivative we want is the product of two functions, which in this case are x^2 and e^x. Thus, $g_1(x) = x^2$ and $g_2(x) = e^x$, and their associated derivatives are $g'_1(x) = 2x$ (from Rule 2) and $g'_2(x) = e^x$, (from Rule 5), respectively. Using Rule 6 we obtain

$$f'(x) = x^2 e^x + e^x(2x) = x^2 e^x + 2x e^x.$$

Example 2 Determine the derivative of the function $f(x) = x^2(x^3 + 3)$.

Solution We can do this problem two ways.

First Way: Use the Product Rule. Because $f(x)$ is the product of two functions, x^2 and $(x^3 + 3)$, we set $g_1(x) = x^2$ and $g_2(x) = (x^3 + 3)$. The respective derivatives of these functions are $g'_1(x) = 2x$ and $g'_2(x) = 3x^2$, respectively. Using Rule 6 we find

$$f'(x) = x^2(3x^2) + (x^3 + 3)(2x)$$
$$= 3x^4 + 2x^4 + 6x$$
$$= 5x^4 + 6x.$$

Second Way: The same answer is obtained by algebraically simplifying the original function $f(x) = x^2(x^3 + 3) = x^5 + 3x^2$, and then differentiating term by term using Rule 5.

At this point we have rules for determining the derivative of functions that are added, subtracted, and multiplied. The next rule provides the details of determining the derivative of two functions that are divided.

Rule 7 (Quotient Rule): If the functions $g_1(x)$ and $g_2(x)$ both have derivatives, with $g_2(x) \neq 0$, then the derivative of the function $f(x) = g_1(x) / g_2(x)$ is

$$f'(x) = \frac{g_2(x)g'_1(x) - g_1(x)g'_2(x)}{[g_2(x)]^2}$$

Interpretation: This rule states how to determine the derivative of a function consisting of one function divided by another. It says, *the derivative of a quotient is the function in the denominator times the derivative of the function in the numerator minus the numerator function times the derivative of the denominator function, with the entire result divided by the square of the denominator function* (note that the derivative of a quotient is *not* equal to the quotient of the individual derivatives).

Example 3 Find the derivative *of* $f(x) = e^x / x^5$.

Solution We first note that the derivative we want is the quotient of two functions, which in this case are e^x and x^5. Thus, $g_1(x) = e^x$ and $g_2(x) = x^5$, and their associated derivatives are $g_1'(x) = e^x$ (from Rule 5) and $g'_2(x) = 5x^4$ (from Rule 2), respectively. Substituting the appropriate terms into Equation 4.10, we obtain

$$f'(x) = \frac{x^5(e^x) - e^x(5x^4)}{[x^5]^2} = \frac{x^5 e^x - 5x^4 e^x}{x^{10}} = \frac{xe^x - 5e^x}{x^6}, x \neq 0$$

Example 4 Find $f'(x)$ for $f(x) = e^x/(x^2 + 4)$.

Solution Again, we first notice that it is a quotient whose derivative is desired, which means we will use the quotient rule (Rule 7). Here, the numerator function, $g_1(x) = e^x$ and the denominator function, $g_2(x) = (x^2 + 4)$. Thus, $g'1(x) = e^x$ (from Rule 5) and $g'_2(x) = 2x$ (from Rule 2). Using Rule 7, we obtain

$$f'(x) = \frac{(x^2 + 4)(e^x) - e^x(2x)}{[x^2 + 4]^2},$$

which, after simplifying, becomes

$$f'(x) = \frac{(x^2 - 2x + 4)e^x}{[x^2 + 4]^2},$$

Occasionally, we have to differentiate a function raised to a power such as $f(x) = (x^2 + 3x + 12)^3$. The following rule provides the method for finding the derivative of this type of function.

Rule 8 (Power Rule): If $f(x) = [g(x)]^n$ where n is a fixed real number and the derivative of g(x) exists, then
$$f'(x) = n[g(x)]^{n-1} g'(x)$$

Interpretation: Although this rule resembles Rule 2, it is quite different. Rule 2 deals with the a single variable raised to a power, as in x^n, where this rule deals with a function that may be made up of many terms raised to a power, such as $(x^2 + 3x + e^x)^3$. The rule states that to find the derivative of a function raised to a power, first treat the function inside the brackets, denoted here by $g(x)$, as a single term and apply Rule 2. Then multiply this result by $g'(x)$, which is simply the derivative of what is inside the brackets.

Example 5 Determine the derivative of $f(x) = (x^2 + 3x + 12)^3$.

Solution First notice that the function consists of the quantity $(x^2 + 3x + 12)$ raised to the third power. As such, it is a function raised to a power, whose derivative can be found using the Power Rule (Rule 8). Therefore, $g(x) = x2 + 3x + 12$, which is the quantity being raised to a power, and the power itself is 3. Thus, $n = 3$ and $g'(x) = 2x + 3$, and it follows from Rule 8 that $f'(x) = 3(x^2 + 3x + 12)^2(2x + 3)$.
     This answer can also be obtained by a second procedure, which firsts cubes the quantity $(x^2 + 3x + 12)$, and then takes the derivative of each term using the Addition Rule (Rule 4). Using Rule 8, however, is quicker.

Example 6 Differentiate $f(x) = \sqrt{x^2 + 1}$

Solution Because $\sqrt{x^2 + 1} = (x^2 + 1)^{1/2}$ we can use Rule 8. Here we set $g(x) = (x2 + 1)$ and take n = ½. Then $g'(x) = 2x$, and it follows from Equation 4.11 that $f'(x) = ½ (x^2 + 1)^{(1/2 - 1)}(2x) = x(x^2 + 1)^{-1/2}$.
Note that in this case the alternative procedure used in Example 5 is not applicable for this function, and Rule 8 provides the only procedure for finding the derivative.

Let us try to apply Rule 8 to the function $f(x) = e^{nx}$, where n is a fixed real number. If we first rewrite $f(x)$ as $f(x) = (e^x)^n$, we have the required form for Rule 8, with $g(x) = e^x$. Now $g'(x) = e^x$ (Rule 5), and Rule 8 yields $f'(x) = n[e^x]^{n-1}(e^x) = ne^{nx}$. We have proven Rule 9.

Rule 9: If $f(x) = e^{nx}$, where n is a fixed real number, $f'(x) = ne^{nx}$.

Interpretation: In fact, Rule 5 is simply a specific case of Rule 9, with n = 1. Rule 9, as do Rules 1, 2, and 5 provides the derivative of a specific class of functions, specifically all functions having the form x^n or e^{nx}.

Example 7 Differentiate $f(x) = e^{8x}$

Solution Using Rule 9, with n = 8, yields, $f'(x) = 8e^{8x}$.

Example 8 Differentiate $f(x) = (3 + 4e^{7x})^{1.95}$

Solution First, notice that $f(x)$ is another function, $g(x) = (3 + 4e^{7x})$, raised to the n = 1.95 power. Using Rule 9 in combination with other appropriate rules, we find $g'(x) = 0 + 4(7)e^{7x} = 28e^{7x}$. It then follows from the power rule that

$f'(x) = 1.95 (3 + 4e^{7x})^{1.95-1} (28e^{7x})$
$\qquad = 54.6 (3 + 4e^{7x})^{.95} (e^{7x})$

To this point, we have considered only functions given by the one equation $y = f(x)$. Frequently, however, business problems are modeled by a set of two equations having the form $y = g_1(u)$ and $u = g_2(x)$. An example of such a set is $y = u^2 + 3u$ and $u = 6x + 2$. Because we can substitute the value for u into the equation for y, it follows that y is ultimately a function of x, and it makes sense to ask for the derivative dy/dx. Interestingly, we can find dy/dx directly without substituting first, if the individual derivatives $g_1(u)$ and $g_2(x)$ are known. The procedure is known as the chain rule.

Rule 10 (Chain Rule): If $y = g_1(u)$ and $u = g_2(x)$, and if both the derivatives dy/du and du/dx are known, then

$$\frac{dy}{dx} = \left(\frac{dy}{du}\right)\left(\frac{du}{dx}\right)$$

 Interpretation: This rule states that the desired derivative of y as a function of x, dy/dx, can be found by multiplying the first derivative, dy/du by the second derivative, du/dx. The term *chain rule* evolves from the ultimate derivative, dy/dx, being a "chain" of two other derivatives, namely, dy/du and du/dx.

Example 9:   Determine dy/dx if $y = u^2 - 5u + 7$ and $u= 7x^2 + 10$.

Solution Using the chain rule, we first determine

$$\frac{dy}{du} = 2u - 5 \qquad and \qquad \frac{du}{dx} = 14x$$

Then,

$$\frac{dy}{dx} = (2u - 5)(14x) = [2(7x^2 + 10) - 5](14x) = 196x^3 + 210x$$

Alternatively, we could first substitute the expression for u into the equation for y, obtaining

$$y = (7x^2 + 10)^2 - 5(7x^2 + 10) + 7 = 49x^4 + 105x^2 + 57.$$

Then, differentiating this expression directly, we again determine

$$\frac{dy}{dx} = 196x^3 + 210x$$

Example 10: A firm's monthly sales revenue S is known to be related to its advertising expenditures by the equation S = 100 - 30E + 0.2E^2, where E represents monthly advertising expenditures in thousands of dollars. The company allocates its monthly advertising expenditure based on the equation $E = 0.1x^2 - 0.3x + 5000$, where x represents thousands of units sold the previous month. Determine the derivative dS/dx, which is the instantaneous rate of change of sales with respect to previous monthly sales.

Solution We are asked to find dS/dx, given S = 100 - 30E + 0.2E^2 and $E = 0.1x^2 - 0.3x + 5000$. Modifying the notation in Equation 4.12 so that it is applicable to this situation, we obtain

$$\frac{dS}{dx} = \frac{dS}{dE} \frac{dE}{dx}$$

Performing the appropriate operations, we have

$$\frac{dS}{dx} = (-30 + 0.4E)(0.2x - 0.3)$$

which, upon substituting $0.1x^2 - 0.3x + 5000$ for E, becomes

$$\frac{dS}{dx} = 0.008x^3 - 0.036x^2 + 394.036x - 591$$

The alternative procedure suggested in Example 9 is applicable here also.

Table 4.9 summarizes all of the general rules for finding the derivatives of combinations of functions presented in this and the previous section.

Table 4.9 General Rules for Finding Derivatives of Combinations of Functions

Combination Type	General Format	Derivative
A Constant times a function	$f(x) = c\, g(x)$	$f'(x) = c\, g'(x)$
Addition	$f(x) = g_1(x) + g_2(x)$	$f'(x) = g_1'(x) + g_2'(x)$.
Subtraction	$f(x) = g_1(x) - g_2(x)$	$f'(x) = g_1'(x) - g_2'(x)$.
Multiplication	$f(x) = g_1(x) \cdot g_2(x)$	$f'(x) = g_1(x)g_2'(x) - g_2(x)g_1'(x)$
Division	$f(x) = g_1(x) / g_2(x)$	$f'(x) = [g_2(x)g_1'(x) - g_1(x)g_2'(x)] / [g_2(x)]^2$
Power	$f(x) = [g(x)]^n$	$f'(x) = n[g(x)]^{n-1} g'(x)$
Chained	$y = g_1(u)$ and $u = g_2(x)$	$dy/dx = (dy/du)(du/dx)$

Section 4.6 Exercises

In Exercises 1 through 18, find $f'(x)$.

1. $f(x) = (x^2 + 3x)(x^5 + x^7 + 2x)$

2. $f(x) = e^{10x}(x^2 + 4)$.

3. $f(x) = x^{-5} + x^{-3} + x^{-2}$

4. $f(x) = (x^{5/2} + x^{1/2})(x^{-4} + x^{-6})$

5. $f(x) = x^{-5/2} + x^{-1/2}$

6. $f(x) = e^x(x^3 + x^{1/2} + x^{-5})$

7. $f(x) = (x^3 + x^5) / (x^2 + x^4)$

8. $f(x) = (x^2 + 3x)/ e^x$

9. $f(x) = e^{4x} / (x^5 - x^3)$

10. $f(x) = e^{7x}/(x^2 + 3)$

11. $f(x) = e^{7x}x^7$.

12. $f(x) = (x^2 + 3) / e^{2x}$

13. $f(x) = (x^6 + 7)/(x^5 + 3x)$

14. $f(x) = (x^2 + 3)^4/(x^7 + x^3)$

15. $f(x) = (x^7 + 6x)^5$.

16. $f(x) = (x^2 + 3x)^6$

17. $f(x) = (x^4 + 3x^2 + 4x + 2)^3$

18. $f(x) = (x^2 + 3e^{4x})^5$

In Exercises 19 through 26, find dy/dx.

19. $y = e^{10x}x^3$.

20. $y = (x^2 + 4x)^5$.

21. $y = x^5 + 3x^{-5}$.

22. $y = x^{-4} + x^{-3} + x^{-2}$.

23. $y = \dfrac{1}{x^5} + \dfrac{1}{x^4}$

24. $y = \sqrt{(x^2 + 4)}$.

25. $y = x^{3/2} + 7x^{5/2}$

26. $y = (x^{10} + 7x^2)(5x^3 + 6x)$.

In Exercises 27 through 29, find dS/dx using the chain rule.

27. $S = E^2 + 3E, \quad E = x^2$.

28. $S = E^2 + 3, \quad E = x^3 + 5$.

29. $S = E/(E + 2), \quad E = 3x^2 + 5$.

4.7 Higher-Order Derivatives

Just as we took the first derivative of a differentiable function, we usually can differentiate the derivative itself. This derivative of the derivative is called the *second derivative* and is commonly denoted by $f''(x)$, y'', d^2y/dx^2, or $d^2[f(x)]/dx^2$. To obtain the second derivative of a function, we treat the first derivative as a new function and differentiate it using the rules of Sections 4.5 and 4.6. Generally, only the first and second derivatives of a function have applications to business problems.

Example 1 Determine the first derivative and second derivative of the function $y = 3x^2 + 2x + 5$.

Solution We initially determine the first derivative, and then take the derivative this function to obtains the second derivative.

The first derivative is obtained, using Rule 4, as

$$f'(x) = \frac{dy}{dx} = 6x + 2$$

The derivative of this function, which is the second derivative, is obtained using Rule 4 once again, as

$$f''(x) = \frac{d^2y}{dx^2} = 6$$

Example 2 Determine d^2y/dx^2 for the function $y = x^2e^x$.

Solution We first find dy/dx and then differentiate it to obtain d^2y/dx^2. Using the product rule (Rule 6), we have

$$dy/dx = x^2e^x + 2xe^x$$

Differentiating dy/dx term-by-term (Rule 4), which requires the product rule for each of the two terms in the sum, we obtain

$$\frac{d^2y}{dx^2} = (x^2e^x + 2xe^x) + (2xe^x + 2e^x)$$

$$= x^2e^x + 4xe^x + 2e^x$$

$$= e^x(x^2 + 4x + 2)$$

Continuing in this manner, we could define third-, fourth-, fifth-, and higher-order derivatives. However, only the first two derivatives of a function have applications to business problems. We consider some of these applications in Chapter 5.

Section 4.7 Exercises

In Exercises 1 through 6, find dy/dx and d^2y/dx^2 and evaluate the second derivative at the points $x = 1$ and $x = 2$.

1. $y = x^5 + 4x^2 + 3x$.   2. $y = x + 3$.
3. $y = x^4 + 3x^2 + 4x + 5$.   4. $y = e^x$.
5. $y = x^3e^{10x}$.   6. $y = 5x^2e^{7x}$.

7. Figure 4.22 represents the distance traveled as a function of time for Mr. Williams' 2-mile trip through the Holland Tunnel, first considered in Exercise 27 in Section 4.5. The equation of the curve illustrated is
$D = -0.05t^3 + 0.25t^2 + 0.3t$, where D is the distance traveled in miles, and t

is measured in minutes from the start of the trip.

a. Determine a general expression for the speed of Mr. Williams' car at any time during the trip.

b. Determine the speed that would be indicated on Mr. Williams' speedometer at $t = 1$ minute.

c. Determine a general expression for Mr. Williams' acceleration at any time during the trip. (*Hint:* Acceleration = $d(speed)/dt = d^2D/dt^2$.)

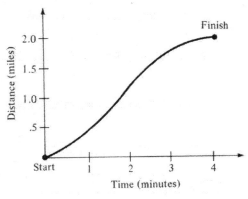

FIGURE 4.22

d. Using your answer for part c., determine Mr. Williams' acceleration at $t = 1$ minute and $t = 3$ minutes. What is the significance of the negative sign at $t = 3$ minutes?

5

Applications of the Derivative

5.1 Optimization through Differentiation
5.2 Modeling
5.3 Maximizing Sales Profit
5.4 Minimizing Inventory Costs
5.5 Econometrics

Optimization, which is the process of either maximizing or minimizing a quantity, is central to most business problems. For example, how many units of a product should be manufactured to maximize profit? How often should material be ordered to minimize total inventory cost? What is the best method for government agencies to control money supplies so as to maximize employment?

In Section 5.1, we develop the theory of optimization based on the derivative. Recall from Chapter 4 that differentiation is a mathematical operation performed on functions. To apply the derivative to business situations, we must first construct mathematical equations that realistically model or represent the situations of interest. The importance of mathematical models is presented in Section 5.2

Once the appropriate equations have been obtained that realistically model the situations being investigated, the optimization technique developed can be applied. Examples of this approach are presented in Sections 5.3 and 5.4.

It is important to realize that not all applications of the derivative deal with optimization. Rates of change have direct applications themselves, many of which were presented in the examples and exercises provided in Chapter 4. An additional, and more advanced example, is presented in Section 5.5.

5.1 Optimization through Differentiation

In this section we introduce a method for finding the high and low values of mathematical functions. The high values are known as *maximum points*, or *maxima*, for short, and the low points as *minimum points*, or *minima*, for short. Together, a function's maxima and minima are referred to as it's *optimal values*. In subsequent sections, we show how to derive a number of important commercial functions, and then how to locate these functions' optimal values using the techniques presented in this section.

As a specific example, assume we know that the relationship between profit P (in dollars) and the number of items manufactured and sold, x, for a particular industry is modeled by the equation

$$P = -x^2 + 120x - 600 \qquad \text{(Eq. 5.1)}$$

We want to know the value(s) of x that will maximize P. That is, how many items should be manufactured if the objective is maximum profit?

One approach is to substitute different values of x into Equation 5.1, calculate corresponding values of P, and determine the values of x that maximizes P. Substituting $x = 10$ into Equation 5.1, we obtain $P = -(10)2 + 120(10) - 600 = \$500$. Substituting $x = 20$ into Equation 5.1 gives $P = \$1,400$. Continuing in this manner, we generate Table 5.1. It appears that $x = 60$ will produce a maximum profit of $P = \$3000$. But can we be sure? Perhaps $x = 61$ will generate a bigger profit. Or, perhaps the maximum profit occurs at $x = 137$.

TABLE 5.1

x (units)	0	10	20	40	60	70	80
P ($)	-600	500	1,400	2,600	3,000	2,900	2,600

The difficulty in calculating the function for only some values of the independent variable, as is done in Table 5.1, is that we are never sure that the optimum does not occur at another value.

A second and more useful procedure for finding maxima and minima is through graphing. Agreeing that the *maximum value* of a function is the largest value the function can obtain, and similarly that the *minimum value* of a function is the smallest value the function can obtain, we conclude that maxima appear as high points and minima appear as low points on the graph of a function.

Plotting the points given in Table 5.1 and realizing that $P = -x^2 + 120x - 600$ is a quadratic equation (see Section 2.5), we draw Figure 5.1 as the graph of Equation 5.1. It is evident from the curve that the maximum profit is \$3,000 from a production run at $x = 60$ units. At this time, Equation 5.1 does not have a minimum, since there is no point in Figure 5.1 that is smaller than every other point.

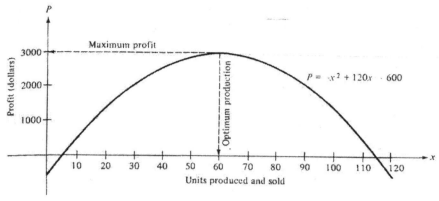

FIGURE 5.1

Example 1 Graph $y = x^2 - 10x + 16$ and determine the maximum and minimum values for y.

Solution This equation is quadratic. Arbitrarily selecting values of x, computing the corresponding values of y, and plotting these points, we obtain Figure 5.2. The minimum value of y is -9 which occurs when $x = 5$. The function does not have a maximum, because there is no point on the graph that is larger than every other point.

In both Figures 5.1 and 5.2 one of the optimal values, either the maximum or the minimum, did not exist. The reason was that the domain, the set of allowable values for the independent variable x, was infinite. The larger we allowed x to become in Figure 5.1, the smaller P became. The larger we allowed x to become in Figure 5.2, the larger y became. Both situations are unrealistic from a business point of view. In business there is always a limit beyond which it is either impossible or not feasible to go.

On an absolute scale, every product is limited in number by the amount of raw material available in the world. Realistically, production runs are also limited by the demand for the product, the time required to make the product, and the capital investment necessary to produce the product. Even under the best conditions, only a finite number (perhaps a large finite number) of each product can be produced. Similarly, every service, on an absolute scale, is limited by the time people have available to perform the service.

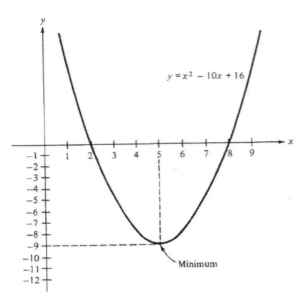

FIGURE 5.2

The point is that every business process has finite limits or boundaries. Therefore every mathematical model of a business situation must reflect these limits. Most often this is done by restricting the domain. Equation 5.1 is not a good model for a commercial situation, because it does not indicate limits on the values of x. A more realistic model is

$$P = -x^2 + 120x - 600 \qquad (0 \leq x \leq 150) \qquad \text{(Eq. 5.2)}$$

We now have the additional information that no less than 0 products and no more than 150 products can be produced. With these restrictions, the graph of Equation 5.2 becomes Figure 5.3, where we have plotted only points associated with the domain $0 \leq x \leq 150$. It now follows that the maximum is $P = \$3000$, occurring at $x = 60$, *and* the minimum is $P = -\$5,100$, occurring at $x = 150$.

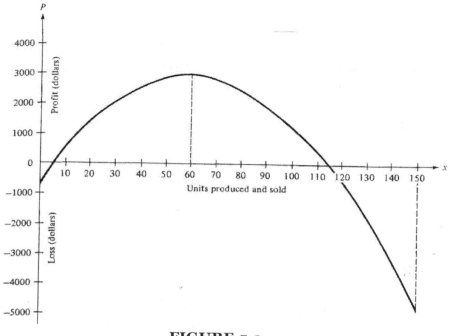

FIGURE 5.3

Example 2 Figure 5.4 represents the relationship between the dollar value of inventory on hand for a distribution center over a 12 month time period t, where t is in months ($0 \le t \le 12$). Find the maximum and minimum dollar values of inventory on hand.

Solution The maximum value of inventory on hand is $7 million which occurs at both $t = 1$ and $t = 12$. The minimum value is $2 million, occurring at $t = 6$.

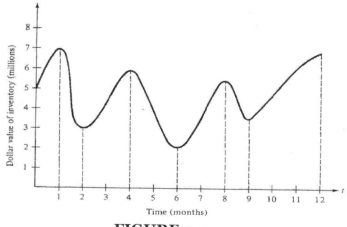

FIGURE 5.4

It follows from Example 2 that optimal values can occur at more than one place. Note that the maximum occurred at both $t = 1$ and $t = 12$.

The peaks at $t = 4$ and $t = 8$ and the valleys at $t = 2$ and $t = 9$ also are interesting. They are not maxima or minima, because there are other points on the graph that are higher $(t = 1)$ and lower $(t = 6)$. Nonetheless, they are high and low points for some small subset of the domain, and, as such, are often called *relative maxima* and *relative minima*. A detailed development of their properties is given in the exercises.

Finding optimal points by graphing has two disadvantages. The first is lack of accuracy. Can we really conclude from Figure 5.2 that the maximum occurs at $t = 6$ and not at $t = 6.1$ or 5.98? No, but as one rarely needs more accuracy than can be obtained from a graph, this disadvantage is not serious. The major difficulty is that the curve must be graphed. Accurately graphing a complicated equation is frequently a difficult and time–consuming procedure which we would like to avoid if possible.

A third approach to optimization, which is more accurate, direct, and eliminates the need for graphing, uses differentiation. This differentiation method is based on the following theorem, the proof of which can be found in most calculus texts.

Theorem 5.1 Let a function be defined on a domain $a \le x \le b$ and have a maximum or minimum at a point c, where $a < c < b$. If the derivative of the function exists at $x = c$, then the derivative must be zero there.

This theorem, after a little thought, is rather obvious. Note in Figures 5.2 and 5.3 that the tangents to each curve at the maximum and minimum points, if drawn, would be horizontal, and therefore have zero slopes. Because the derivative is the slope of the tangent line, it follows that the derivative at such maximum or minimum points is zero.

This theorem simplifies the search for optimal points. Maxima and minima can occur only where the first derivative is zero or where the theorem is not applicable. The theorem is not applicable in two cases. First, it says nothing about optimal points at the boundaries of the domain, usually called the *end points*. In Theorem 5.1, the end points are $x = a$ and $x = b$. Second, the theorem says nothing about optimal points at places where the derivative does not exist. Accordingly, maxima and minima of functions can occur at only one of three points, and nowhere else:

1. Points where the first derivative is zero
2. Points where the first derivatives do not exist
3. End points.

To locate maximum and minimum points for any function, first find all points where the first derivative is zero, then all points where the derivative does not exist, and finally all end points. These points, taken together, are referred to as *candidate points*, or *candidates*, for short. Substituting each of the candidate points into the given equation will determine which of the points optimize it.

Example 3 Determine the maximum and minimum values of the function

$$P = -x^2 + 120x - 600 \quad (0 \le x \le 150)$$

Solution Differentiating the given function, we have $dP/dx = -2x + 120$. To find values of x for which this derivative equals zero, we set the derivative equal to zero and solve for x. Accordingly,

$$-2x + 120 = 0$$
$$-2x = -120$$
$$x = 60$$

The first derivative exists everywhere, because for each value of x the quantity $dy/dx = -2x + 120$ is defined; thus, there are no points where the first derivative does not exit (category 2). The end points are $x = 0$, $x = 150$. Thus, the candidates for the points at which the function's maximum and minimum values occur are $x = 60$, $x = 0$, and $x = 150$.

Gathering these candidate points together, we substitute each into the given function and evaluate the corresponding values for P. This is done in Table 5.2. It is now clear that the maximum is $P = \$3{,}000$, which occurs at $x = 60$, and the minimum is $P = -\$5{,}100$, which occurs at $x = 150$.

TABLE 5.2

x	$P = -x^2 + 120x - 600$	
0	-600	
60	3,000	← Maximum
150	-5,100	← Minimum

Example 4 Determine the maximum and minimum values of the function

$$y = x^3 - 21x^2 + 120x - 100 \quad (1 \le x \le 12).$$

Solution Differentiating the given function, we find $dy/dx = 3x^2 - 42x + 120$. To locate all values of x for which this derivative is zero, we set the derivative equal to zero and solve for x. Thus,

$$3x^2 - 42x + 120 = 0$$
$$x^2 - 14x + 40 = 0 \quad \text{(dividing by 3)}$$
$$(x - 10)(x - 4) = 0 \quad \text{(factoring)}$$
$$x = 10 \quad \text{and} \quad x = 4.$$

Thus, the first derivative is zero at $x = 10$ and $x = 4$.

There are no points for which the first derivative does not exist, because $dy/dx = 3x^2 - 42x + 120$ can be evaluated at all values of x. The end points for this problem are $x = 1$ and $x = 12$.

Evaluating the given function at the candidate points, $x = 10$, $x = 4$, $x = 1$, and $x = 12$, we obtain Table 5.3. It follows that the maximum is $y = 108$ which occurs at $x = 4$, and the minimum is $y = 0$ which occurs at two places, $x = 10$ and $x = 1$.

TABLE 5.3

x	$y = x^3 - 21x^2 + 120x - 100$	
1	0	←Minimum
4	108	← Maximum
10	0	← Minimum
12	44	

Example 5 Determine the maximum and minimum of $y = t^3 - 9t^2 - 120t + 1{,}500$ ($0 \le t \le 30$).

Solution Differentiating the given function, we find $dy/dt = 3t^2 - 18t - 120$. To locate all values of t for which this derivative is zero, we set the derivative equal to zero and solve for t. Thus

$$3t^2 - 18t - 120 = 0$$
$$t^2 - 6t - 40 = 0 \quad \text{(dividing by 3)}$$
$$(t + 4)(t - 10) = 0 \quad \text{(factoring)}$$
$$t = -4 \quad \text{and} \quad t = 10.$$

The first derivative is zero at $t = -4$ and $t = 10$. Because $t = -4$ is outside our domain and not an allowable point for this problem, we disregard it.

The first derivative exists everywhere, because for each value of t the quantity $3t^2 - 18t - 120$ is defined. The end points for this problem are at $t = 0$ and $t = 30$. Evaluating the given function at the candidate points, $t = 0$, $t = 10$, and $t = 30$, we obtain Table 5.4. It follows that the maximum is $y = 16{,}800$ occurring at $t = 30$, and the minimum is $y = 400$, which occurs at $t = 10$.

TABLE 5.4

t	$y = t^3 - 9t^2 - 120t + 1500$	
0	1,500	
10	400	← Minimum
30	16,800	← Maximum

Example 6 Determine the maximum and minimum values of the function

$$D = (P - 20)^2(P - 30)^2 \qquad (20 \leq P \leq 35)$$

Solution Differentiating this function with the product rule for differentiation, we obtain

$$\frac{dD}{dP} = (P - 20)^2 2(P - 30) + (P - 30)^2 2(P - 20)$$
$$= 2(P - 20)^2(P - 30) + 2(P - 30)^2(P - 20)$$

Setting this quantity equal to zero and solving for P, we have

$$2(P - 20)^2 (P - 30) + 2(P - 30)^2(P - 20) = 0$$
$$2(P - 20)(P - 30)[(P - 20) + (P - 30)] = 0$$
$$2(P - 20)(P - 30)(2P - 50) = 0.$$
$$P = 20, \quad P = 30, \quad \text{and} \quad P = 25.$$

The derivative exists everywhere, and the end points are $P = 20$ and $P = 35$. It follows from Table 5.5, where all of the candidates are evaluated, that the maximum is $D = 5{,}625$, which occurs at $P = 35$, and the minimum is $P = 0$, which occurs at both $P = 20$ and $P = 30$.

TABLE 5.5

P	$D = (P - 20)^2 (P - 30)^2$	
20	0	←Minimum
25	625	
30	0	←Minimum
35	5,625	← Maximum

Section 5.1 Exercises

In Exercises 1 through 5 find the maximum and minimum values of the given functions two ways: First, graph the functions, visually locating the optimal points and, second, use differentiation.

1. $y = 3x^2 - 24x - 5$, $(0 \le x \le 6)$
2. $y = -x^2 + 25x - 3.5$, $(4 \le x \le 16)$
3. $y = 7x^2 + 56x + 25$, $(0 \le x \le 5)$
4. $y = -5x^2 + 100x$, $(0 \le x \le 20)$
5. $y = 2x - 1$, $(25 \le x \le 50)$

In Exercises 6 through 15 use the first derivative to determine maximum and minimum values of the given functions.

6. $D = t^3 - 12t + 7$, $(-3 \le t \le 3)$
7. $D = t^3 - 12t + 7$, $(-4 \le t \le 4)$
8. $D = t^3 - 12t + 7$, $(-5 \le t \le 5)$
9. $D = t^3 - 12t + 7$, $(0 \le t \le 3)$
10. $P = 2n^3 - 54n + 2800$, $(-3 \le n \le 5)$
11. $y = t^3 + 3t^2 - 105t + 20$ $(-10 \le t \le 10)$
12. $y = x^3 - 48x + 57$, $(0 \le x \le 4)$
13. $x = (1/3)t^3 - 4t^2 + 12$, $(0 \le t \le 9)$
14. $T = c^3 - 10c^2 + 12c + 10$, $(0 \le c \le 10)$
15. $y = (x - 10)(x - 20)$, $(5 \le x \le 25)$

16. A television manufacturer has found that the profit P (in dollars) obtained from selling x television sets per week is given by the formula $P = -x^2 + 300x - 5,000$. Determine how many television sets the manufacturer should produce to maximize profits. What is the maximum profit that can be realized?

17. A manufacturing company has found that the profit P (in dollars) realized in selling x items is given by $P = 22x - \dfrac{x^2}{2,000} - 10,000$.
    a. How many items should the manufacturer produce to maximize profit?
    b. Find the maximum profit.

18. The manufacturer described in Exercise 16 also has determined that the total cost of producing x items, denoted by TC (in dollars) is given by
    $$TC = \dfrac{x^2}{2,000} - 7x + 10,000.$$
    a. Determine the number of items that should be produced if the

    manufacturer's goal is to minimize total cost rather than to maximize profit. .

    b. What is the minimum total cost? Is this answer reasonable?

19. In the course of a week, a refrigerator manufacturer can sell x refrigerators at a unit price of $300. The total cost TC (in dollars) is given as $TC = 2.5x^2 - 200x + 20{,}000$.

    a. How many units should the firm produce each to maximize profits?

    b. Determine the maximum profit.

    c. Determine the total cost associated with achieving maximum profit?

20. A firm has found that the total cost TC (in dollars) of producing x items is given by the equation $TC = \frac{1}{3}x^3 - 10x^2 - 800x + 12{,}000$. Determine the number of units this firm should produce to **minimize** its total production cost.

21. Assume that the firm described in Exercise 20 can sell all units it produces at a fixed price of $325 per unit. Determine how many units this firm should produce to maximize its profit.

22. Find the maximum and minimum values of the function given by

$$y = \begin{cases} -x^2 + 2x + 5 & (0 \le x \le 2) \\ x + 1 & (2 < x \le 3) \end{cases}$$

23. Find the maximum and minimum values of the function given by

$$y = \begin{cases} -x^2 + 2x + 5 & (0 \le x \le 2) \\ x^2 - 8x + 16 & (2 < x \le 5) \end{cases}$$

24. A function $y = f(x)$ has a *relative* maximum at $x = c$ if there exists an interval (perhaps very small) centered around $x = c$ such that the maximum value of $f(x)$ over this interval occurs at $x = c$. Determine the relative maxima for the function drawn in Figure 5.4.

25. A function $y = f(x)$ has a *relative minimum* at $x = c$ if there exists an interval (perhaps very small) centered around $x = c$ such that the minimum value of $f(x)$ over this interval occurs at $x = c$. Determine the relative minima for the function drawn in Figure 5.4.

26. Can a relative maximum also be a maximum?

27. Can a relative maximum occur at an end point? Must a maximum be a relative maximum?

28. Theorem 5.1 remains true if the words "maximum" and "minimum" are replaced by "relative maximum" and "relative minimum." In addition, the following result is also valid. *If $f'(c) = 0$ and if the second derivative exists at $x = c$, then $x = c$ is a relative maximum if $f''(c) < 0$, and $x = c$ is a relative minimum if also $f''(c) > 0$.* Use this second–derivative test to show that $f(x) = -x^2 + 2x + 5$ has a relative maximum at $x = 1$.

29. Use the second–derivative test given in Exercise 28 to find all relative maxima and minima for $y = x^3 - 21x^2 + 120x - 100$, $1 \leq x \leq 13$.

30. If both the first and second derivatives of $f(x)$ are zero at $x = c$, no conclusions can be drawn from the second–derivative test. Show that both derivatives are zero at $x = 0$ for the three functions $y = x^4$, $y = -x^4$ and $y = x^3$. Graph each function and verify that $y = x^4$ has a relative minimum at $x = 0$, $y = -x^4$ has a relative maximum at $x = 0$, and $y = x^3$ has neither at $x = 0$.

5.2 Modeling

A *model* is a representation of a particular situation. A map is a model of a geographical region, a college transcript is a model of a person's academic achievement, and an organization chart is a model of a company's management structure. Many situations, especially dynamic ones that change with time, can be modeled by mathematical equations.

Very few models are ever complete; that is, the model does not reveal every aspect of the situation it represents. A map does not detail weather conditions (unless it is a weather map, in which case it does not detail road construction), a college transcript does not indicate the ease in which grades were achieved, and an organization chart does not detail the personalities of the people filling the slots. Generally, this is of little consequence.

Each model is built for a particular purpose, which usually requires representing only part of a situation. For a person planning a car trip, a road map may be an adequate model. For a person trying to locate the appropriate individual to see in a company, an organization chart is a good model. These models fit the needs of the people using them. This then is the criteria on which models are judged: Does the model adequately fit the needs of the person using the model?

The word "adequate" is important. What is considered adequate by one person may not be adequate to another. Consequently, a good model for one person may be either an inadequate or bad model for someone else. This is a fact of life. There are no absolutes in modeling. The usefulness of a model is relative to its purpose.

Because many commercial situations are too complex to be modeled in their entirety, simplifying assumptions are usually made that neglect minor contributions. A model of price fluctuations for a given product may not include the effects of a possible strike in the industry supplying raw materials. A model of consumer spending may not include psychological factors. The choice of which factors should be omitted is often subjective and depends on what factors are relevant for the situation being investigated. Omitting a factor is reasonable if the resulting model adequately represents the given situation.

Models are important to management as an aid in decision making because questions often arise as to which course of action out of many possible ones is the best. By applying each action to the model and observing the effects of these decisions on the model, an optimal decision often can be found. In the succeeding sections, we model specific business situations with mathematical equations. We then use differentiation methods on the models to ascertain an optimal strategy for the business problem at hand.

One simplification we make throughout this chapter is the modeling of discrete variables with continuous ones. Most business quantities can assume only integer values. Automobile sales are given in whole cars; profits are reported to the nearest dollar; the number of employees in an industry is a whole number. A production run of 19.73 cars, a profit of \$195.73869, and 30,198.7 employees are not commercially realistic.

More formally, we say that a quantity or variable is *continuous* if, whenever it assumes two different values, it can assume all numbers between these values.§§§§§ Car sales is not a continuous variable; one can sell 2 cars or 3 cars, but not 2.78 cars which is a number between 2 and 3. Profits are not continuous variables. A profit of \$1.95 is realistic, as is a profit of \$1.96, but a profit of \$1.9557 is not realistic. A good example of a continuous variable is time. An order may be placed at 8:07 or at 8:08, and also at 8:07396, although we may have difficulty in measuring it to this accuracy. Variables that are not continuous are called *discrete*. Car sales and profits are *discrete variables*.

Consider again Equation 5.2:

$$P = -x^2 + 120x - 600 \qquad (0 \le x \le 150),$$

which related the profit, P, to the number of units, x, produced for a particular

---

§§§§§ The concept of continuous variables is different from that of continuous functions. A rigorous definition of a continuous function can be found in any good calculus text.

commodity. We assumed that x could be any value between 0 and 150. Realistically, this is not the case, because sales are discrete variables which must be whole numbers. One cannot let $x = 49.8$. For the model, however, $x = 49.8$ is a perfectly good number within the domain. It can be substituted into Equation 5.2 with little difficulty.

Equation 5.2 models a discrete variable (number of units sold) by a continuous variable x. The reason for doing this is that differentiation techniques cannot be applied to discrete variables, only to continuous ones. If we wish to optimize a commercial situation with the derivative, we first must convert all discrete independent variables to continuous ones. We consider a model, for example Equation 5.2, to be valid if it adequately agrees with reality when the dependent variable assumes integer values. Thus, replacing discrete variables by continuous ones is a simple conceptual process made to the final result obtained by the model, should such a replacement make practical sense.

5.3 Maximizing Sales Profit

Profit maximization is a major goal of for-profit businesses. For companies that sell a physical product, this problem becomes one of determining the quantity of the product that is either produced or purchased, and then subsequently sold, to maximize the profit on the sale of the items. Mathematically solving this problem requires first creating an appropriate model and then, using the optimization techniques developed in the previous section, determining the maximum profit point

The Model

The mathematical model used for profit maximization is an extremely simple one, it is based on the standard definition of profit as the revenue received in sales minus the cost of either producing or purchasing the items sold. Using the notation developed in Section 2.4 (Break-Even Analysis), we have

R = total sales revenue

C = total cost incurred in producing or purchasing the items sold

Now, letting

P = profit
the mathematical model for profit is

$$P = R - C \qquad\qquad \text{(Eq. 5.3)}$$

In this model, P, R, and C are all taken to be functions of x, which is the number of items either produced or purchased and then subsequently sold.

There are two methods employed in using Equation 5.3 to determine the value of x that maximizes profit. Both methods rely on the simplifying assumption, used in this section, that all items, x, produced or purchased, can subsequently be sold.

The most common method is to first derive equations that accurately model R and C. These equations are then substituted into Equation 5.3, the derivative of the resulting single equation for P is taken, and then set to zero. This method is presented first.

A second method is to symbolically take the derivative of the profit equation, as it is written in Equation 5.3, and set it to zero. The resulting equation is then used to determine the relationship between the derivatives of R and C for maximum profit. This second method, quickly and easily, establishes one of the cornerstone theories in economics, that profit maximization is achieved when marginal revenue equals marginal cost. This second method is presented at the end of this section.

Method I: Maximizing a Single Profit Equation

The simplest revenue and cost equations are the ones previously presented in Section 2.4.****** These are:

$$R = px,$$

(Eq. 5.4)

where p the price per unit, and x is the number of items sold, and

$$C = ax + F$$

(Eq. 5.5)

where the a is the cost per item , F is the fixed costs, and x is the number of items produced or purchased. Because of the assumption that all items produced or purchased can be sold, x is the same variable in both Equation 5.4 and 5.5.

Example 1 How many items should a manufacturer make and sell to maximize profit if fixed costs are $10,000, each item costs $1.25 to make and sells for $1.50. Due to physical considerations, the manufacturer can produce a maximum of 100,000 units.

****** It should be noted that in Section 2.4 the value determined to be the break-even point was based on achieving no profit and no loss (that is $P = 0$). Here we are determining the number of items produced or purchased and subsequently sold to make P a maximum.

Solution We first determine the total revenue and cost equations. From Equation 5.4, the revenue received from selling x items, in dollars, is

$$R = 1.50x$$

Similarly, we use Equation 5.5 to obtain the cost equation In dollars, the total cost for producing x items is

$$C = 1.25x + 10,000.$$

Because $P = R - C$, we have

$$P = 1.50x - (1.25x + 10,000)$$
$$= 0.25x - 10,000 \qquad (0 \leq x \leq 100,000)$$

Taking the derivative of this function yields

$$P' = 0.25.$$

Clearly, this derivative can never be zero, because there is no value of x that will cause this to happen. Other points where a maximum can occur are the end points $x = 0$ and $x = 100,000$ and points where the first derivative does not exist, of which there are none. Thus, there are only two candidate points, $x = 0$ and $x = 100,000$.

Evaluating the function $P = 0.25x - 10,000$ at the candidate points, we obtain Table 5.6. It follows from this table that the maximum profit is 15,000 , which occurs the end point of 100,000 items (that is, the largest number of items that can physically be produced). This is reasonable, because the profit, P, increases for increasing values of x, the profit is maximized by producing and selling as many items as possible.

TABLE 5.6

x	$P = 0.25x - 10,000$
0	-10,000 <--End Point
100,000	15,000 <-- Maximum

The result found in this first example will always be true when the revenue and cost equations are determined by Equations 5.4 and 5.5. The reason is that each additional item produced and sold adds a fixed amount (the difference between the unit price and unit cost) to the profit. However, in practice, these two equations do not always accurately model revenue and cost, and maximum profits do not occur at maximum sales. The reasons for this are

1. The revenue can be a more complicated relationship than given by Equation 5.4. For example. there may be a discount for each item sold.

2. At some stage in an actual operation the added costs incurred in producing or purchasing additional items become higher due to such things as personnel costs , and increased insurance, equipment, lighting, security and space requirements. This means that the simple relationship given by Equation 5.5 does not apply.

Examples of these more complicated revenue and cost equations are considered next.

Example 2 Consider that the optimal number of widgets to be produced and sold is to be determined. Due to physical space and machine requirements, a maximum of 100,000 widgets can be manufactured. The units have the following cost and revenue equations, in dollars:

$$C= 0.25x + 10,000$$

and

$$R = (2.25 - .000025x)x = 2.25x - 0.000025x^2$$

That is, the cost equation is still determined as a combination of variable and fixed costs, but the unit price, p, has a discount of 0.000025 for each unit sold.
    Using Equation 5.3, the profit equation becomes

$$P = R - C = (2.25x - 0.000025x^2) - (0.25x + 10,000)$$

$$= -0.000025x^2 +2.00x - 10,000 \qquad (0 \le x \le 100,000)$$

Using the differentiation procedure detailed in Section 5.1, we first find
$$\frac{dP}{dx} = -.00005x + 2.00$$

Setting this derivative equal to zero, we calculate

$$-.00005x + 2.00 = 0$$

$$.00005\, x = 2.00$$

$$x = \frac{2.00}{.00005}$$

$$x = 40,000$$

Again, other points where a maximum can occur are the end points $x = 0$ and $x = 100,000$ and points where the first derivative does not exist, of which there are none. From Table 5.7 it can be seen that the largest monthly profit is $P = 30,000$ at a production run of 40,000 units, far from capacity.

TABLE 5.7

x	$P = -0.000025x^2 + 2x - 10,000$	
0	-10,000	<--End Point
40,000	30,000	<--Maximum
100,000	-60,000	<-- End Point

Example 3 A publishers sells a certain soft-cover book for $15 per copy. The revenue and cost equations for this book, in dollars are

$$R = 15x$$

and

$$C = \frac{x^2}{5,000} + 8x + 12,000$$

Determine the weekly production run that will generate maximum profit. Assume that all books published can be sold, the capacity of the publishing house is 20,000 copies per week, and the publisher has contractual obligations to a distributor for 5,000 copies per week.

Solution The profit equation for this example is

$$P = R - C = 15x - \left(\frac{x^2}{5,000} + 8x + 12,000\right) = -\frac{x^2}{5,000} + 7x - 12,000$$

To determine a suitable domain, we note that production capacity limits production to 20,000 copies, so $x \leq 20,000$. Contractual obligations require a run of at least 5,000 copies, hence $x \geq 5,000$. Together, we have $5,000 \leq x \leq 20,000$, and the problem becomes one to find values of x that will maximize

$$P = -\frac{x^2}{5,000} + 7x - 12,000 \qquad (5,000 \leq x \leq 20,000)$$

The first derivative of this function is

$$\frac{dP}{dx} = -\frac{2x}{5,000} + 7$$

Setting this first derivative to zero, we calculate

$$\frac{2x}{5,000} = 7$$

$$2x = 35,000$$

$$x = 17,500$$

Other points where the maximum may exist include the end points $x = 5000$ and $x = 20,000$, and points where dP/dx does not exist, of which there are none. It then follows from Table 5.8 that the maximum profit of $P = 49,250$ is realized with a production run of $x = 16,500$ copies per week.

TABLE 5.8

x	$P = -x^2/5,000 + 7x - 12,000$	
5,000	18,000	<--End Point
17,500	49,250	<--Maximum
20,000	48,000	<-- End Point

Method 2: Marginal Revenue Equals Marginal Cost

In this second method Equation 5.3 is used to determine a general relationship between revenue and cost that produces the same result as obtained using Method 1. This second method is presented as it easily and simply establishes one of the cornerstones of modern economic theory.

Consider Equation 5.3, which, for convenience is reproduced below

$$P = R - C \qquad\qquad \text{(Eq. 5.3)}$$

We know that, in the absence of any constraints on the production or purchase of the items being sold, the maximum profit point is found at the point for which the derivative of P, that is P', is zero. Taking the derivative of Equation 5.3 and setting it equal to zero yields

$$P' = R' - C' = 0$$

Solving this equation, the derivative is zero when

$$R' = C'$$

That is, the maximum profit is achieved when the derivative of the revenue function equals the derivative of the cost function. In economics, the derivative of revenue is referred to as **marginal revenue,** and the derivative of cost is referred to as **marginal cost**. Thus, in economic terms, maximum profit is achieved when marginal revenue equals marginal cost, barring any physical limitations on production (that is, without any restrictions defining end points)

From a mathematical perspective, this also provides a second method of maximizing profit. Once a revenue and cost equation have been determined, the derivative of each equation can be taken separately and these derivatives set equal and solved for x. The value obtained is the same as that produced by setting the derivative of the profit equation equal to zero.

Example 4 Find the optimal value of x for Example 3 by setting the marginal revenue equal to the marginal cost.
Solution The revenue and cost equations, from Example 3 are

$R = 15x$

and

$$C = \frac{x^2}{5,000} + 8x + 12,000$$

Thus, the marginal revenue, which is the derivative of the revenue function is

$R' = 15.$

Similarly, the marginal cost, which is the derivative of the cost function is

$$C' = \frac{2x}{5,000} + 8$$

.

Setting marginal revenue equal to marginal cost, we obtain

$$15 = \frac{2x}{5,000} + 8$$

Solving for x yields

$x = 16,00$

.

This is the same value that was obtained in Example 3 by setting the first derivative of the profit equation equal to zero. As in Example 3 (see Table 5.8), the end points would also have to be considered.

Section 5.3 Exercises

1. A television manufacturer can sell all units produced at $200 per unit. The total cost C (in dollars) in producing x units per week is given by $C = 5,000 + 20x + \frac{1}{2} x^2$.

    a. Determine an expression (model) for profit as a function of x.
    b. Determine an appropriate domain for x if the weekly production

capacity is limited to 300 units.
c. Determine the maximum weekly profit.

2. Redo Exercise 1 if the weekly production capacity is only 150 units.

3. A company can sell all units of a particular product. The cost equation (in dollars) of producing x units is given by

$$C = \frac{x^2}{4,000} - 5x + 50,000 .$$

The unit price is fixed at $10 per item.
a. Determine an expression for the profit as a function of x,
b. Determine an appropriate domain for x if the production capacity is limited to 50,000 units.
c. Find the maximum profit.

4. Redo Exercise 3 if in addition the manufacturer has contractual obligations for 40,000 units per week.

5. Assume that the manufacturer described in Exercise 3 is interested in minimizing costs rather than maximizing profits. How many units should be produced to achieve this objective?

6. A refrigerator manufacturer can sell all the refrigerators it can produce. The total cost for producing x refrigerators per week is given by the equation $C = 300x + 900$. The unit price, p, is related to the number of refrigerators sold by the equation $p = 700 - 2x$.
a. Determine an equation for the revenue equation.
b. Determine an equation for the profit.
c. Determine an appropriate domain if the production capacity is *100* units per week.
d. How many units should be produced in a week to maximize profits?

7. Redo Exercise 6 if the production capacity is only 40 refrigerators per week.

8. A clothing manufacturer can sell all the suits produced each month up to a limit of 500. The unit cost per suit is $150, and the fixed costs are $15,000. The unit price, in dollars, is given as $UP = 200 - 0.25x$. Determine the maximum profit the company can realize each month.

9. Determine the marginal revenue if
   a. $R = 15x$

b. $R = 200x - (1/4)x2$

.c. $R = 2.25x - 0.000025x^2$.

10. Evaluate the marginal revenue found in Exercise 9c for both $x = 30,000$ and $x = 50,000$.

11. Determine the marginal cost if
    a. $C = (x^2/5,000) + 8x + 12,000$
    b. $C = 50x + 5,000$
    c. $C = 10,000 + 0.25x$.

12. Evaluate the marginal cost found in Exercise 11c. for both $x = 30,000$ and $x = 50,000$.

13. Redo Example 2 by setting the marginal revenue equal to the marginal cost.

14. Find the optimal value of the quantity x in Exercise 3 by setting the marginal revenue equal to the marginal cost.

15. Find the optimal value of the refrigerators in Exercise 6 by setting the marginal revenue equal to the marginal cost.

5.4 Minimizing Inventory Costs

Optimizing techniques are used in inventory problems for minimizing the total of storage and ordering costs while simultaneously ensuring that enough items are on hand to meet current demand. In this section, we present a simplified inventory model and then determine the optimum number of items to stock to minimize the costs of ordering and storing inventory items. Inherently, we wish to avoid both over-stocking, with its resulting increase in storage costs, and under-stocking, with its resulting loss in sales. Table 5.9 presents the parameters that are assumed known; they are used to determine the optimum amount of items to be ordered with each order placed throughout the year.

TABLE 5.9 KNOWN INVENTORY PARAMETERS

Notation	Meaning	Comments
D	Annual demand for all of the items	A known amount.
m	Cost of placing a single order	A known dollar amount.
k	Cost of storing one item for one year.	Either given or calculated as the cost of financing times the cost of a single item.
f	Cost of financing, as a percent	Used to calculate k, if k is not given.
c	Cost of a single item	Used to calculate k, if k is not given.
t	Lead time	The delivery time, in days, between when an order is place and when it is received.

Table 5.10 lists the quantities that we will be calculating, with the last item in the table being the critical one – the EOQ.

TABLE 5.10 CALCULATED INVENTORY PARAMETERS

Notation	Meaning	Formula
x	Number of items to be ordered with each order	The unknown variable
N	Number of orders placed in a year	$N = \left(\dfrac{D}{x}\right)$
AI	Average items in inventory	$AI = \left(\dfrac{x}{2}\right)$
k	Annual storage cost for one item	$k = (f)(c)$, or it is given directly
TOC	Total Annual Ordering Cost	$TOC = (m)(N) = m\left(\dfrac{D}{x}\right)$
TSC	Total Annual Storage Cost	$TSC = k\left(\dfrac{x}{2}\right)$
TC	Total Annual Cost	$TC = TOC + TSC$
EOQ	Economic Order Quantity (Optimum Order Size)	$EOQ = x = \sqrt{\dfrac{2mD}{k}}$

The Model

In this problem, the goal is to determine the optimum order size, referred to as the **Economic Order Quantity**, **(EOQ)**, that minimizes the total yearly inventory costs, while maintaining sufficient inventory at all times to meet the daily demand for the inventoried items.

In addition to the quantities that are assumed known (see Table 5.9) two additional assumptions are made. These are:

1. The demand for items is uniform throughout the year. That is, as many items are sold during the first day as are sold during the 200th day, and as many items are sold during the fourth week as are sold during the seventeenth week.
2. Inventory is reordered at equal time intervals and in equal lots. For example, 700 cases every 2 weeks.

These two assumptions imply a depletion of inventory as shown in Figure 5.5

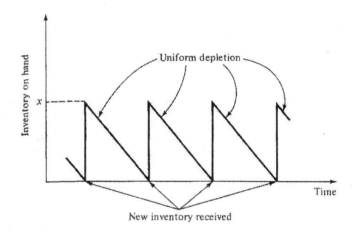

FIGURE 5.5

In this model, it is the total yearly cost, *TC*, that we want to minimize. This total cost is simply the sum of the total yearly ordering costs, *TOC*, and the total yearly storage cost, *TSC*, for the items. Mathematically,

$$TC = TOC + TSC \tag{Eq. 5.6}$$

The total yearly ordering cost, *TOC*, is determined as

TOC = (Cost of placing one order)(Number of orders placed in a year)
Thus,

$$TOC = m\left(\frac{D}{x}\right) \tag{Eq. 5.7}$$

The second cost needed to minimize total cost is the yearly storage costs, *TSC*. This cost is determined as

TSC = (Cost of storing one item for a year) (Average items in inventory)

Thus,

$$TSC = k\left(\frac{x}{2}\right) \tag{Eq. 5.8}$$

Substituting for *TOC* and *TSC* into Equation 5.6 yields

$TC =$ m(D/x)+k (x/2) $(1 \leq x \leq D)$

The domain of $1 \leq x \leq D$ is determined as follows: Realistically, no fewer than one item can be ordered at a time, and the maximum number of items that can be ordered is D, the amount of items needed in a year (Ordering D items at one time means that only one order is placed in a year).

How Much to Order

Before taking the derivative of the total cost function and setting it equal to zero,, we first re-write it as follows

$TC =$ mDx^{-1} + (k/2)x $(1 \leq x \leq D)$ (Eq. 5.9)

Taking the derivative of Equation 5.9 and setting it equal to 0, we have,

$d(TC)/dx$ = -mDx^{-2} + (k/2) = 0

Solving for *x* results in

x^2 = 2mD/k

or

$$x = \pm\sqrt{\frac{2mD}{k}}$$

Because $x = -\sqrt{2mD/k}$ is negative, and therefore not in the domain defined by

Equation 5.9, we disregard it. Although the first derivative $d(TC)/dx$ does *not* exist at $x = 0$ (because the quantity $(mD)/x$ is undefined at this point), this point is also not in the domain, and is disregarded. Thus, a minimum value of total cost can occur only at the end points $x = 1$ and $x = D$, or at

$$x = \sqrt{\frac{2mD}{k}}$$

This value of x is referred to as both the *optimum order size* and the *Economic Order Quantity, EOQ*. Thus,

$$EOQ = \sqrt{\frac{2mD}{k}}$$

(Eq. 5.10)

Example 1 A distributor estimates annual demand for television sets to be 1,000 units over the next year. The cost of placing a single order is $10, and storage costs per unit per year are $8. To minimize total inventory costs, determine
a. the optimum order size, and
b. the number of orders that will be placed in a year.

Solution For this problem $D = 1,000$, $m = 10$, and $k = 8$, where all monetary figures have been expressed as dollars. With these values,
a. From Equation 5.10 the Economic Order Quantity is:

$$EOQ = \sqrt{\frac{2mD}{k}}$$

$$= \sqrt{\frac{2(10)(1,000)}{8}} = \sqrt{2,500} = 50$$

Thus, the minimum occurs either at $x = 50$ or at the end points $x = 1$ and $x = 1,000$.[††††††] Substituting these values of x into the equation for TC, we generate Table 5.11, from which it follows that the optimal order size is $x = 50$, which is the Economic Order Quantity, EOQ.

[††††††] The minimum will always occur at the EOQ. The only time order size is limited occurs when the EOQ is larger than the maximum amount that can be ordered, due to physical restrictions on the order.

TABLE 5.11

x	$TC = m\left(\dfrac{D}{x}\right) + k\left(\dfrac{x}{2}\right) = 10\left(\dfrac{1,000}{x}\right) + 8\left(\dfrac{x}{2}\right)$
1	$10,004.
50	$400. <--Minimum
1000	$4010.

b. The total number of orders placed in a year, N, is determined from the equation N = D/x = 1,000/50 = 20 (see Table 5.10). That is, one thousand units are required over the year and each order is for 50 items; hence, the distributor must place 1000/50 = 20 orders.

Example 2 A soda distributor's annual demand for cases of soda is 2,000 a year. The cost of placing a single order is $9.66 and the storage costs per case per year is $1.40. To minimize total inventory costs, determine:
a. the optimum order size, and
b. the number of orders that will be placed in a year.

Solution Here D = 2,000 m = 9.66 and k = 1.40, where all monetary figures have been expressed as dollars. With these values,
a. From Equation 5.10 the Economic Order Quantity, rounded to the nearest single unit, is:

$$EOQ = \sqrt{\frac{2mD}{k}} = \sqrt{\frac{2(9.66)(2,000)}{1.40}} = \sqrt{27,600} = 166$$

Unless there is a restriction that limits an order to below this amount, the EOQ will produce the minimum cost. That is, the end points need not be checked because they do not restrict an order to be less than 166 cases, or at the end points of 1 and 2,000.

Substituting the value of 166 into the total cost equation

$$TC = m\left(\frac{D}{x}\right) + k\left(\frac{x}{2}\right),$$

which yields a total cost of

$$TC = 9.66\left(\frac{2,000}{166}\right) + 1.40\left(\frac{166}{2}\right) = \$232.58$$

b. The total number of orders placed in a year, N, is determined as D/x = 2000/166 = 12.04. Thus, rounded to the nearest unit, the minimum inventory cost is achieved by placing 12 orders throughout the year.

When to Order

In addition to determining *how many items* to order with each order, and *how many orders* will be needed in a year, it is also important to know *when* to place an order. This determination depends on the *lead time*, which is the estimated time between when an order is place and when it is received.

Take a look at Figure 5.5 again, reproduced below for convenience.

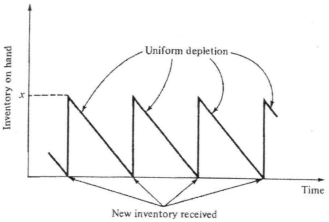

FIGURE 5.5

The model repesented by Figure 5.5 shows that new inventory is received exactly when the existing inventory goes to zero. In practice this is never true because daily demand is never exactly uniform. To compensate for this, orders are typically placed when inventory falls below a pre-determined point, and based on the fact that there is a delay between when an order is placed and when it is received.

The point at which an order is placed is referred to as the *reorder point, RP,* and it is calculated as daily demand, *d*, times the lead time, *t*. Thus,

RP = (d)(t)   (Eq. 5.11)

where the daily demand, *d*, is calculated as

$$d = \frac{D}{Working\ days\ in\ a\ year}$$

Because the reorder point also assumes an exact daily demand, in practice the reorder point is raised slightly from the number determined in Equation 5.11. Doing this adjusts for any spikes that can occur in the daily demand before a new order is received in inventory.

The last quantity of interest is the cycle time, T, which is just the time between when orders are placed. The formula for cycle time is

$$T = \frac{Working\ days\ in\ a\ year}{Number\ of\ orders\ placed\ in\ a\ year}$$

Table 5.12 summarizes these additional formulas.

TABLE 5.12 ADDITIONAL CALCULATED INVENTORY PARAMETERS

Notation	Meaning	Formula
d	Daily demand	$d = \dfrac{D}{Working\ days\ in\ a\ year}$
RP	Reorder Point	RP =(d)(t)
T	Cycle time (the time between the placement of when orders.)	$T = \dfrac{Working\ days\ in\ a\ year}{Number\ of\ orders\ placed\ in\ a\ year}$

Section 5.4 Exercises

1. The cost of placing an order is $10, and the cost of storing one item for one year is $3. Determine the optimum order size if 540 items are required during a year.

2. The cost of placing an order is $1, and the cost of storing one item for one year is $25. Determine the economic order quantity if 31,250 items are required in a year.

3. The cost of placing an order is $4.80, and the storage cost per unit for one month is $2. Find the optimum order size if 1,000 units are needed each year. (Hint: convert all parameters to yearly values.)

4. For the Economic Order Size determined in Exercise 3, determine:
   a. the total reorder costs over the course of a year.
   b. the total storage costs over the course of a year.
   c. the total costs incurred over the course of a year.

5. The cost of placing an order is $9.60. One thousand units are required during a year, and the cost of carrying one item for 1 year is $1.92.
   a. Determine the economic order quantity.
   b. Find the number of orders that will be placed during a year.

6. For the situation described in Exercise 5 and the results obtained in parts a. and b., construct a figure similar to Figure 5.5.

7. Assume that Figure 5.6 adequately describes the inventory situation of a medium sized appliance dealer.
   a. Determine the economic order quantity for the dealer.
   b. Find the total number of orders placed during a year.
   c. Determine the total number of appliances sold during a year.

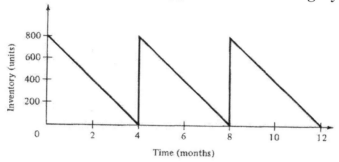

FIGURE 5.6

8. Determine the reorder point and cycle time for Exercise 1, assuming the lead time is 4 days.

9. Determine the reorder point and cycle time for Exercise 2, assuming the lead time is 2 days.

10. Determine the reorder point and cycle time for Exercise 3, assuming the lead time is 3 days.

11. Using the second–derivative test described in Exercise 28 in Section 5.1, show that the economic order quantity $x = \sqrt{2mD/k}$ is a relative minimum for Equation 5.9. From this, conclude that whenever the economic order quantity lies in the domain $1 \le x \le D$ it is also the minimum.

12. Equation 5.9 presupposes a linear relationship between the order size x and the individual order cost, TOC. Derive an expression for the total storage cost TC if the relationship between x and TOC is quadratic; that is, find a formula for TC if $TOC = mx + px^2$. What is the economic order quantity in this case?

5.5 Econometrics

Econometrics is the branch of economics that uses mathematical methods to model economic systems. Although econometrics relies heavily on statistical methods, an important but simple application of the derivative as a rate of change is also used. By applying differentiation techniques to a simplified model of a national economy, for example, we can gain interesting insights into the effect of an increase in overall business investment on the total economy. These insights are the beginnings of Keynesian Economic theory.

Our first assumption is that the economy being modeled consists of only consumers (i.e., individuals) and businesses, ignoring the effects of government and foreign sectors. Such a model approximates conditions in the United States during the previous century. In the exercises, we refine this model to include the government.

Our second assumption is that businesses do not save money. All money received by business is distributed to banks to repay past loans or to stockholders in the form of dividends. Banks, being themselves businesses, return their receivables to individuals as interest payments. Therefore all money received by businesses is eventually distributed to individuals as dividends or interest. Our second assumption can be restated as, "All money spent by consumers and businesses is received only by consumers."

Each dollar received by consumers is either spent or saved. Because, by our second assumption, banks cannot save money, they are assumed to lend all available funds to businesses to use for commercial expenditures. Businesses borrow money from banks for investment. As these investments produce money, the profits are used to both repay loans from the banks and as share-holder dividends. Consumers receive money from other consumers, or from banks in the form of interest payments, or from businesses in the form of dividends. This money is either re-spent directly or saved. Saved money is lent to business for investment, and the cycle begins again.

In summary, we are making the following simplifying assumptions:

1. The economy consists of only consumers and businesses.
2. All money is received only by consumers.
3. Businesses borrow from consumer savings to obtain funds for business expenditures.

We are interested in the question, What are the effects of a change in business investment on the total economy?

Before attempting an answer, we must determine how we will measure the total economy. A reasonable measure is the *gross national product* which is simply the total amount of money spent within the economy. We denote this quantity by T. If we let B denote the amount of money spent by businesses, the question of interest can be restated: What is the change in T with respect to a change in B? Or, mathematically, what is dT/dB?

The Model

To calculate this derivative, we first must express T as a function of B. That is, we must model our economy in such a way that we can ultimately obtain one equation for T in terms of B. We have already

T = total expenditures within the economy

and

B = total business expenditures.

In addition, we now define

C = total consumer expenditures.

It then follows directly from the first assumption that

$T = C + B.$ (Eq. 5.12)

Equation 5.12 is a model of the economy, but it is not sufficient for our purpose. We need an equation for T strictly in terms of B (so we can differentiate), whereas Equation 5.12 relates T to both B and C. More information is needed.

From all available data, it appears that consumer spending C can be decomposed into two parts, necessities and luxuries. Necessities are the absolute basic necessities, and luxuries are everything else. For example, a family may have to spend $100 per week for food to survive but, if more funds were available, they might spend $200 per week for food. This additional $100 for food would be classified as a luxury. Expenditures for basic necessities, which we denote as C_o, are reasonably fixed. Expenditures for luxuries are a function of the amount of money available; the more money available, the more money spent on luxuries.

Because all money spent by consumers and businesses T is received by consumers [2nd assumption], we see that expenditure for luxuries is a function of T. Furthermore, if we assume that this portion of consumer spending is proportional to the amount of money available, we have

$$C = mT + C_o, \hspace{6cm} \text{(Eq. 5.13)}^{++++++}$$

where m denotes the fraction of total income spent on luxuries.

To simplify the problem even further, we assume we are modeling an affluent society in which expenditures for basic necessities are much less than expenditures for luxuries. In such a case, we can replace Equation 5.13 with

$$C = mT, \hspace{6cm} \text{(Eq. 5.14)}$$

with little error. In economic theory, the term m is known as the *marginal propensity to consume*. Substituting Equation 5.14 into Equation 5.12 and rearranging, we find

$$T = mT + B.$$

Solving for T yields,

$$T = \left(\frac{1}{1 - m}\right) B \hspace{5cm} \text{(Eq. 5.15)}$$

Equation 5.15 is the model we were seeking. Differentiating it with respect to B, we obtain the desired rate of change

$$\frac{dT}{dB} = \left(\frac{1}{1 - m}\right) \hspace{5cm} \text{(Eq. 5.16)}$$

Equation 5.15 is the equation of a straight line, and Equation 5.16 is its slope. It follows directly from our knowledge of slopes (Section 2.3) that an increase in business expenditures B by an amount Q forces a corresponding increase in T by $1/(1-m)$ times Q. In economic theory, the term $1/(1 - m)$ derived in Equation 5.16 is known as the **multiplier**.

Example 1 Determine the effect of a \$10,000 increase in business investment on the total national income if individuals as a group spend 75% of the national income.

Solution Because all monies spent within the economy are received by consumers [assumption 2], total national income is the same as total expenditures T. A

++++++ This was one of the key assumptions made by Lord Keynes in his general theory of employment, interest, and money.

$10,000 increase in business investment is the same as an increase in business expenditures B of $10,000. From Equation 5.16, the change in T with respect to B is $1/(1 - m)$. Here $m = 0.75$, hence

$$\frac{1}{1 - m} = \frac{1}{1 - 0.75} = \frac{1}{0.25} = 4$$

That is, T increases 4 units with every one-unit change in B. A $10,000 change in B results in a theoretical change of $40,000 in T.

At first glance, this result is startling. Example 1 indicates that the total income for society as a whole can be increased by $4 with only a $1 increase in business investment, assuming $m = 0.75$. A little thought reveals why this is so.

After the initial expenditure of $1, the recipient, a consumer, receives a dollar as income. He or she spends 75¢ (75% of $1) and saves the rest. A second consumer receives the 75¢ spent by the first consumer. He or she in turn spends 56¢ (75% of 75¢) and saves the rest. A third consumer receives the 56¢ spent by the second consumer and continues the cycle. As this income is received and re-spent, the net effect will be an increase of $4 in the total income of society.

Of course these results are valid only to the extent that our model adequately represents a given society. It is unlikely that any economy, including the United States economy during the previous century, can be adequately modeled by Equations 5.12 and 5.14. The model does not include the time period required to re-spend increased income, the economic state of the people receiving this income, or the ability of society to produce the extra goods demanded by consumers having additional money. Unemployment and inflation are not parts of our model. Population growth, food supplies, and available resources have also been neglected. Nevertheless, the construction presented here is typical of that applied to other more sophisticated models.

Section 5.5 Exercises

1. Determine the increase in the total national income of a society modeled by Equation 5.12 and Equation 5.14 if $m = 0.6$ and business investment is increased by $25 million.

2. Determine the decrease in the total national income of a society modeled by Equation 5.12 and Equation 5.14 if $m = 0.7$ and business investment is decreased by $10 million.

3. Redo Exercise 1 for a society modeled by Equations 5.12 and 5.13.

4. As was noted in the text, the constant m used in Equation 5.14 is referred to as

the ***marginal propensity to consume***. The term $1/(1-m)$ derived in Equation 5.16 is known as the ***multiplier***. Determine the value of the multiplier if the marginal propensity to consume is 0.8. Why do you think the term "multiplier" is used?

5. Determine the net effect on the income of a society after a $1,000 increase in business expenditures has been cycled through five people if $m = 0.6$.

6. Consider a three–sector economy consisting of individual consumers, businesses, and governments each making expenditures denoted as C, *B,* and G, respectively. Assume that the following three equations adequately describe the relationship between these quantities:

$T = C + B + G$

$C = mT + C_o$

and

$B = B_o,$

where B_o denotes a constant business expenditure and the other symbols are as previously defined in the text. For this model, determine the rate of change in total expenditures with respect to a change in government expenditures.

28. Determine the decrease in the total national income of a society modeled by Equations 5.12 and 5.14 if $m = 0.75$ and business investment is decreased by $8 millions.

29. Redo Problem 27 for a society modeled by Equations 5.12 and 5.13.

Chapter

Curve Fitting and Trend Lines

6.1 Constant Curve Fit
6.2 Linear Least-Squares Trend Lines
6.3 Quadratic and Exponential Trend Lines
6.4 Selecting an Appropriate Curve

Throughout this book we have used equations to model and represent various business situations without mentioning, for the most part, how the equations were obtained. In practice, such equations are not immediately available to the user but must be derived. The derivations are generally one of two types, theoretical or empirical.

In the theoretical approach, known principles are used to generate the equations. Indeed, this was the approach taken in Chapter 5 to mathematically model the problems presented there. A specific example is given in the beginning of Section 5.3. There we used the accepted principle that profit, P, is the total revenue received from all sales, R, minus the total cost, C.

In the empirical approach, one uses past data to generate the equations. Although such methods are no better than the accuracy of the data, they are often the only ones available, especially if there are no theoretical results that apply. As an example, a certain business, knowing that sales volume depends on *advertising expenditures, may want to know the relationship between these quantities. Does volume increase linearly (as a straight line) with advertising expenditures or perhaps exponentially? Obviously, there is no theoretical principle that can answer this question, because the answer differs from product to product. In this chapter, we present an introduction to curve fitting which is one method of extracting meaningful mathematical equations from a set of data points. Also presented is how spreadsheet programs, such as Excel®"§§§§§§, can be used to both graphically display and provide these mathematical equations.*

6.1 Constant Curve Fit

The simplest curve fit occurs when the data are relatively constant. For this case, a horizontal straight line (see Section 2.2) may represent a good approximation to the given situation.

Definition 6. 1 Let a denote the average value of a set of data. The line $y = a$ is the average-value, straight-line fit for these data points.

Example 1 The yearly gross sales of a manufacturing firm for the past decade are plotted in Figure 6.1. Determine the average-value, straight-line fit for these data.

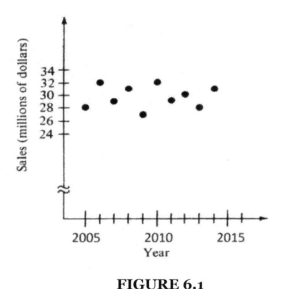

FIGURE 6.1

Solution For convenience, we first tabulate the given data points in Table 6.I.

TABLE 6.1

Year	Sales (millions)	Year	Sales (millions)
2005	28	2010	32
2006	32	2011	29
2007	29	2012	30
2008	31	1013	28
2009	27	2014	31

Because the data are relatively constant, a straight-line fit is a reasonable approximation. Here the average yearly sales are

$$a = \frac{28 + 32 + 29 + 31 + 27 + 32 + 29 + 30 + 28 + 31}{10} = 29.7$$

The average-value, straight-line fit is $y = 29.7$ which is drawn in Figure 6.2.

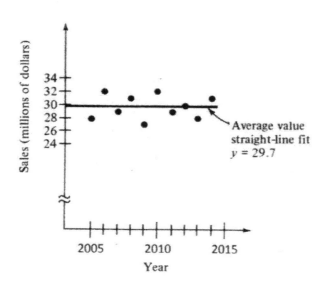

FIGURE 6.2

Obviously, if the data are not reasonably constant, the average-value method is a poor approximation that can lead to erroneous conclusions. We would have little confidence in a 2018 projection based on the average-value, straight-line fit for the data given in Figure 6.3.

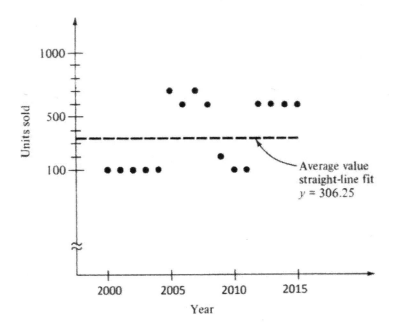

FIGURE 6.3

A useful modification to an average-value, straight-line fit is the concept of moving averages. Here several averages are calculated for different time periods, resulting in a set of averages which "move with the data."

Example 2 Determine consecutive 5-year moving averages for the data previously listed in Table 6.1.

Solution The first 5-year average a_1, includes data for 2004 through 2009, is

$$a_1 = \frac{28 + 32 + 29 + 31 + 27}{5} = 29.4$$

The second 5-year average for the years 2006 through 2010 is

$$a_2 = \frac{32 + 29 + 31 + 27 + 32}{5} = 30.2$$

Using the data for the years 2007 through 2011, we compute the third 5-year moving -average as

$$a_3 = \frac{29 + 31 + 27 + 32 + 29}{5} = 29.6$$

Continuing in this manner, we also find that $a_4 = 29.8$, $a_5 = 29.2$, and $a_6 = 30.0$.

The arithmetic for computing consecutive moving averages can be simplified if we note that each average differs from its predecessor by the addition and deletion of two pieces of data. In Example 2, a_2 differed from a_1 by the addition of the 2010 data and the deletion of the 2005 data. Similarly, a_3 differed from a_2 by the addition of the 2011 data and the deletion of the 2006 data. In general, each new average can be calculated from the previous average by adding the difference between the new data point and the oldest data point divided by the time span under consideration. Thus, in Example 2, a_2 can be determined from a_1 as

$$a_2 = a_1 + \left(\frac{32-28}{5}\right)$$

and

$$a_3 = a_2 + \left(\frac{29 - 32}{5}\right)$$

Example 3 Compute and graph consecutive 4-year moving averages for the years 2009 through 2015, inclusive, for the data given in Figure 6.3.

Solution The first 4-year moving average that is being calculated now starts at 2009 and ends at 2012. Reading the appropriate points from the graph, we find

$$a_1 = \frac{200 + 100 + 100 + 600}{4} = 250.$$

Then,

$$a_2 = a_1 + \left(\frac{600 - 200}{4}\right) = 250 + 100 = 350,$$

$$a_3 = a_2 + \left(\frac{600 - 100}{4}\right) = 350 + 125 = 475,$$

and

$$a_4 = a_3 + \left(\frac{600 - 100}{4}\right) = 475 + 125 = 600.$$

These averages are drawn in Figure 6.4

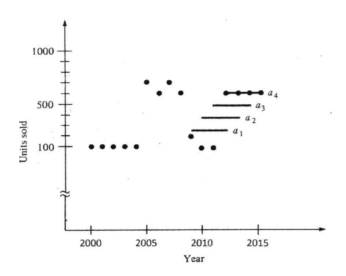

FIGURE 6.4

Section 6.1 Exercises

1. Find the average-value, straight-line fit for the data given in Table 6.2.

TABLE 6.2

Price ($)	1	2	3	4	5	6	7	8	9	10
Demand (hundreds)	12	13	9	8	11	10	9	13	8	10

2. Compute consecutive 5-year moving averages for the data given in Table 6.2.

3. The gross sales for a small furniture store are given in Table 6.3 for a 9-year period. Find the average-value, straight-line fit for these data.

TABLE 6.3

Year	2006	2007	2008	2009	2010	2011	2012	2013	2014
Sales ($1000)	28	29	32	27	26	31	28	27	30

4. Compute consecutive 4-year moving averages for the data given in Table 6.3, starting with years 2006 through 2009.

5. The Spencer Food Company is considering an increase in its advertising budget to bolster sales of its Kitty-Kat high-protein cat food, a product which has particular appeal to upper-income cat owners. As a manager of the company, you are asked for a preliminary opinion on the advisability of such an increase. What is your initial reaction based on the information listed in Table 6.4?

TABLE 6.4

Year	2006	2007	2008	2009	2010	2011	2012	2013	2014
Advertising ($1000)	140	150	160	170	180	160	160	170	170
Sales ($1000)	28	29	32	26	26	27	28	27	30

6.2 Linear Least-Squares Trend Line

Empirically obtained data on supply, demand, sales, cost, and other commercial quantities rarely are represented adequately by average-value straight lines. Many times, however, such data can be modeled by the more general straight line $y = mx + b$, with $m \neq 0$.

If the data consist of only two points, we can use the methods developed in Section 2.3 (see Example 5) to fit a straight line through them. If more than two data points are given, one of two situations can occur. First, all the data points can lie on the same straight line. In such a case, which almost never occurs in practice, we simply pick two of the points and construct a straight line through them, as before.

The more common situation involves a set of data that do not lie on any straight line but which, nonetheless, seem to be adequately represented by such a curve. A case in point involves the data plotted in Figure 6.5. Although a straight line appears to be a reasonable approximation to the data, no one line of the form $y = mx + b$ contains all the given points. Therefore we seek the straight line that best fits the data.

Any straight-line approximation has one y-value on the line for each value of x. This y-value may or may not agree with the given data. Thus, for the values of x at which data are available, we generally have two values of y: one value from the data and a second value from the straight-line approximation to the data. This situation is illustrated in Figure 6.6. The error at each x- is simply the difference between the y-value of the data point and the y-value obtained from the straight-line approximation. We designate this error as $e(x)$.

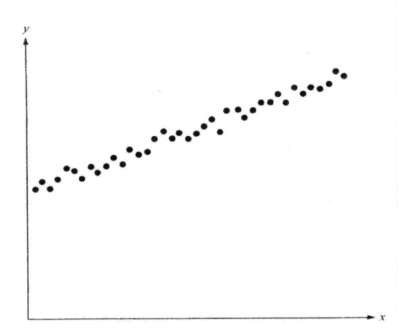

FIGURE 6.5

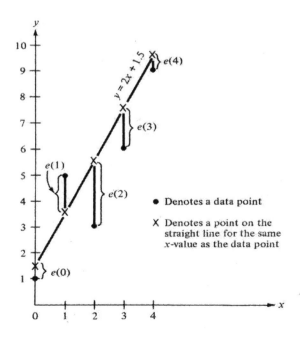

FIGURE 6.6

Example 1 Calculate the errors made in approximating the data shown in Figure 6.6 by the line y = 2x + 1.5.

Solution The line and the given data points are plotted in Figure 6.6. There are errors at $x = 0$, $x = 1$, $x = 2$, $x = 3$, and $x = 4$. Evaluating the equation $y = 2x + 1.5$ at these values of x, we compute Table 6.5.

TABLE 6.5

Given data		Evaluated from y = 2x + 1.5
x	y	y
0	1	1.5
1	2	3.5
2	3	5.5
3	6	7.5
4	9	9.5

It now follows that

$e(0) = 1 - 1.5 = -0.5$
$e(1) = 5 - 3.5 = 1.5$
$e(2) = 3 - 5.5 = -2.5$
$e(3) = 6 - 7.5 = -1.5$

and

$e(4) = 9 - 9.5 = -0.5.$

Note that these errors could have been read directly from the graph.

We can extend this concept of errors to the more general situation involving N data points. Let (x_1, y_1), (x_2, y_2), (x_3, y_3), ..., (x_N, y_N) be a set of N data points for a particular situation. Any straight-line approximation to this data generates errors $e(x_1)$, $e(x_2)$, $e(x_3)$, ... , $e(x_N)$ which individually can be positive, negative, or zero. The latter case occurs when the approximation agrees with the data at a particular point. We define the overall error as follows.

Definition 6.2 The least-squares error, E, is the sum of the squares of the individual errors. That is,

$$E = [e(x_1)]^2 + [e(x_2)]^2 + [e(x_3)]^2 + \cdots + [e(x_N)]^2 \qquad \text{(Eq. 6.1)}$$

Using this definition, the only way the total error, E, can be zero is for each of the individual errors to be zero. The reason for this is that each term in Equation 6.1 is squared, which ensures that an equal number of positive and negative individual errors cannot sum to zero.

Example 2 Compute the least-squares error for the approximation used in Example 1.

Solution

$E = [e(0)]^2 + [e(1)]^2 + [e(2)]^2 + [e(3)]^2 + [e(4)]^2$
$\quad = (-0.5)^2 + (1.5)^2 + (-2.5)^2 + (-1.5)^2 + (-0.5)^2$
$\quad = 0.25 + 2.25 + 6.25 + 2.25 + 0.25 = 11.25.$

Definition 6.3 The least-squares straight line is the line that minimizes the least-squares error.

It can be shown (although not considered here) that the least-squares straight line is given by the equation $y = mx + b$, where m and b simultaneously satisfy the two equations

$$bN + m \sum_{i=1}^{N} x_i = \sum_{i=1}^{N} y_i \qquad \text{(Eq. 6.2)}$$

and

$$b \sum_{i=1}^{N} x_i + m \sum_{i=1}^{N} (x_i)^2 = \sum_{i=1}^{n} x_i y_i \qquad \text{(Eq. 6.3)}$$

Here x_i and y_i denote the values of the ith data point and N is the total number of data points being considered. We also have used the sigma notation introduced in Section 1.7.

Example 3 Find the least-squares straight line for the data listed in Table 6.6.

TABLE 6.6

x	0	1	2	3	4
y	1	5	3	6	9

Solution A good procedure for calculating the least-squares straight line is to first construct an expanded table similar to Table 6.7.

TABLE 6.7

x_i	y_i	$(x_i)^2$	$x_i y_i$
0	1	0	0
1	5	1	5
2	3	4	6
3	6	9	18
4	9	16	36
Sums: 10	24	30	65

Once this table is constructed, the following sums can be directly obtained as:

$$\sum_{i=1}^{5} x_i = 10$$

$$\sum_{i=1}^{5} y_i = 24$$

$$\sum_{i=1}^{5} (x_i)^2 = 30$$

and

$$\sum_{i=1}^{5} x_i y_i = 65$$

Substituting the appropriate sums into Equations 6.2 and 6.3, with $N = 5$ (because there are 5 data points), we have

$$5b + 10\,m = 24$$

and

10b + 30m = 65.

Solving these two equations simultaneously for m and b, we obtain $m = 1.7$ and $b = 1.4$. Thus, the equation of the least-squares line is

y = 1.7x + 1.4

The graph of this line, along with the original data is shown in Figure 6.7.

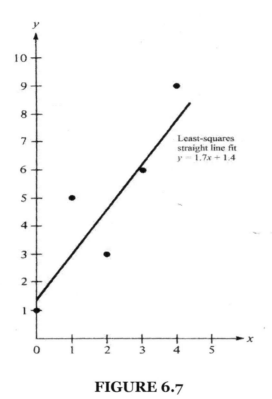

FIGURE 6.7

Creating Least-Squares Lines with Excel

Figure 6.8 illustrates how the least squares line developed in Example 1 looks when it is created using Excel. Notice that the equation provided on the graph is identical to that found in Example 1. This is to be expected, as Excel creates the equation as a linear least-squares line.

In business and economic applications a line use to fit empirically obtained data is referred to as a *trend line*. A trend line *need not* be linear – any least squares line, including the quadratic and exponential, presented in the next section is a trend line because it minimizes the sum of the squared error terms

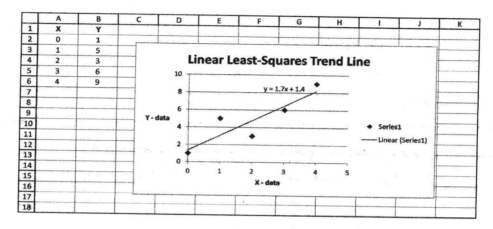

FIGURE 6.8

The step-by-step procedure for creating a linear least squares line, such as that shown in Figure 6.8, is as follows.

First, the actual data must be entered into a spreadsheet, as shown in Figure 6. Here, the data has been entered into columns A and B, respectively. Although any two consecutive columns can be used for the data, the data entered in the left-most column is taken by Excel to be the domain set and the data in the right-most column as the range set. Alternatively, the data can be entered in any two consecutive rows, but the domain set data must be above that of the range set data.

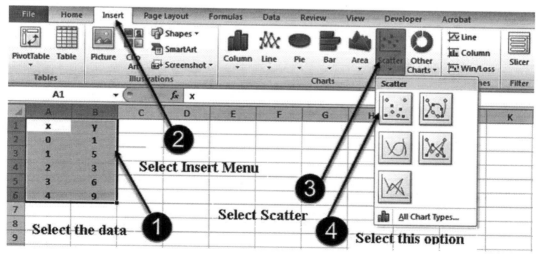

FIGURE 6.9

Once the data has been entered into the spreadsheet, it must be highlighted. Then, selecting the Insert menu option, followed by the Scatter options, as shown in Figure 6.9 creates a scatter diagram of the data, as shown in Figure 6.10.

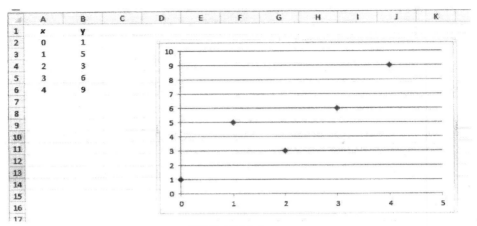

FIGURE 6.10

To create a linear least-squares trend line, click on the Layout option in the Chart Tools ribbon, shown in Figure 6.11 (if the Chart Tools are not shown, clicking anywhere within the scatter diagram will cause it to be displayed). At this point, you can also use the Chart Title and Axis Titles to enter a title for the chart and to label the x and y axes.

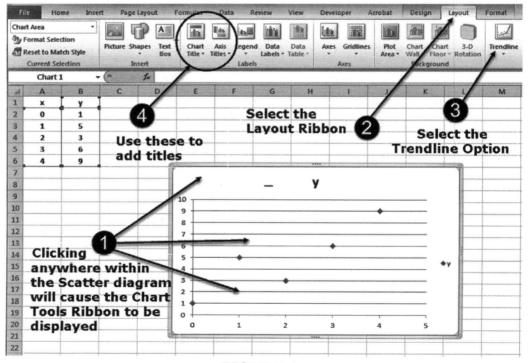

FIGURE 6.11

Selecting the Trendline option shown in Figure 6.11, will cause the drop-down menu shown in Figure. 6.12.

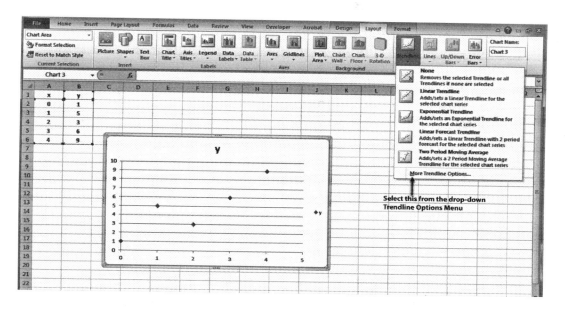

FIGURE 6.12

When the Trendline drop-down menu shown in Figure 6.12 is displayed you are ready to add the trend line and its equation onto the scatter diagram. To do so, click on the last option, which is labeled More Trendline Options. Selecting this option will bring up the last menu needed, which is that shown on Figure 6.13.

From the menu shown in Figure 6.13, select Linear as the Trend/Regression Type and then check the next to last option, which is Display Equation, as shown on the figure. Then click close, and the completed scatter diagram, complete with a trend line and its equation will appear, as previously shown in Figure 6.8, and reproduced as Figure 6.14.

Notice in Figure 6.14 that the linear trend line equation computed and displayed by Excel is the same as the least-squares equation developed by hand in Example 3.

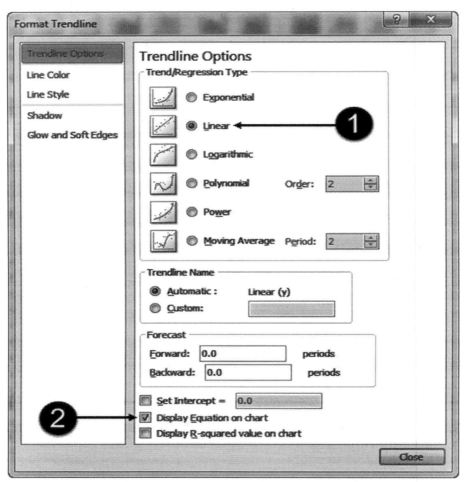

FIGURE 6.13

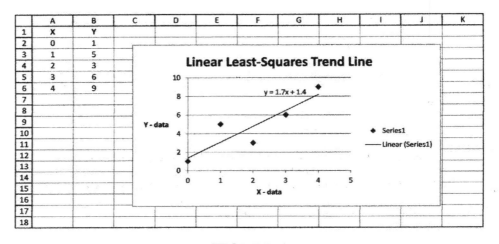

FIGURE 6.14

Example 4 Find the linear least-squares linear trend line for the data given in Table 6.8, both by hand and then using a spreadsheet.

TABLE 6.8

x	0	1	2	3	4	5	6
y	2.0	1.0	3.5	5.5	4.5	5.5	6.5

Solution Following the procedure suggested in Example 3, we construct Table 6.9.

TABLE 6.9

	x_i	y_i	$(x_i)^2$	$x_i y_i$
	0	2.0	0.0	0.0
	1	1.0	1.0	1.0
	2	3.5	4.0	7.0
	3	5.5	9.0	16.5
	4	4.5	16.0	18.0
	5	5.5	25.0	27.5
	6	6.5	36.0	39.0
Sums:	21	28.5	91.0	109.0

The following sums can now be read directly from the table.

$$\sum_{i=1}^{7} x_i = 21$$

$$\sum_{i=1}^{7} y_i = 28.5$$

$$\sum_{i=1}^{7} (x_i)^2 = 91$$

$$\sum_{i=1}^{7} x_i y_i = 109$$

Substituting the appropriate sums into Equations 6.2 and 6.3, with N = 7 (because there are 7 data points) yields

7b + 21m = 28.1

and

21b + 91m = 109

Solving these two equations simultaneously for m and b, we obtain $m = 0.839$ and $b = 1.56$. Thus, the equation of the least-squares line is $y = 0.839x + 1.56$, which is drawn with the original data in Figure 6.15.

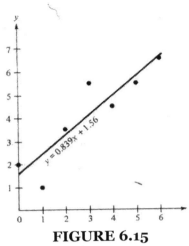

FIGURE 6.15

Using the procedures previously illustrated in Figures 6.8 through 6.14 to develop an Excel based linear least-squares trend line for the data in Table 6.8 produces the trend line shown in Figure 6.16. As expected, the equation developed in Excel matches the equation developed and shown in Figure 6.15.

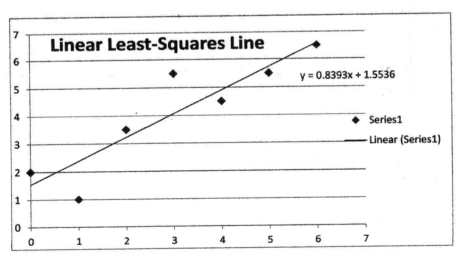

FIGURE 6.16

Example 5 Verify that the least-squares line derived in Example 4 yields a smaller least-squares error for the data than the line $y = x + 1$.

Chapter 6: Curve Fitting and Trend Lines   **Mathematics for Business**

Solution The line $y = x + 1$ and the individual errors are drawn in Figure 6.17. Reading directly from this graph, we obtain

$$E = [e(0)]^2 + [e(1)]^2 + [e(2)]^2 + [e(3)]^2 + [e(4)]^2 + [e(5)]^2 + [e(6)]^2$$
$$= (1)^2 + (-1)^2 + (0.5)^2 + (1.5)^2 + (-0.5)^2 + (-0.5)^2 + (-0.5)^2$$
$$= 1 + 1 + 0.25 + 2.25 + 0.25 + 0.25 + 0.25$$
$$= 5.25.$$

To compute the error for the least-squares line $y = 0.839x + 1.56$ we could also read the individual errors directly from Figure 6.15. More accurately, we first evaluate the equation of the line at the appropriate x-values and then calculate

$$E = (2 - 1.56)^2 + (1 - 2.399)^2 + (3.5 - 3.238)^2 + (5.3 - 4077)^2$$
$$+ (4.5 - 4.916)^2 + (5.3 - 5.755)^2 + (6.5 - 6.594)^2$$
$$= 0.19 + 1.96 + 0.07 + 2.02 + 0.16 + 0.07 + 0.01$$
$$= 4.49.$$

As expected, the least-squares error is less for the least-squares straight line.

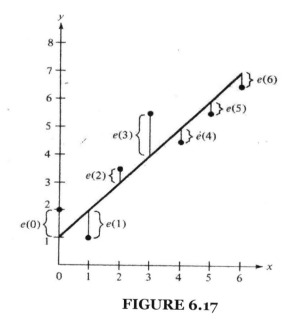

FIGURE 6.17

Example 6 Find the least-squares straight line for the data in Table 6.10 and use this line to determine the average yearly increase in sales for 2010 through 2014.

TABLE 6.10

Year	2010	2011	2012	2013	2014
Sales ($millions)	10	13	11	15	14

Solution Here we will directly create the linear least-squares trend equation and its graph using Excel, as shown in Figure 6.18. As we are looking for a relationship between Sales and Years, the independent (x-variable) is the year, and the dependent variable is Sales. The slope of the trend line is one, which means that sales have increased, on average, 1-million dollars per year between the years 2010 and 2014.

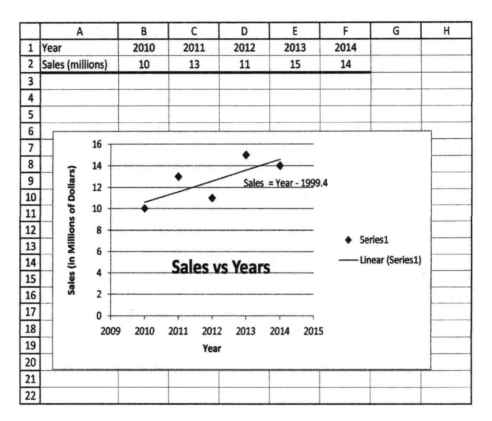

FIGURE 6.18

Section 6.2 Exercises

1. Determine the least-squares straight line for the data given in Exercise 5 on page 241. Based on this straight line, determine if an increase in the advertising budget seem worthwhile

2. Consider the data given in Table 6. 11.

TABLE 6.11

x	0	1	2	3	4	5	6
y	1	5	8	7	12	14	13

a. Plot the data points, either by hand or using a scatter diagram, and determine whether a straight-line approximation for the trend line seems reasonable.
b. Determine the least-squares straight line for the data, either by hand or using a spreadsheet program.

3. Consider the data given in Table 6.12.

TABLE 6.12

x	0	1	2	3	4	5	6	7
y	36	49	55	56	67	69	76	85

a. Plot the data points, either by hand or using an Excel scatter diagram, and determine whether a straight-line approximation for the trend line seems reasonable.
b. Determine the least-squares straight line for the data, either by hand or using Excel.
c. Calculate the least-squares error for this line.
d. Draw any other straight line that appears to fit the data reasonably well and compare the least-squares error of this line to the result from part (c).

4. Repeat Exercise 3 for the data given in Table 6.13.

TABLE 6.13

x	0	1	2	3	4
y	10	13	20	13	52

5. The annual sales receipts for television sets for one department in a chain store are given in Table 6.14.

TABLE 6.14

Year	2007	2008	2009	2010	2011	2012	2013
Sales (thousands)	15	18	16	20	18	22	19

a. Determine the least-squares straight line for these data, either by hand or using Excel.

b. Determine the sales for 2011 that the line found in part a provides.

c. Predict the sales for 2018 using the line found in part a.

6. The number of air conditioners sold each year by one department in a chain store are given in Table 6.15

TABLE 6.15

Year	2008	2009	2010	2011	2012	2013
Units	19	16	21	19	23	20

a. Find the least-squares straight line for these data, either by hand or using Excel.

b. Use this line to project the number of units that will be sold in 2018.

7. A farmer in Madison, Iowa, collected the data in Table 6. 16, which relates the number of bushels of wheat obtained from a test plot of land to the amount of rainfall in Madison during the growing season. Find the least-squares straight line for this data, either by hand or using Excel, and use it to estimate the amount of wheat that could be expected from a rainfall of 3.5 inches.

TABLE 6.16

Rain (inches)	2.0	2.2	2.3	3.2	3.8	4.9	5.6
Yield (bushels)	25	25	30	30	40	50	50

8. Using the results from Example 6 in the text , complete Table 6.17 and then compute the least-squares error. Here y_c denotes the y-value obtained from the least-squares straight line by evaluating the equation at the corresponding values of x.

· **TABLE 6.17**

x_i	y_i	y_c	$e(x)$	$[e(x)]^2$
-2	10			
-1	13			
0	11			
1	15			
2	14		28	

Sums:

6.3 Quadratic and Exponential Trend Lines

In a majority of business situations a linear least-squares line provides the most appropriate fit between the variables under consideration. However, there are cases where other, non-linear least-squares curves fit the data better, in that the non-linear curve produces a smaller squared error than a straight line. Two of the most common of these additional curve types are a quadratic curve (see Section 2.5) and an exponential curve (see Section 2.7).

For example, consider Figure 6.19 , where the data points clearly follow a quadratic pattern. In cases like this it is appropriate to fit the data with a quadratic equation of the form

$y = ax^2+bx+c.$ (Eq. 6.4)

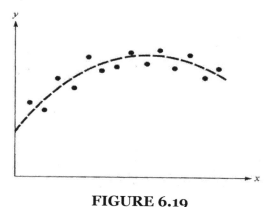

FIGURE 6.19

Similarly, Figure 6.20 illustrates a case where a better fit is provided by an exponential equation of the form

$y = e^x$ (Eq. 6.5)

Although the equations necessary to determine a quadratic curve fit are presented at the end of this section (those for an exponential fit are beyond the scope of this text), it is much simpler and easier to determine the exact trend equation using a spread sheet program, such as Excel, rather than by hand calculations. However, before presenting the steps necessary to create least-squares quadratic and exponential equations, the definition of these curve types is given, as follows:

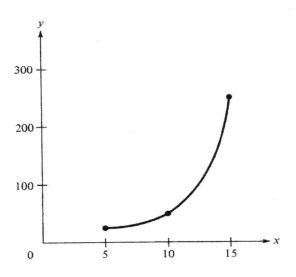

FIGURE 6.20

Definition 6.4 The *least-squares quadratic curve* is a quadratic curve of the form $y = ax^2 + bx + c$ that minimizes the least-squares error (see Definition 6.2).

Definition 6.5 The *least-squares exponential curve* is an exponential curve of the form $y = e^x$ that minimizes the least-squares error (see Definition 6.2).

Using Excel For Non-Linear Trend Lines

To use Excel for determining and graphing the equation for both quadratic and exponential least-squares trend lines, as well a number of other non-linear trend lines, requires the same steps used in determining a linear curve fit, with one modification, which is noted in Step 5 below. Recall that the steps for creating linear trend lines are as follows:

A. Produce the Scatter Diagram

Step 1: List the independent variable data (*x*-values) and dependent variable data (*y*-values) in either two consecutive columns or rows. If columns are used, the x-values must be in the column to the left of the *y*-values; otherwise, if rows are used, the *x*-values must be in the row above the *y*-values.

Step 2: Highlight the x and y data, click on the Insert menu option, and select Scatter Diagram, as previously shown on Figure 6.9. This will produce a scatter diagram of the data.

B. Create the Trend Line

Step 3: Click on the Layout option in the Chart Tools ribbon, as shown on Figure 6.11 (if the Chart Tools option is not shown, clicking anywhere within the scatter diagram will cause it to be displayed). This will cause the drop-down menu, previously shown as Figure 6.12 to appear.

Step 4: Select the Trendline option and then click on the last option shown in Figure 6.12, which is More Trendline Options. This will cause the drop-down menu shown in Figure 6.13, and reproduced below as Figure 6.21, to appear.

Step 5: When the menu shown in Figure 6.21 is displayed, click on the Exponential radio button if an exponential least squares line is desired, or click on the Polynomial radio button with order 2 if a quadratic least squares line is desired. This is the only difference between creating a linear trend line and the other types of trend lines provided by Excel.

Step 6. Check the Display Equation on Chart checkbox at the bottom of the menu shown on Figure 6.21 and click on the Close button. This will produce a display of the selected trend line type with its associated equation directly on the scatter diagram of the data.

Step 7: Add a Chart Title and Axis Titles using the appropriate menu options circled in Figure 6.11.

Example 1 Determine and plot the data and least-squares quadratic trend line for the data given in Table 6.18.

TABLE 6.18

x	0	1	2	3	4
y	10	14	18	30	50

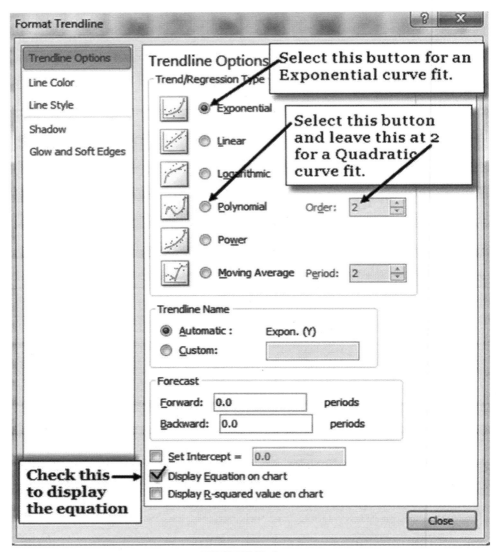

FIGURE 6.21

Solution The graph of the data and the quadratic least-squares trend line, along with its equation, using the seven steps presented above, is shown in Figure 6.22

Example 2 Determine and plot the data and least-squares exponential trend line for the data given in Table 6.19:

Table 6.19

x	0	1	2	3	4	5
y	3.5	5.3	7.4	11.2	14.9	22.7

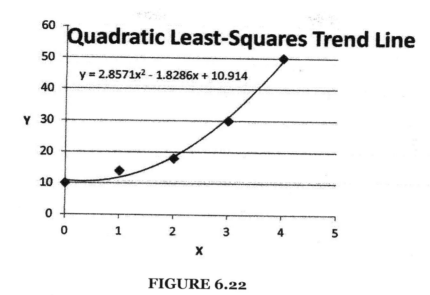

FIGURE 6.22

Solution The graph of the data and the exponential least squares trend line, along its equation, using the seven steps presented above, is shown in Figure 6.23

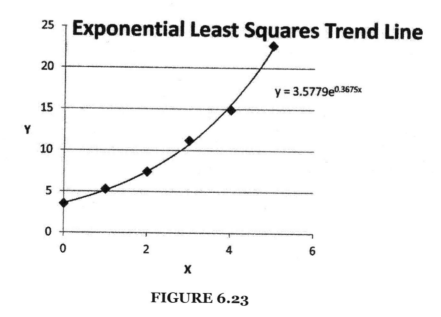

FIGURE 6.23

Derivation of Quadratic Least Squares Equation

Being quadratic, the least-squares quadratic curve must satisfy the quadratic equation, $y = ax^2 + bx + c$ given in Definition 6.4. Because there are three unknowns in this equation, specifically the constants a, b, and c, we expect three equations for these unknowns similar to Equations 6.2 and 6.3 for the linear least-squared curve. This is indeed the case. The equations are

$$cN + b\sum_{i=1}^{N} x_i + a\sum_{i=1}^{N} (x_i)^2 = \sum_{i=1}^{N} y_i \qquad \text{(Eq. 6.6)}$$

and

$$c\sum_{i=1}^{N} x_i + b\sum_{i=1}^{N} (x_i)^2 + a\sum_{i=1}^{N} (x_i)^3 = \sum_{i=1}^{n} x_i\, y_i \qquad \text{(Eq. 6.7)}$$

and

$$c\sum_{i=1}^{N} (x_i)^2 + b\sum_{i=1}^{N} (x_i)^3 + a\sum_{i=1}^{N} (x_i)^4 = \sum_{i=1}^{n} (x_i)^2\, y_i \qquad \text{(Eq. 6.8)}$$

Here x_i and y_i are the coordinates of the ith data point, and N is the total number of data points under consideration.

Example 3 Determine the least-squared quadratic trend line for the data previously given in Example 1 and reproduced as Table 6.20:

TABLE 6.20

x	0	1	2	3	4
y	10	14	18	30	50

Solution A good procedure for calculating the least-squares quadratic curve is to first construct an expanded table as shown in Table 6.21

Substituting the appropriate sums from the table into Equations 6.6 through 6.8 with $N = 5$ (because there are 5 data points), we obtain:

$5c + 10b + 30a = 122$

$10c + 30b + 100a = 340$

$30c + 100b + 354a = 1156.$

TABLE 6.21

	x_i	y_i	$(x_i)^2$	$(x_i)^3$	$(x_i)^4$	$x_i y_i$	$(x_i)^2 y_i$
	0	10	0	0	0	0	0
	1	14	1	1	1	14	14
	2	18	4	8	16	36	72
	3	30	9	27	81	90	270
	4	50	16	64	256	200	800
Sums:	10	122	30	100	354	340	1156

These three equations can be solved with a number of algebraic or matrix methods that are beyond the scope of this book. The solution, however, is $a = 2.86$, $b = -1.83$, and $c = 10.91$. Thus, the equation of the quadratic curve is $y = 2.86x^2 - 1.83x + 10.91$, which is the same equation previously illustrated in Figure 6.22.

Section 6.3 Exercises

1. Using Excel find the least-squares quadratic trend line for the data listed in Table 6.22.

TABLE 6.22

x	0	1	2	3	4
y	10	11	15	16	23

2. Complete Table 6.23 for the data given in Table 6.22 and show that the least-squares error is 4.9. Here y_c denotes the y-value obtained from evaluating the least-squares quadratic curve, $y = 0.6429x^2 + 0.5286x + 10.086$, at the appropriate values of x.

TABLE 6.23

x_i	y_i	y_c	$e(x)$	$[e(x)]^2$
0	10			
1	11			
2	15			
3	16			
4	23			
Sums:				

3. Find the least-squares straight line for the data given in Table 6.22 and then calculate the least-squares error for this line. How does this error compare with the error found in Exercise 2? Draw both the least-squares quadratic curve and the least-squares straight line on the same graph and compare visually.

4. Using Excel find the least-squares quadratic trend line for the data listed in Table 6.24.

TABLE 6.24

x	-2	-1	0	1	2
y	10	11	15	16	23

5. Using Excel find the least-squares quadratic trend line for the data listed in Table 6.25.

TABLE 6.25

x	-3	-2	-1	0	1	2	3
y	8.1	2.9	0	-1	0	3.1	7.8

6. Graph the curve $y = x^2 - 1$ on the same graph produced for Exercise 5 and determine the least-squares error for both of the curves. Note that three of the data points in Table 6.25 actually lie on the curve $y = x^2 - 1$.

7. Consider the three data points (-1, 0), (0, 7), and (1, 10).
   a. Using Equations. 6.6 through 6.8, determine the three simultaneous equations required to fit a least-squares quadratic curve to these data.
   b. Verify that the solutions to the equations found in part a are a= -2, b = 5, and c = 7.

8a. Redo Exercise 2a for the data points (1, 0), (2, -1), and (3, 0).

b. Verify that the solutions to the equations found part a are $a = 1$, $b = -4$, and $c = 3$.

9. Using a spread sheet program, find the least-squares exponential trend line for the data listed in Table 6.26.

TABLE 6.26

x	0	1	2	3	4
y	2	16	90	500	2,500

10. Using a spread sheet program, find the least-squares exponential trend line for the data listed in Table 6.27.

TABLE 6.27

x	0	1	2	3	4	5
y	16	20	38	60	90	130

11. Sales of a rapidly growing manufacturing firm for its first five years of operation are given in Table 6.28.
   a. Using a spread sheet program, find the least-squares exponential trend line for this data.
   b. Use the trend equation found in Part a to project sales for 2016.

TABLE 6.28

Year	1	2	3	4	5
Sales	0.9	2.9	9.5	28.8	100.0

12. Census figures for a Midwestern city are given in Table 6.29.
   a. Using a spread sheet program, find the least-squares exponential trend line for this data.
   b. Use the trend equation found in Part a to project the population in 2020.
   c. Determine the year when the population was 1,000.

TABLE 6.29

Year	1975	1985	1995	2005	2015
Population	4,953	7,389	11,023	16,445	24,532

6.4 Selecting an Appropriate Curve

In this chapter, only empirical data that lent themselves to either constant, linear, quadratic, or exponential fits were presented. Fortunately, the majority of business problems of interest typically assume one of these forms.

In actual practice, one is first presented the data, and the initial problem is to determine which, if any, of the curve types considered in this chapter best fits the data. The starting point is always the same: Plot the given data on a scatter diagram and then take a long, hard look at the resulting plot.

Typically, a pattern develops. Based on the emergent pattern and knowledge of various curves, a curve type that appears to fit the data reasonably well is then selected. Once this selection has been made, its associated least-squares equation determined, the final step is to test whether or not the resulting curve does in fact model the data adequately. Such tests fall under the areas of statistical inference and hypothesis testing, which are both beyond the scope of this book.

Appendix A

Determining Valid Settlement Dates

A financial settlement date refers to the date on which the trade of a stock, bond, or other financial instrument, is legally completed. On this date the transfer of funds and the corresponding financial instrument's title between buyer and seller takes place (see the Point of Information box on page 273). For stocks and bonds the settlement date typically occurs within one to three business days after the trade date. As such, Saturdays, Sundays, and holidays are excluded from the time counted between the trade and settlement dates.

In this appendix two commonly used methods are presented to determine if a date is either a Saturday or Sunday. The first method illustrates Excel's WEEDAY() function, while the second method, referred to as Zeller's algorithm, shows how to determine weekend days either by hand or by program code. A method is then presented for determining if a date falls on a holiday.

A.1 Day-Of-The-Week Determination

Excel's WEEKDAY() function can be used to determine the day of the week corresponding to any date. This function accepts a date within its parentheses[*******] and returns a number from 1 to 7 corresponding to the days Sunday through Saturday, respectively. For the WEEKDAY( ) function to work correctly, the date provided to it must be in a valid Excel Date format. Figure A.1 illustrates an Excel spreadsheet that uses this function to determine the day-of-the week corresponding to a user input date.

Note that the spreadsheet in Figure A.1 displays the value provided by the WEEKAY() function, with the correspondence between values and day names provided by the table listed in the spreadsheet. You will shortly see how to display the actual day name corresponding to this value.

	A	B	C	D	E	F	G
1	Spreadsheet for Determing the Day-of-The Week						
2							
3	Enter the date:	1/10/2016					
4					Correspondence		
5	DAY-OF-WEEK=	1		1	=	Sunday	
6				2	=	Monday	
7				3	=	Tuesday	
8				4	=	Wednesday	
9				5	=	Thursday	
10				6	=	Friday	
11				7	=	Saturday	
12							

FIGURE A.1 Determining the Day-of-the-Week

The formula used to determine the day-of –the week value shown in Figure A.1 is displayed in cell C3 within the spreadsheet shown in Figure A.2.

[*******] Data contained within the parentheses of a function are formally referred to as *arguments* of the function.

POINT OF INFORMATION

BONDS

A **bond** an agreement with legal force, which is a promise or pledge between a borrower to a lender defining the terms under which a loan will be repaid.

In finance, a bond, which is also known as a **fixed-income security**, is used for the purpose of raising funds. Here a corporation or government (local or national) borrows money from an investor for a defined period of time at a fixed interest rate. As such, the bonds are loan agreements between the bond issuer and an investor.

Bonds issued by corporations are referred to as **corporate bonds**, and those issued by state or city governments or agencies are referred to as **municipal bonds**, or **munis**, for short. Bonds issued by a national government are referred to as **government bonds**. The amount of an individual bond, which is typically either $1,000 or $5,000, is referred to as the bond's **face amount**. The date specified on the bond for the return of the full face amount is referred to as the bond's **maturity date**.

Bonds are always issued with an interest rate, which is referred to as the **coupon rate**. The bond includes provisions in which the issuer is required to pay the interest rate on the bond's face amount at fixed periods of time, until the bond's maturity date.   Typically, these interest payments, referred to as **coupon payments** are made at equal six-month month periods. At the maturity date the last interest payment is made and the face amount of the bond is returned to the bond holder.[††††††††] The **dated date** refers to the date when the calculation of the first interest payment begins, although the bond itself is typically sold or delivered on a different date.

After bonds are issued they can be traded on what is referred to as the **secondary market**. Here the original owner of the bond can freely sell the bond to any buyer. The date on which the buyer and seller formally and legally agree to the sale, is referred to as the **trade date**. The date upon which the transfer of the bond to the buyer's account and the transfer of funds to the seller's account occurs is referred to as the **settlement date**.

[††††††††] The term coupon is derived from a time when corporate and government bonds were issued as physical documents with dated coupons attached. On or after each date on the coupon , the holder of the coupon would tear the coupon from the bond and deposit it into a bank or hand in back to the bond's issuer to receive the amount printed on the coupon.

	A	B	D	E	F
1	Spreadsheet for Determing the Day-of-The Week				
2					
3	Enter the date:	42379			
4					Correspondence
5	DAY-OF-WEEK=	=WEEKDAY(B3)	1	=	Sunday
6			2	=	Monday
7			3	=	Tuesday
8			4	=	Wednesday
9			5	=	Thursday
10			6	=	Friday
11			7	=	Saturday
12					
13	This date is a	=VLOOKUP(B5,D5:F11,3)			

FIGURE A.2 The Formulas used to create Figure A.1

Typically, the actual day's name rather than its corresponding WEEKDAY() value is more useful than simply displaying the value returned by this function. This additional information is provided in Cell B6 within the spreadsheet shown in Figure A.3.

	A	B	C	D	E	F	G
1	Spreadsheet for Determing the Day-of-The Week						
2							
3	Enter the date:	1/10/2016					
4						Correspondence	
5	DAY-OF-WEEK=	1		1	=	Sunday	
6	This date is a	Sunday		2	=	Monday	
7				3	=	Tuesday	
8				4	=	Wednesday	
9				5	=	Thursday	
10				6	=	Friday	
11				7	=	Saturday	
12							

Figure A.3
A Spreadsheet that Displays a Date's Day-of-the-Week Name

Figure A.4 provides the formula used in cell B6 that produces the day name corresponding to the DAY-OF-THE-WEEK value displayed in cell B5. Because the data within the table is arranged vertically, with each column containing the same type of data, the table is referred to as a vertical table. Here, the first column contains the possible integer values that can be returned by the WEEKDAY( ) function and the third column the day names corresponding to each value. For tables arranged in this manner, Excel provides a VLOOKUP( ) function. [†††††††]

As shown in cell B6, the first item provided within the function's parentheses is B5. [§§§§§§§] This item identifies the location of the value that is to be searched for within the table. By design, the VLOOKUP( ) function always compares the searched for value (in this case the date in cell B5) to each value in the first column of the table. The location of the table itself is the second item within the function's parentheses, which in this case is D5:F11. Notice this provides the range of table by listing the table's first and last cell address. The last entry provided to the VLOOKUP() function, which in this case is a 3, tells the VLOOKUP () function to return the entry in the third column of the table that corresponds to the match found in the first column. If no match is found the entry closest to, but lower than the searched for value, is considered a match. As seen in Figure A.3, the VLOOKUP( ) function has correctly identified the WEEKDAY( ) value of 1 in cell B5 as a Sunday.

	A	B	C	D	E	F	G
1	Spreadsheet for Determing the Day-of-The Week						
2							
3	Enter the date:	42379					
4					Correspondence		
5	DAY-OF-WEEK=	=WEEKDAY(B3)		1	=	Sunday	
6	This date is a	=VLOOKUP(B5,D5:F11,3)		2	=	Monday	
7				3	=	Tuesday	
8				4	=	Wednesday	
9				5	=	Thursday	
10				6	=	Friday	
11				7	=	Saturday	
12							

Figure A.4 The Formulas used to create Figure A.3

[†††††††] For horizontally constructed tables, where each row contains the same data type, Excel's HLOOKUP( ) function is used.

[§§§§§§§] A more direct entry for cell B6, which avoids the display of the value returned by the WEEKDAY() function in cell B5, is = VLOOKUP(WEEKDAY(B3),D5:F11,3).

A.2 Zeller's Algorithm

Zeller's algorithm provides a series of steps that can be used for either writing a computer program or manually determining the day of the week corresponding to a given date. The steps required for this algorithm provide an integer number, referred to as the *Zeller value*, between 0 and 6. Here, the number 0 corresponds to Saturday, 1 to Sunday, 2 to Monday, and so on. Zeller's algorithm is as follows:
    Starting with a date of the form M/D/Y, where

> M = the month of the year
> D = the day of the year
> Y = the four digit year

the procedure for determining the Zeller value for this date is:

Step 1: If the month, M, is less than 3 then subtract 1 from the 4-digit year.

Step 2: If the month, M, is less than 3, add 12to the value of M.

Step 3: Set the century equal to the first two digits of the 4-digit year.

Step 4: Set the two-digit year equal to the last two digits of the 4-digit year.

Step 5: Determine the value of the following expression:
> D + the integer value of 2.6 * (month +1)
>> + the 2-digit year
>> + the integer value of (the two-digit year/4)
>> + the integer value of (the century /4)
> − 2 * century

Step 6: The Zeller value is the remainder when the value found in step 5 is divided by 7.

Example: Determine the Zeller value for the date 1/10/2016.

Solution

Step 1: Because M is less than 3, the 4-digit year, Y, becomes 2016 - 1 = 2015.

Step 2: Because M is less than 3, M becomes 1+ 12 = 13.

Step 3: Set the century = 20, which is the first 2 digits of 2015 (see Step 1).

Step 4: Set the year = 15, which is the last two digits of 2015 (see Step 1).

Step 5: The value of the required expression is

$$10 + \text{integer of } (2.6 * 14) + 15 + \text{integer of } (15/4)$$
$$+ \text{integer of } (20/4) - 2 * 20$$
$$= 10 + 36 + 15 + 3 + 5 - 40 = 29$$

Step 6: The remainder when 29 is divided by 7 is 1. This is the Zeller value, which corresponds to a Sunday. Notice that this indicates the same day displayed in Figure A.4.

Figure A.5 illustrates an Excel spreadsheet that illustrates how Zeller's algorithm can be coded. Clearly, you would only code this algorithm within a more extensive computer program that required a day-of-the-week function or subroutine. For comparison purposes, the date shown in the figure corresponds to the date used in the previous example, while also displaying the values obtained for each step required by Zeller's algorithm.

	A	B	C	D	E
1	Spreadsheet for Determing the Day-of-The Week using Zeller's Algorithm				
2					
3	Enter the date:	1/10/2016			
4					
5	Month =	1			
6	Day =	10			
7	Year =	2016			
8					
9		The Intermediate Step Values For Determining the Zeller Value			
10		Step 1	2015		
11		Step 2	13		
12		Step3	20		
13		Step 4	15		
14		Step 5	29		
15		Step 6	1	<-- This is the Zeller value	
16					

Figure A.5 Determining a Day-of-the-Week Zeller Value

	A	B	C	D	E
1		Spreadsheet for Determing the Day-of-The Week using Zeller's Algorithm			
2					
3	Enter the date:	42379			
4					
5	Month =	=MONTH(B3)			
6	Day =	=DAY(B3)			
7	Year =	=YEAR(B3)			
8					
9			The Intermediate Step Values For Determining the Zeller Value		
10		Step 1	=IF(B5<3,B7 -1, B7)		
11		Step 2	=IF(B5<3,B5 +12, B5)		
12		Step3	=INT(C10/100)		
13		Step 4	=MOD(C10,100)		
14		Step 5	=B6+INT(2.6*(C11+1))+C13+INT(C13/4)+INT(C12/4)-2*C12		
15		Step 6	=MOD(C14,7)	<-- This is the Zeller value	
16					

Figure A.6 The Formulas used to create Figure A.5

As illustrated in Figure A.7, a lookup table can also be added to the spreadsheet shown in Figure A.5 to display the day name corresponding to the calculated Zeller value (the construction of this spreadsheet is left as Exercise 6 at the end of this section).

	A	B	C	D	E
1	Spreadsheet for Determing the Day-of-The Week using Zeller's Algorithm				
2					
3	Enter the date:	1/10/2016			
4					
5	Month =	1			
6	Day =	10			
7	Year =	2016			
8					
9			The Intermediate Step Values For Determining the Zeller Value		
10		Step 1	2015		
11		Step 2	13		
12		Step3	20		
13		Step 4	15		
14		Step 5	29		
15		Step 6	1	<-- This is the Zeller value	
16					
17	This date is a	Sunday			
18			A Look-up Table		
19			0	Saturday	
20			1	Sunday	
21			2	Monday	
22			3	Tuesday	
23			4	Wednesday	
24			5	Thursday	
25			6	Friday	
26					

Figure A.7 Displaying a Date's Day-of-the-Week Name

A.3 Holiday Determination

In addition to the restriction that the calculation of a settlement day cannot include or occur on either a Saturday or Sunday, the same restriction applies to holidays. Unlike weekend days, which occur on a regular basis and for which algorithms exist to determine these days, such as Zeller's algorithm just presented, no such algorithm exists for determining each year's holiday dates .

To make a determination that a date falls on a holiday requires a table of holidays, referred to as a *Holiday Table*, that lists the date of each holiday for each year. As an example of such a table, Tables A.1 lists the official 2015 holidays for the United State. Except for New Year's Day, Independence Day, and Christmas, all of the other dates change, depending on the year. (the holiday names are for convenience; it is the actual dates that are needed). Similarly, Table A.2 provides a 2015 Canadian Holiday Table.

TABLE A.1 United States Holiday Table for 2015

Date	Holiday
1/1/2015	New Year's day
1/19/2015	Martin Luther King Jr.'s Birthday
2/16/2015	President's Day
4/3/2015	Good Friday
4/5/2015	Easter Sunday
5/25/2015	Memorial Day
7/4/2015	Independence Day
9/7/2015	Labor Day
10/12/2015	Columbus Day
11/26/2015	Thanksgiving Day
12/25/2015	Christmas

Once a Holiday Table is available, the determination of a given date falling on a holiday is made by comparing the date to each date in the Holiday Table. If a match is found, the date corresponds to a holiday and cannot be used as a settlement date.

Figure A.8 illustrates a spreadsheet that compares a user-entered date to entries in a vertical table (as noted in the prior section, what makes the table vertical is that each column in the table, rather than each row, contains a given data type; in this case the first column in the table consists of dates and the second column contains text). As shown in Figure A.8, an entered date of 7/4/2015 in cell B3 is correctly identified as Independence Day in cell B5.

TABLE A.2 Canadian Holiday Table for 2015

Date	Holiday
1/1/2015	New Year's day
2/16/2015	Family Day
4/3/2015	Good Friday
4/5/2015	Easter Sunday
4/6/2015	Easter Monday
5/18/2015	Victoria Day
7/1/2015	Canada Day
8/3/2015	Civic Holiday
9/7/2015	Labour Day
10/12/2015	Thanksgiving Day
11/11/2015	Remembrance Day
12/25/2015	Christmas
12/26/2015	Boxing day

Figure A.9 provides the formula used in cell B5 that produces the holiday date look-up. As indicated, a VLOOKUP() function is used. The first cell address within the parentheses, B3, identifies the location of the value that is to be searched for within the table. The location of the table, B9:C30 provides the first and last cell of the table, and is the second item in the parentheses. By design, VLOOKUP( ) compares the searched for value (in this case the date in cell B3) to each value in the first column of the table. The last entry provided to the VLOOKUP() function, which in this case is a 2, tells the VLOOKUP() function to return the entry in the second column of the table, corresponding to the match found in the first column.

If no exact date match is found, the entry closest to, but lower than the value in B3, is considered by VLOOKUP ( ) to be a match. Thus, any date value between two holiday dates is reported back as a match to the closest, earlier holiday date. To prevent this, the **Not a Holiday** entries were inserted between each valid holiday. Thus, any date that does not fall exactly on a holiday will be correctly identified as **Not a Holiday.**

	A	B	C	D
1			**Holiday Determination**	
2				
3	Enter a Date:	7/4/2015		
4				
5	This is	Independence Day		
6				
7				
8		**Date**	**Holiday**	
9		1/1/2015	New Year's day	
10		1/2/2015	Not a Holiday	
11		1/19/2015	Martin Luther King Jr.'s Birthday	
12		1/20/2015	Not a Holiday	
13		2/16/2015	President's Day	
14		2/17/2015	Not a Holiday	
15		4/3/2015	Good Friday	
16		4/4/2015	Not a Holiday	
17		4/5/2015	Easter Sunday	
18		4/6/2015	Not a Holiday	
19		5/25/2015	Memorial Day	
20		5/26/2015	Not a Holiday	
21		7/4/2015	Independence Day	
22		7/5/2015	Not a Holiday	
23		9/7/2015	Labor Day	
24		9/8/2015	Not a Holiday	
25		10/12/2015	Columbus Day	
26		10/13/2015	Not a Holiday	
27		11/26/2015	Thanksgiving Day	
28		11/27/2015	Not a Holiday	
29		12/25/2015	Christmas	
30		12/26/2015	Not a Holiday	
31				

Figure A.8 A Spreadsheet that Determines if a Date is a Holiday

	A	B	C	D
1			Holiday Determination	
2				
3	Enter a Date:	42189		
4				
5	This is	=VLOOKUP(B3,B9:C31,2)		
6				
7				
8		Date	Holiday	
9		42005	New Year's day	
10		42006	Not a Holiday	
11		42023	Martin Luther King Jr.'s Birthday	
12		42024	Not a Holiday	
13		42051	President's Day	
14		42052	Not a Holiday	
15		42097	Good Friday	
16		42098	Not a Holiday	
17		42099	Easter Sunday	
18		42100	Not a Holiday	
19		42149	Memorial Day	
20		42150	Not a Holiday	
21		42189	Independence Day	
22		42190	Not a Holiday	
23		42254	Labor Day	
24		42255	Not a Holiday	
25		42289	Columbus Day	
26		42290	Not a Holiday	
27		42334	Thanksgiving Day	
28		42335	Not a Holiday	
29		42363	Christmas	
30		42364	Not a Holiday	
31				

Figure A.9 The Formulas used to create Figure A.8

Appendix A Exercises

1. Create the spreadsheet shown in Figure A.3. Use this spreadsheet to determine the day of the week corresponding to the United States holidays dates listed in Table A.1.

2. Create the spreadsheet shown in Figure A.3. Use this spreadsheet to determine the day of the week corresponding to the Canadian holidays dates listed in Table A.2

3. Table A.3 lists the national holidays of Mexico for 2015. Create the spreadsheet shown in Figure A.3. Use this spreadsheet to determine the day of the week corresponding to the Mexican holidays dates listed in Table A.3.

TABLE A.3 Mexican Holiday Table for 2015

Date	Holiday
1/1/2015	New Year's day
2/2/2015	Constitution Day
3/16/2015	Benito Jaurez Birthday
4//2/2015	Maunday Thursday
4/3/2015	Good Friday
5/11/2015	Labour Day
5/5/2015	Cinco de Maya
9/16/2015	Independence Day
10/12/2015	Revolution Day Memorial
11/16/2015	Day of the Dead
11/16/2015	Revolution Day
12/1/2/2015	Day of the Virgin of Gaudalupe
12/25/2015	Christmas

4. Create the spreadsheet shown in Figure A.8.
   a. Use this spreadsheet to verify that all of the dates listed in Table A.1 are correctly identified as holidays.
   b. Enter the dates 1/7/2015, 4/10/2015, and 7/16/2016 to verify that these dates are correctly identified as non-holiday dates.

5.a. Create an Excel spreadsheet identical to that shown in Figure A.8, but remove all of the rows in the look-up table that are listed as Not a Holiday (adjust the second operand in the VLOOKUP() function to correctly identify the last table entry. Then complete the following spreadsheet.

Date	Output in Cell B5
'71/4//2015	
1/18/2015	
1/31/2015	
2/15/2015	
2/25/2015	
4/4/2015	
5/24/2015	
7/3/2015	
9/5/2015	
10/5/2015	
11/25/2015	
11/28/2015	
12/31/2015	

b. Using either the Excel spreadsheet shown in Figure 3.18, or the spreadsheet created for part a., what text will appear in cell B5 for all entered dates greater than 12/25/2015.

6. Construct the Excel spreadsheet shown in Figure A.7.

Appendix B
Day Counts and Leap Year Determination

*In calculating the portion of the interest payment that is due the seller when a bond is sold between two coupon payment dates (see the Point of Information box on page 288) a number of allocation methods are provided. Two of the most commonly used and legally required for most bonds traded in the United States are presented in this section. It should be noted that in all date calculations between two dates, the last day (that is, the day in the second date) is **not** counted.*

B.1 30/360 Day Count Method

For municipal, and corporate bonds, a 30/360 day count method is used, unless otherwise specified at the time of the trade.

As its name suggests, the 36/360 day count method considers each month to have 30 days and each year 360 days. A consequence of this is that each six-month coupon period consists of exactly 180 days.

Although a few variations of this method exist, the one used in the United States is referred to as the United States 30/360 method, or 30/360 US, for short. Using this method, the number of days between two dates is determined as follows, where the first date is denoted as $M_1/D_1/Y_1$ and the second date as $M_2/D_2 Y_2$ and the following steps are applied in sequence:[********]

Step1: If the first day, D_1, is the last day of the month, set D1 to 30.

Step2 If the second day, D_2, is the last day of the month, and the first day, D_1, is earlier than the 30th day of the month change the second date to the 1st day of the next month (change the year if necessary); otherwise change D_2 to 30.

Step 3: The number of days, N, between the two date is then determined as
$$Number-of-Days = 360\,(Y_2 - Y_1) + 30(M_2 - M_1) + (D_2 - D_1)$$

[********] As other 30/360 procedures are defined (they mainly differ in how the treat the end-of-month days), you should always check with the method defined for the particular 30/360 financial instrument under consideration .

POINT OF INFORMATION

ALLOCATING INTEREST PAYMENTS

The full interest due on a bond coupon payment date is paid to whoever owns the bond on that date. However, when an existing bond is sold from one investor to another between coupon payment dates, this interest payment rightfully belongs to each owner based on the number of days within the coupon period that each person owned the bond. That is, the bond's current owner is only entitled to the interest for the period when he or she actually owned the bond, and the seller is entitled to the interest for the time he or she owned the bond.

Because the buyer, who is the current bond owner, receives the full coupon payment when it is made, the proportion of the interest due the seller is paid by the buyer to the seller on the settlement date. This proportion is calculated as the days the seller owned the bond divided by the total number of days in the coupon period (that is, the number of days between the prior and next interest payment date).

For purpose of allocating the interest between the seller and buyer, the days that the seller owned the bond, as shown in Figure B.1, is the number of days from the prior coupon date to the settlement date (recall from the prior section that the settlement date is the date on which ownership of the bond is officially transferred from seller to buyer). This number of days is referred to as the **accrued days**.

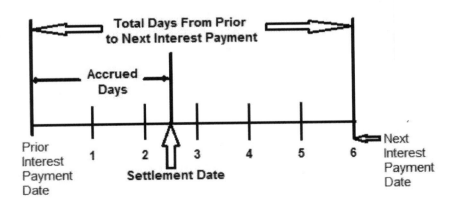

FIGURE B.1 Determining the Accrued Days

A number of examples using these steps are shown in Table B.1.

TABLE B.1 Examples of 30/360 US Day Count Calculations

1st Date	2nd Date	Comments and Calculation
3/1/2016	3/15/2016	Neither date is changed, and Number-of-Days $= 15 - 1 = 14$
2/28/2016	3/15/2016	Because this is a leap year, the start day, 28, is NOT the last day of the month, and is left as 28, and Number-of-Days $= 30(3-2) + (15 - 28) = 17$
2/28/2017	3/15/2017	Because the start day, 28, is the last day of the month (for a leap year this would be $D_1 = 29$), D_1 is set to 30, as per Step 1, and Number-of-Days $= 30(3-2) + (15 - 30) = 15$
1/1/2016	7/1/2016	Neither date is changed, and Number-of-Days $= 30(7-1) = 180$ (Note, that as expected, a half year contains 180 days.)
7/1/2016	7/31/2016	The second date is changed 10 8/1/2016, as per Step 2, and July is assumed to have 30 days. Thus, Number-of-Days $= 30(8 - 7) + (1 - 1) = 30$
7/1/2016	7/30/2016	Neither date is changed, and Number-of-Days $= (30-1) = 29$ (Note, that as expected, this result is one day less than the previous example.)
7/30/2016	8/1/2016	Neither date is changed, and July is assumed to have 30 days, and Number-of-Days $= 30(8 - 7) + (1 - 30) = 1$

Excel® Implementation

Excel's 30/360 day count function is named DAYS360( ). This function can computes both the 30/360 US and 30/360 European methods depending on the third argument provided to the function. When the third argument is omitted, the United States convention is used.

Figure B.2 illustrates using an Excel spreadsheet to calculate the 30/360 day difference between the first two dates listed in Table B.1.

	A	B	C
1	**30/360 Day Count Spreadsheet**		
2			
3	Enter the First Date:	3/1/2016	
4	Enter the Second Date:	3/15/2016	
5	The 30/360 Day Difference is:	14	
6			

FIGURE B.2 30/360 Day Count Spreadsheet

To calculate a 30/360 US day difference, the formula located in cell B5 in the spreadsheet is:

$$=DAYS360(B4,B4)$$

which provides the function with a required starting and ending date. In using this function you must ensure that the dates have both been formatted as Dates. Although the format for the starting and ending date need not be the same , it would be unusual to use different formats for them.

To use the European 30/360 day count convention, which is beyond the scope of this text, the text TRUE must be entered as the function's third argument.

B.2 Actual/Actual Day Count Method

For United States government bonds, the method known as the actual/actual, day count method must be used, unless otherwise specified at the time of the trade.

To compute the actual number of days between two dates each date must first be converted to the actual number of days from a base date. Once both dates have been converted to the number of actual days from a base date, the number of actual days between the two dates is found by subtracting the converted earlier date from the converted later date.

Commonly, the converted actual number of days from a base date are referred to as Julian dates, although the term formally refers to one method of determining the actual days from a base date after October 15, 1582 (this is the day the modern Gregorian calendar went into effect). In computing actual Julian dates, the base year selected for the calculation must be the

In this section a quicker method is presented that determines the number of days from the base date of 0/0/0000. Although the actual days computed are not true Julian individual day dates, the day difference between the two computed days provides the same number of actual days as is found using a true Julian days method. The steps used for this quicker method are as follows:

Starting with a date of the form M/D/Y, where

M = the month of the year
D = the day of the year
Y = the four digit year

the procedure for determining the actual number of days between two dates is:

Step 1: If the month, M, is less than 3 then set the variable MP = 0
and YP = Y - 1; otherwise, set M = the integer value of $(0.4 + M + 2.3)$
and Yp = Y

Step 2:[†††††††] Set the variable   T = the integer value of $(Yp/4)$
$$- \text{ the integer value of } (Yp/100)$$
$$+ \text{ the integer value of } (Yp/400)$$

Step 4: The number of actual days since the base date of 0/0/000 is
$$\text{Days} = 365*Y + 31 * (M - 1) + D + T - MP$$

Figure B.3 illustrates an Excel spreadsheet that determines the number of actual days for the entered date of 1/31/2016 using this four step procedure.
For convenience, the intermediate variables and values defined in the above steps are also provided. As shown in Figure B.3, the actual day count corresponding to the date 1/31/2016 is 736,360 days.

	A	B	C	D	E	F
1	Actual Date Count					
2						
3	Enter the Date:	1/31/2016				
4						
5	The month is:	1		MP =	0	
6	The Day is:	31		YP =	2016	
7	The year is:	2016		T =	489	
8						
9	The Actual Day Count is:	736360				
10						

FIGURE B.3 Actual Day Count Spreadsheet

Figure B.4 provides the formulas that were used to produce Figure B.3, while Figure B.5 expands the spreadsheet to provide for the entry of a second date., and then determines the actual day count for this second entered date. Using the two calculated day counts, the actual day difference between the two dates is obtained (see cell B20) by subtracting the second day count in B18 from the first day's count in cell B9. Thus, as seen in Figure B.5 the total number of actual days between the

---

[†††††††] The interested reader will see that this is a determination of the number of leap years, as presented later in this section.

dates 2/15/2016 and 1/31/1999 is 6225 days. As in all day difference computations, the difference between dates includes the first date but not later date.

	A	B	C	D	E
1		Actual Date Count			
2					
3	Enter the Date:	42400			
4					
5	The month is:	=MONTH(B3)		MP =	=IF(B5<3,0,INT(0.4*B5+2.3))
6	The Day is:	=DAY(B3)		YP =	=IF(B5<1,B7-1,B7)
7	The year is:	=YEAR(B3)		T =	=INT(E6/4) -INT(E6/100)+INT(E6/400)
8					
9	The Actual Day C	=365*B7 +31*(B5-1)+ B6 +E7-E5			
10					

FIGURE B.4 The Formulas Used to Create Figure B.3

	A	B	C	D	E	F
1		Actual Date Count				
2						
3	Enter the First Date:	1/31/1999				
4						
5	The month is:	1		MP =	0	
6	The Day is:	31		YP =	1999	
7	The year is:	1999		T =	484	
8						
9	The Actual Day Count is:	730150				
10						
11						
12	Enter the Second Date:	2/15/2016				
13						
14	The month is:	2		MP =	0	
15	The Day is:	15		YP =	2016	
16	The year is:	2016		T =	489	
17						
18	The Actual Day Count is:	736375				
19						
20	The Actual Days between the dates is =	6225	days			
21						

FIGURE B.5 Determining the Actual Days Between Two Dates

B.3 Leap Year Determination

A leap year is any year that is evenly divisible by 4 but not evenly dividable by 100, with the exception that all years divisible by 400 are leap years. For example, the year 2012 was a leap year because it is evenly divisible by 4 but not evenly divisible by 100. The year 2000 was a leap year because it is evenly divisible by 400. Thus, the steps for determining a leap year are:

Step 1: Determine if the year is evenly divisible by 4 (that is, there is a remainder of zero).

Step 2: Determine if the year is NOT evenly divisible by 100 (that is, there is a non-zero remainder).

Step 3: Determine if the year is evenly divisible by 400 (that is, there is a remainder of zero).

Step 4: If the year is evenly divisible by 4 and not evenly divisible by 100 (Steps 1 and 2), or the year is evenly divisible by 400 (Step 3), then the year is a leap year.

Example 1: Determine if the year 2000 is a leap year.

Solution:

Step 1: The year 2000 divided by 4 is 500, with a remainder or zero. Thus, the year is evenly divided by 4.

Step 2: The year 2000 divided by 100 is 20. Thus, the year is evenly divisible by 100 because it has a remainder of zero.

Step 3: The year 2000 divided by 400 is 5. Thus, the year is evenly divisible by 400 because it has a remainder of 0.

Step 4: Because the year is evenly divisible by 400 (Step 4), it is a leap year.

Example 2: Determine if the year 2016 is a leap year.

Solution:

Step 1: The year 2016 divided by 4 is 504, with a remainder of zero . Thus, the year is evenly divided by 4.

Step 2: The year 2016 divided by 100 is 20.16. Thus, the year is NOT evenly divisible by 100, because it has a remainder of 0.16.

Step 3: This is not needed because Steps 1 and 2 have already determined the year is a leap year. That is,

Step 4: Because the year is evenly divisible by 4 (Step 1) and not evenly divisible by 100 (Step 2), it is a leap year.

Example 3: Determine if the year 2017 is a leap year.

Solution:
Step 1: The year 2017 divided by 4 is 504.25. Thus, the remainder is 0.25, and the year is not evenly divided by 4.
Step 2: The year 2017 divided by 100 is 20.17. Thus, the year is NOT evenly divisible by 100, because it has a remainder of 0.17.
Step 3: The year 2017 divided by 400 is 5.0425. Thus, the year is not evenly divisible by 400, because it has a remainder of 0.0425
Step 4: Because the year is not evenly divisible by 4 (Step 1) and not evenly divisible by 400 (Step 3), it is a not leap year.

Figure B.6 shows an Excel Spreadsheet that determines whether a user-input year is, or is not, a leap year.

	A	B	C	D
1	Spreadsheet for Determining Leap Years			
2				
3	Enter the Year:	2001		
4				
5	This year	IS NOT	a Leap Year.	
6				

FIGURE B.6 A spreadsheet for Determining Leap Years

The formula used in Cell B5 that makes this determination is:

=IF(OR(AND(MOD(B3,4)=0,MOD(B3,100)<>0),MOD(B3,400)=0),"IS","IS NOT")

This statement uses the OR( ) function to select between two expressions; if either of these expressions is true, the entered year is a leap year. The first expression in the OR( ) function,

AND(MOD(B3,4)=0,MOD(B3,100)<>0

determines if both the year divided by 4 has a remainder of zero AND the year divided by 100 has a non-zero remainder. This completes Steps 1 and 2 of the leap year procedure listed previously. The second expression in the OR( ) function,

MOD(B3,400)= 0

determines if the year divided by 400 has a remainder of zero, which completes Step 3 of the leap year procedure. The OR( ) function checks both of these expressions, and if either one is true, the text IS is placed in cell B5; otherwise, the text IS NOT is placed in cell B5. This determination corresponds to Step 4 in the leap year procedure.

Table B.3 lists all of the leap years form 1600 until 2196.

TABLE B.3 Leap Years from 1600 – 2196

1600	-	-	-	2000	-
1604	1704	1804	1904	2004	2104
1608	1708	1808	1908	2008	2108
1612	1712	1812	1912	2012	2112
1616	1716	1816	1916	2016	2116
1620	1720	1820	1920	2020	2120
1624	1724	1824	1924	2024	2124
1628	1728	1828	1928	2028	2128
1632	1732	1832	1932	2032	2132
1636	1736	1836	1936	2036	2136
1640	1740	1840	1940	2040	2140
1644	1744	1844	1944	2044	2144
1648	1748	1848	1948	2048	2148
1652	1752	1852	1952	2052	2152
1656	1756	1856	1956	2056	2156
1660	1760	1860	1960	2060	2160
1664	1764	1864	1964	2064	2164
1668	1768	1868	1968	2068	2168
1672	1772	1872	1972	2072	2172
1676	1776	1876	1976	2076	2176
1680	1780	1880	1980	2080	2180
1684	1784	1884	1984	2084	2184
1688	1788	1888	1988	2088	2188
1692	1792	1892	1992	2092	2192
1696	1796	1896	1996	2096	2196

Appendix B Exercises

1. Create an Excel Spreadsheet that accepts two dates and computes the days between these dates using the 30/360 US day count method. Verify that your spreadsheet works correctly by using the dates provided in Table B.1.

2. Either by hand or using the Excel spreadsheet created for Exercise 1, determine the days between the following dates using the 30/360 US day count method.

    a. 1/31/2016 and 1/31/2017
    b. 2/17/2016 and 7/18/2016
    c. 3/5/2016 and 9/20/2016
    d. 4/1/2016 and 6/1/2016
    e. 5/15/2016 and 8/16/2016

3. Create the Excel Spreadsheet shown in Figure B.3, and verify that your spreadsheet works correctly by using the dates shown in the figure.

4. Starting with the Spreadsheet formulas shown in Figure B.4, create the Excel Spreadsheet shown in Figure B.5. Using this spreadsheet determine the days between the dates listed in Exercise 2.

5. Either by hand or using the Excel spreadsheet created for Exercise 4, determine the actual number of days between the dates listed in Table B.1.

6. Create the Excel Spreadsheet shown in Figure B.6, and verify that your spreadsheet works correctly by using the dates shown in the figure.

7. Either by hand or using the Excel spreadsheet created for Exercise 2, determine if the following years are leap years.
    a. 1600
    b. 1607
    c. 1712
    d. 1774
    e. 1800
    f. 1812
    g. 1900
    h. 1998
    i. 2000
    j. 2018

Solutions to Selected Odd–Numbered Problems

Chapter 1

Section 1.1 (Exercises on page 6)

1. -3 3. 1.6 5. $-9\,1/2$ 7. 162 9. -162 11. $-2/3$ 13. -14.03
15. 4 17. -4 19. $-4/5$ 21. -5.5 23. -4 25. 4 27. -4
29. -7.7 31. 4 33. 2 35. -6.62 37. 30 39. $246/497$

Section 1.2 (Exercises on page 12)

1. Yes   3. No   5. No   7. Yes   9. $x = 5$ 11. $x = -2$ 13. $p = -4$
15. $t = 7$ 17. $x = -3$ 19. $p = -\,23/6$ 21. $a = 13/3$ 23. $y = 1/3$
25. $t = -172/7$

Section 1.3 (Exercises on pages 18 and 19)

1. 81 3. π^{15} 5. $(1.7)^{5.1}$ 7. y^{10} 9. $(3.1)^{24}$ 11. $2^{-5} = 1/32$
13. $10^{-3} = 1/1000$ 15. $27^{1/3} = 3$ 17. $2^{-9} = 1/512$ 19. $2/3$ 21. $6/5$

Section 1.4 (Exercises on page 23)

1. $x = 2$ 3. $y = \pm 3$ 5. $b = \pm 2$ 7. $p = 1.3^{1/5}$ 9. $t = (9.3)^{1/9.3}$
11. $x = 3, x = 2$ 13. $p = 0.56, p = -3.56$ 15. $x = -3$
17. $n = 1/3, n = -1$ 19. $t = .558, t = -0.3583$ 21. $x = 0, x = 2$

Section 1.5 (Exercises on pages 29, 30, and 31)

1. a. A: $(3, 2)$ B: $(9, 6)$ C: $(10,0)$ D: $(4, -6)$ E: $(8, -4)$
    F: $(-6, 5)$ G: $(-2, 1)$ H: $(0, 5)$ I: $(-5, -3)$
    J: $(-1, -4)$ K: $(0, -7)$
   b. Points A and B

3.

a.

b.

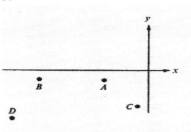

c.

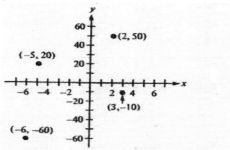

5.

7. a. All points on the *x*-axis have a *y*-coordinate of 0.
   b. All points on the *y*-axis have an *x*-coordinate of 0.

9. Each point on the line has the same *y*-coordinate.

Section 1.6 (Exercises on page 39)

1.

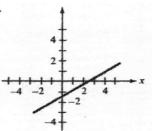

3.

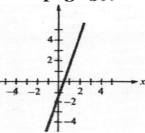

5.

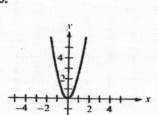

7.

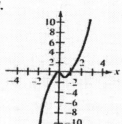

9.

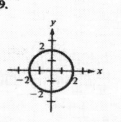

11. (a)

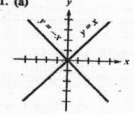

b. The curves have opposite slopes.

13. All three points lie on the same graph.

15 a.

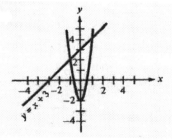

b. Points of intersection: $(1.105, 4.105)$, $(-0.905, 2.095)$

Section 1.7 (Exercises on pages 43 through 46)

1. a. $(x_1)^2 + (x_2)^2 + (x_3)^2$
   b. $2x_3 + 2x_4 + 2x_5 + 2x_6 + 2x_7 + 2x_8 + 2x_9 + 2x_{10} + 2x_{11}$
   c. $+ (x_1 + y_1) + (x_2 + y_2) + (x_3 + y_3) + (x_4 + y_4) + (x_5 + y_5) + (x_6 + y_6)$
   d. $(3)M_{99} + 4) + (3)M_{100} + 4) + (3)M_{101} + 4) + (3)M_{102} + 4)$
      $+ (3)M_{103} + 4) + (3)M_{104} + 4) + (3)M_{105} + 4)$

3. a. $\displaystyle\sum_{i=2}^{29} 3i^2$ b. $\displaystyle\sum_{i=2}^{29} i(3^2)$ c. $\displaystyle\sum_{i=2}^{29} 2(3^i)$ d. $\displaystyle\sum_{i=2}^{29} (-1)^i(3i^2)$

5. a. 15   b. 31   c. 151   d. 3   e. 26   f. 465
   g. They are not equal.

9. Average $= 1/n \sum_{i=1}^{n} G_i$

Section 1.8 (Exercises on pages 48 and 49)

1. 0.67	3. 0.24	5. 2.87
7. 0.667	0.235	2.871
9. 3356.42	11. .003356	13. 3,300,000,000,000

Chapter 2

Section 2.1 (Exercises on page 55)

1.a. Yes   b. No   c. No   d. Yes   e. Yes   f. Yes   g. No
   h. Yes   i. No   j. Yes
3. $V = \$6,000 - \$1,500t$ is a linear equation.

Section 2.2 (Exercises on pages 62 and 63)

1. a.

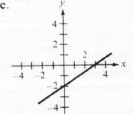

b.

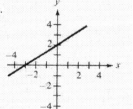

c.

d.

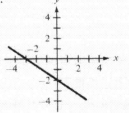

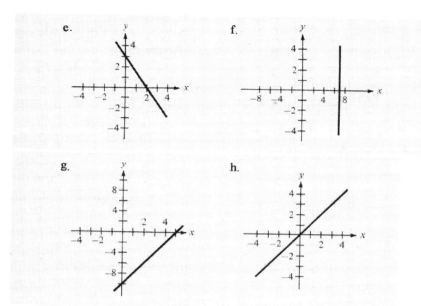

3. $3.93 million

5. $2.00 (200 cents)

Section 2.3 (Exercises on pages 72, 73, and 74)

1. a. −2/3   b. 2/3   c. 2/3   d. −2/3
   e. −3/2   f. ∞   g. 2   h. 1
3. $A = (2/11)t + 1$
5. $P = 0.05S + 2000$

Section 2.4 (Exercises on pages 79 and 80)

1. a. $C = 10x + 20,000$ b. $R = 12x$
   c. $14,000 loss   d. 10,000 units
3. Break-even point = $15,000/ ($12.00 - $2.00) = 1,500 units

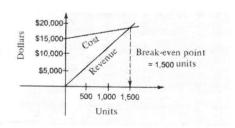

5. a. 9,375   b. 6,383
c. Yes, the higher the price the greater profit on each unit. This means break-even will occur at a lower number of units sold.

7. The variable cost per bookend is $9.00

Section 2.5 (Exercises on pages 85 and 86)

1.a. Yes   b. No   c. Yes   d. Yes
   e. No   f. Yes   g. Yes   h. Yes

3. a. $x = 3, -2$ b. $x = 5/3, -1$

c. $x = -\dfrac{\sqrt{7}}{2}, +\dfrac{\sqrt{7}}{2}$

d. $x = \dfrac{3 \pm \sqrt{21}}{2}$

e. $x = \dfrac{1 \pm \sqrt{17}}{2}$ f. $x = \dfrac{4 \pm \sqrt{8}}{2} = \dfrac{4 \pm \sqrt{4 \cdot 2}}{2} = \dfrac{4 \pm 2\sqrt{2}}{2} = 2 \pm \sqrt{2}$

5. a. $15,125   b. $20,000   c. 6 years

Section 2.6 (Exercises on page 88)

1. a. Yes; 5th degree in x b. No   c. Yes; 4th h degree in x
   d. No   e. Yes, 2nd degree in x f. No

Section 2.7 (Exercises on pages 90 and 91)

1. Yes   3. No   5. Yes   7. No   9. Yes
11. a.738.91   b. 12,151.04   c. 133,943.08   d. 1,476,478.16
13. b. 88.69 grams   b. 235.44 grams

Chapter 3

Section 3.1 (Exercises on pages 100 and 101)

1. a. i = .02, n = 4, P(0) = $2,000
   b. $2,164.86
3. $2,812.16
5. $2,901.89
7. $1,853.94
9. $3,033.40
11. $P(1460) = \$3{,}500\,(1 + .025/365)^{1460} = \$3{,}868.08$
13. $P(1095) = \$2{,}500(1 + .03/365)^{1095} = \$2{,}735.43$

Section 3.2 (Exercises on pages 107, 108, and 109)

1. a. $7,401.22   b. $7,429.74   c. $7,444.32   d. $7,458.96
3. $16,991.90
5. At 2% compounded quarterly, $1,000 is worth $1,020.15 after a year.
   At 4% compounded annually, $1,000 is worth $1,040 after a year.
   Therefore, the 4% annually is the better investment alternative.
7. a. $12,802.36   b. $10,960.35   c. $8,104.03
   d. The Present value of a Future Value amount goes down (that is, decreases) as the interest rate increases.
9. $8,367.55
11. In the friend's business she will receive $12,000 in three years. Investing it in the 4% account yield $11,268.25. Therefore, assuming equal credit risk for both alternative, she gets a better return from her friend's business.
13. PV of Buyer A = $20,000 + $4,274.02 = $24,274.02
    PV of Buyer B = $15,000 + $8,889.96 = $23,889.96
    PV of Buyer C= $10,000 + $14,225.66 =$24,225.66
    Assuming equal credit risk, Buyer A has made the best offer.
15. 1st Opportunity: PV = $6,336.75
    2nd Opportunity: PV = $6,229.98
    3rd Opportunity: PV = $6,650.57
    Assuming equal credit risk, the 3rd opportunity is better.

19. $i = \left(\frac{1,350}{1,000}\right)^{1/3} - 1 = 1.1052 - 1 = 0.1052 = 10.52\%$

21. $i = \left(\frac{2x}{x}\right)^{1/10} - 1 = (2)^{0.1} - 1 = 1.07177 - 1 = 0.07177 = 7.18\%$

Section 3.3 (Exercises on page 114)

1. NPV = $735.29 + 1,057.29 + $1,847.69 − $2,500
       = $3,640.27 − $2,500 = $1,140.27

3. NPV = 493.80 +$969.26 + $1,855.63 − $2,900 = $418.69

Section 3.4 (Exercises on pages 123 and 124)

1. $PV = \$50 \left[\frac{1 - \left(1 + \frac{0.04}{4}\right)^{-40}}{\frac{0.04}{4}} \right] = \$1,641.73$

3. Net PV $= \$750 \left[\dfrac{1 - (1 + 0.08)^{-3}}{0.08} \right] - \$1,500 = \$1,932.82 - \$1,500$

  $= \$432.82$

5. $\text{NPV}_1 = \$2,000 \left[\dfrac{1 - \left(1 + \frac{0.04}{12}\right)^{-24}}{\frac{0.04}{12}} \right] + \$38,000 \left(1 + \dfrac{.04}{12}\right)^{-24} - \$70,000$

  $= \$46,056.50 + \$35,083.09 - \$70,000 = \$11,139.59$

$\text{NPV}_2 = \$3,500 \left[\dfrac{1 - \left(1 + \frac{0.04}{12}\right)^{-24}}{\frac{0.04}{12}} \right] - \$70,000$

  $= \$80,598.88 - \$70,000 = \$10,598.88$

On a strictly monetary basis, and assuming equal credit risk for both
  investments, the first investment is more profitable.

7. $\text{NPV}_1 = \$2,300 \left[\dfrac{1 - \left(1 + \frac{0.04}{4}\right)^{-12}}{\frac{0.04}{4}} \right] - \$20,000$

  $= \$25,886.68 - \$20,000 = \$5,886.68$

$\text{NPV}_2 = \$1,500 \left[\dfrac{1 - \left(1 + \frac{0.04}{4}\right)^{-16}}{\frac{0.04}{4}} \right] + \$2,000 - \$18,000$

  $= \$22,076.81 + \$2,000 - \$18,000 = \$6,076.81$

On a strictly monetary basis, and assuming equal credit risk for both
  investments, the second investment is more profitable (Note: to compare
  investments the same amount must be considered in both NPVs. Thus, in the
  second alternative, after investing $18,000, there is still $2,000 of immediate,
  or Present Value, funds available, which must be added to the NPV).

9. PV $= \$80 \left[\dfrac{1 - \left(1 + \frac{0.06}{2}\right)^{-20}}{\frac{0.06}{2}} \right] + \$1,000 \left(1 + \dfrac{.06}{2}\right)^{-20}$

$$= \$1,190.20 + \$553.68 = \$1,743.88$$

11. $FV = \$400 \left[\dfrac{\left(1 + \dfrac{0.04}{4}\right)^{12} - 1}{\dfrac{0.04}{4}} \right] = \$400(12.682503) = \$5,073.00$

13. $FV = \$20 \left[\dfrac{\left(1 + \dfrac{0.05}{52}\right)^{48} - 1}{\dfrac{0.05}{52}} \right] = \$20(49.100757) = \$982.02$

Section 3.5 (Exercises on pages 131 and 132)

1. $171.87

3. ($171.87)(360) − $36,000 = $25,873.20

7. a. $1,016.06

   b. ($1,016.06)(48) − $45,000 = $48,770.88 - $45,000 = $3,770.88

c.

	A	B	C	D	E	F	G
1	Amount of Loan:		$45,000				
2	Length of Loan (in years):		4				
3	Annual Interest Rate:		4%				
4	Montly Payment:		$1,016.06				
5							
6			Payment Number	Payment Amount	Interest Paid	Principal Paid	Outstanding Balance
7			0	-	-	-	$45,000.00
8			1	$1,016.06	$150.00	$866.06	$44,133.94
9			2	$1,016.06	$147.11	$868.95	$43,265.00
10			3	$1,016.06	$144.22	$871.84	$42,393.16

9.

	A	B	C	D	E	F	G
1	Amount of Loan:		$800				
2	Length of Loan (in years):		1				
3	Annual Interest Rate:		4%				
4	Montly Payment:		$68.12				
5							
6			Payment Number	Payment Amount	Interest Paid	Principal Paid	Outstanding Balance
7			0	-	-	-	$800.00
8			1	$68.12	$2.67	$65.45	$734.55
9			2	$68.12	$2.45	$65.67	$668.88
10			3	$68.12	$2.23	$65.89	$602.99
11			4	$68.12	$2.01	$66.11	$536.88
12			5	$68.12	$1.79	$66.33	$470.55
13			6	$68.12	$1.57	$66.55	$404.00
14			7	$68.12	$1.35	$66.77	$337.23
15			8	$68.12	$1.12	$67.00	$270.23
16			9	$68.12	$0.90	$67.22	$203.01
17			10	$68.12	$0.68	$67.44	$135.57
18			11	$68.12	$0.45	$67.67	$67.90
19			12	$68.12	$0.23	$67.90	$0.00

Section 3.6 (Exercises on pages 136, 137 and 138)

1. a. ($480 + $3,000) / 24 = $145.00
   b. ($720 + $3,000) / 24 = $103.33
   c. 14.677% for the 2 year loan, 14.546% for the 3 year loan

3. a. Total Interest = (0.06)($4,000)(1year) = $240.00
   b. Monthly payment = ($240+ $4,000)/ (12 months) = $353.33
   c. For a PV of $4,000, a payment of $353.33 for 12 months (1 year), the true interest rate is 10.895%.

5. a. Monthly payment = $9,000/36 months = $250
   b. Total Interest charge = (0.06) ($9,000) (3 years) = $1,620
   c. Cash Received = $9,000 - $1,620 = $7,380
   d. For a PV of $7,380, a payment of $250 for 36 months, the true interest rate is 13.376%.

7. a. Required loan amount = ($15,000) / [1 − (0.04)(5)] =$18,750

b. Payment = $18,750/60 = $312.50

c. Total interest = $18,750 - $15,000 = $3,750

d. For a PV of $15,000, a payment of $312.50 for 60 months (5 years), the true interest rate is 9.154%.

Section 3.7 (Exercises on pages 143 and 144)

1. $PV = \$1{,}000 + \$1{,}000 \left[\dfrac{1 - (1 + 0.04)^{-9}}{0.04} \right]$

$= \$1{,}000 + \$1{,}000(7.435332) = \$8{,}435.33$

3. $PV = \$20 + \$20 \left[\dfrac{1 - \left(1 + \dfrac{0.02}{12}\right)^{-179}}{\dfrac{0.02}{12}} \right]$

$= \$20 + \$20[154.6570781] = \$3{,}113.14$

5. $FV = \$40 \left(1 + \dfrac{0.04}{4}\right) \left[\dfrac{\left(1 + \dfrac{0.04}{4}\right)^{12} - 1}{\dfrac{0.04}{4}} \right]$

$= \$40(1.01)[12.682503] = \$512.37$

7. $FV = \$20 \left(1 + \dfrac{0.05}{52}\right) \left[\dfrac{\left(1 + \dfrac{0.05}{52}\right)^{48} - 1}{\dfrac{0.05}{52}} \right]$

$= \$20(1.000961541)[49.10075664] = \$982.96$

9. $FV = \$1\left(1 + \dfrac{0.05}{365}\right)\left[\dfrac{\left(1 + \dfrac{0.05}{365}\right)^{730} - 1}{\dfrac{0.05}{365}}\right]$

$= \$(1.000961541)[767.6906738] = \$767.80$

11. $FV = \$1,000(1 + 0.08)\left[\dfrac{(1 + 0.08)^7 - 1}{0.08}\right]$

$= \$1.000(1.08)[8.92280335] = \$9,636.63$

Section 3.8 (Exercises on page 146)

1. 2.0150%
3. 2.0201%
5. 4.0811%
7. 8.2432%

Chapter 4

Section 4.1 (Exercises on pages 152, 153, and 154)

1. Yes   3. No   5. Yes   7. No
9. Yes   11. Yes   13. Yes
15. a. Yes   b. Yes   c. No
    d. Yes   e. No   f. No (consider two-tone cars)
    g. No

Section 4.2 (Exercises on page 159)

1. a. 0, 1, 2, 3, 4, 5, 6, 7, 8, 9, 10
   b. Integer numbers
   c. 225, 196, 169, 144, 121, 100, 81, 64, 49, 36, 25
3. Yes; the inverse is also a function.
5. Yes, the inverse is not a function.
7. a. 4   b. 34   c. −6   d. $(a + b)^2 + 3(a + b) - 6$
   e. $x^2 + 3x - 6 + (2x + 3)\Delta x + (\Delta x)^2$

9. a. 18   b. d + 2d² +d³   c. $(x + y) + 2(x + y)^2 + (x + y)^3$
   d. $(2a) + 2(2a)^2 + (2a)^3 = 2a + 8a^2 + 8a^3$

Section 4.3 (Exercises on page 166)

1. a. 7   b. 5   c. −5   d. −8
3. a. 3   b. 12   c. 31   d. −18
5. $\dfrac{-1}{(x_1)(x_2)}$

   a. $-1/[(4)(6)] = -0.04167$ b. $-1/[(3)(7)] = -0.04762$ c. $-1/[(2)(4)] = -0.125$

Section 4.4 (Exercises on page 178, 179, and 180)

5. −3   −3 and −3
7. $2x - 2$ 0 and −12
9. $6x^2 - 4x + 3$ 5 and 173
11. $2/(x + 2)^2$ 2/9 and 2/9
13. $-2/x^3$ −2 and 2/125
15. From the left instantaneous rate of change equals zero;
    from the right instantaneous rate of change equals zero.
17. a. $[\{3(7) + (1/2)(7)^2\} - 0]/7 = 6.5$ million *per year*
    b. $10 million *per year*   c. $80 million   d. $75.5 million

Section 4.5 (Exercises on pages 186, 187, and 188)

1. $f'(x) = 5x^4 - 21x^2 + 4$ 3. $f'(x) = 7x^6 + 18x^2 - 8x$
5. $f'(x) = x^4 - x^2 - x$ 7. $f'(x) = 7x^6 + 20x^4 + 6x$
9. $f'(x) = 10e^x$ 11. $f'(x) = 4x^3 - 14x + 7e^x$
13. $f'(x) = 3x^2 + 4x + 8e^x$ 15. $f'(x) = 1$
17. $dy/dx = 7x^6 + 30x^4 + 3$ 19. $dy/dx = 5x^4 - x^3 + 7e^x$
21. $dy/dx = x^3 - x^2 - x$ 23. $dy/dx = 3x^2 - 6x + 2$
25. a. $ds/dx = 6000 - 100x$ b. Yes; *yes*
27. a. 2 miles per 4 minutes = 30 miles per hour
    b.

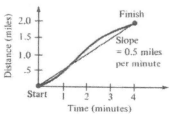

c. 0.65 miles per minute = 39 miles per hour

d.

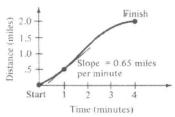

29. a. No   b. Yes   c. No   d. No

Section 4.6 (Exercises on page 196)

1. $f'(x) = (x^2+3x)(5x^4 + 7x^6 + 2) + (x^5 + x^7 + 2x)(2x + 3)$
3. $f'(x) = -5x^{-6} - 3x^{-4} - 2x^{-3} = -5/x^6 - 3/x^4 - 2/x^3$
5. $f'(x) = -(5/2)x^{-7/2} - (1/2)x^{-3/2} = -5/2x^{7/2} - 1/2x^{3/2}$
7. $f'(x) = [(x^2 + x^4)(3x^2 + 5x^4) - (x^3 + x^5)(2x + 4x^3)]/(x^2 + x^4)^2$
9. $f'(x) = (x^5 - x^3)4e^{4x} - e^{4x}(5x^4 + 3x^{-4})/(x^5 - x^3)^2$
11. $f'(x) = e^{7x}7x^6 + x^77e^{7x} = 7e^{7x}(x^6 + x^7) = 7e^{7x}x^6(1 + x)$
13. $f'(x) = [(x^5 + 3x)6x^5 - (x^6 + 7)(5x^4 + 3)]/(x^5 + 3x)^2$
15. $f'(x) = 5(x^7 + 6x)^4(7x^6 + 6)$
17. $f'(x) = 3(x^4 + 3x^2 + 4x + 2)^2(4x^3 + 6x^2 + 4)$
19. $dy/dx = e^{10x}3x^2 + x^3 10 e^{10x} = e^{10x}(3x^2 + 10x^3)$
21. $dy/dx = 5x^4 - 15x^{-6} = 5/x^4 - 15/x^6$
23. $dy/dx = -5x^{-6} - 4x^{-5} = -5/x^6 - 4/x^5$
25. $dy/dx = (3/2)x^{1/2} + (35/2)x^{3/2}$
27. $dS/dx = (dS/dE)(dE/dx) = (2E + 3)(2x) = (2x^2 + 3)(2x) = 4x^3 + 6x$
29. $dS/dx = (dS/dE)(dE/dx) = \{[(E + 2) - E]/(E + 2)^2\}(6x)$
    $= \{2/(3x^2 + 5 + 2)^2\}6x = 12x/(3x^2 + 7)^2$

Section 4.7 (Exercises on pages 197 and 198)

1. $y' = 5x^4 + 8x + 3$ $y'' = 20x^3 + 8$ 28 and 168
3. $y' = 4x^3 + 6x + 4$ $y'' = 12x^2 + 6$ 18 and 54
5. $y' = (10x^3 + 3x^2)e^{10x}$ $y'' = (100x^3 + 60x^2 + 6x)e^{10x}$ 166 e^{10} and 1052 e^{20}
7. a. $-0.15t^2 + 0.5t + 0.3$
   b. 0.65 mile per minute = 39 miles per hour
   c. $-0.3t + 0.5$
   d. 0.2 mile per minute^2, -0.4 mile per minute^2
      at $t = 3$ the car is decelerating or slowing down

Chapter 5

Section 5.1 (Exercises on page 208, 209, and 210)

1.
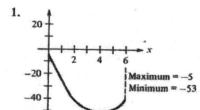

3.
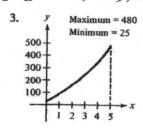

5.
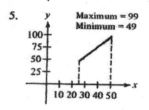

7. Maximum = 23; minimum = −9

9. Maximum = 7; minimum = −9

11. Maximum = 559; Minimum = − 305

13. Maximum = 12; minimum = − 220/3

15. Maximum = 75; minimum = −25

17. a. 22,000   b. $232,000

19. a. 100 units   b. $5000   c. $25,000

21. 45 units

23. Maximum = 6; Minimum = 0

25. 5, 3, 2, 3.5

27. No; No

29. Relative minimum at $x = 10$, relative maximum at $x = 4$

Section 5.3 (Exercises on pages 219 and 220)

1. a. $P = -1/2x^2 + 180x - 5,000$ b. $0 \leq x \leq 300$ c. $11,200

3. a. $P = 10x - (x^2/4,000 - 5x + 50,000) = -x^2/4,000 + 15x - 50,000$
   b. $0 \leq x \leq 50,000$
   c. $175,000

5. 10,000 units

7. a. $TR = 500x - 2x^2$ b. $P = -2x^2 + 200x - 2,000$
   c. $0 \leq x \leq 40$ d. 40 units

9. a. 15   b. $200 - x/2$ c. $2.25 - .00005x$

11. a. $MC = x/2500 + 8$ b. $MC = 50$ c. $MC = 0.25$

13. $R = 200x$, therefore, $MR = R' = 200$

$C = 5000 + 20x + (1/2) x^2$ therefore, MC = C' = $20 + x$
Setting $MR = MC$ yields $x = 180$

15. $R = 500x - 2x^2$, therefore, $MR = R' = 500 - 4x$
   $C = 300x + 2,000$, therefore, MC = C' = 300   Setting $MR = MC$ yields $x = 50$

Section 5.4 (Exercises on pages 228, 229, an 230)

1. 60   3. 20   5. a. 100   b. 10   7. a. 800   b. 3   c. 2,400

9.

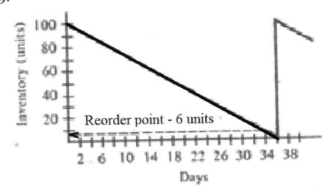

Section 5.5 (Exercises on pages 233 and 234)

1. $62.5 million   3. $62.5 million   5. $2,383.36 increase

Chapter 6

Section 6.1 (Exercises on pages 240 and 241)

1. $y = 10.3$
3. $y = 28.67$
5. An increase does not seem advisable, as sales appear to
   decrease as advertising is increased. (In the next section, the
   average rate of change of sales with respect to advertising can
   be determined, which will show that sales do, in fact, decrease
   with an increase in advertising – see the solution to Exercise 1
   in Section 6.2.)

Section 6.2 (Exercises on pages 254, 255, and 256)

1. The linear-least squares straight line is
      sales = -.0538(advertising) + 36.846

Because sales go down as advertising is increased, it does not make sense to increase the advertising budget.

3.b. $y = 6.3214x + 39.5$

c. E = 49.54

5. a. sales = 0.7857 (year) − 15.61

b. 19.04

c. 24.54

7. Yield = 7.5546 (rain) + 9.8126, Yield = 36.2537.

Section 6.3 (Exercises on page 263, 264, and 265)

1. The least-squares quadratic line is
$y = 0.6429x^2 + 0.5286x + 10.086$

3. The least−squares straight line is $y = 3.1x + 8.8$ with E = 9.9.

5. The least-squares quadratic line is
$y = 0.994x^2 − 0.0179x − 0.9905$

7.a. $3c + 2a = 17$
$2b = 10$
$2c + 2a = 10$ (Sol: c = 7, b = 5,. a = −2)

9. $y = 2.3633e^{1.7704x}$

11. $y = 0.278e^{1.17173x}$

Appendix A (Exercises on pages 279, 280, and 281)

1. Use the Formulas shown in Figure 3.16. In doing so, make sure that all cells that are used to store dates are in the same Date format.

3.

Day	Date	Holiday
Thursday	1/1/2015	New Year's day
Monday	2/2/2015	Constitution Day
Monday	3/16/2015	Benito Jaurez Birthday
Thursday	4//2/2015	Maunday Thursday
Friday	4/3/2015	Good Friday
Friday	5/11/2015	Labour Day
Tuesday	5/5/2015	Cinco de Maya
Wednesday	9/16/2015	Independence Day
Monday	10/12/2015	Revolution Day Memorial
Monday	11/16/2015	Day of the Dead
Monday	11/16/2015	Revolution Day
Saturday	12/1/2/2015	Day of the Virgin of Gaudalupe
Friday	12/25/2015	Christmas

5. a. Note: Any entered date that does not exactly match a date in the table is

matched with the closest date that is earlier than the entered date.

Date	Output in cell B5
1/7/2015	New Year's day
1/18/2015	New Year's day
1/31/2015	Martin Luther King Jr.'s Birthday
2/15/2015	Martin Luther King Jr.'s Birthday
2/25/2015	President's Day
4/4/2015	Good Friday
5/24/2015	Easter
7/3/2015	Memorial Day
9/5/2015	Independence Day
10/5/2015	Labor Day
11/25/2015	Columbus day
11/28/2015	Thanksgiving
12/31/2015	Christmas

b. For all dates after 12/25/2015 cell B5 will contain the text Christmas.

Appendix B (Exercises on page 293)

1.

	A	B	C
1	30/360 Day Count Spreadsheet		
2			
3	Enter the First Date:	42430	
4	Enter the Second Date:	42444	
5	The 30/360 Day Difference is:	=DAYS360(B3,B4)	
6			

3.

	A	B	C	D	E
1		Actual Date Count			
2					
3	Enter the Date:	42400			
4					
5	The month is:	=MONTH(B3)		MP =	=IF(B5<3,0,INT(0.4*B5+2.3))
6	The Day is:	=DAY(B3)		YP =	=IF(B5<1,B7-1,B7)
7	The year is:	=YEAR(B3)		T =	=INT(E6/4) -INT(E6/100)+INT(E6/400)
8					
9	The Actual Day C	=365*B7 +31*(B5-1)+ B6 +E7-E5			
10					

5.

	A	B	C	D	E	F
1		Actual Date Count				
2						
3	Enter the Date:	42581				
4						
5	The month is:	=MONTH(B3)		MP =	=IF(B5<3,0,INT(0.4*B5+2.3))	
6	The Day is:	=DAY(B3)		YP =	=IF(B5<1,B7-1,B7)	
7	The year is:	=YEAR(B3)		T =	=INT(E6/4) -INT(E6/100)+INT(E6/400)	
8						
9	The Actual Day Count is:	=365*B7 +31*(B5-1)+ B6 +E7-E5				
10						
11						
12	Enter the Date:	42583				
13						
14	The month is:	=MONTH(B12)		MP =	=IF(B14<3,0,INT(0.4*B14+2.3))	
15	The Day is:	=DAY(B12)		YP =	=IF(B14<1,B16-1,B16)	
16	The year is:	=YEAR(B12)		T =	=INT(E15/4) -INT(E15/100)+INT(E15/400)	
17						
18	The Actual Day Count is:	=365*B16 +31*(B14-1)+ B15 +E16-				
19						
20	Day Dif =	=B18-B9				
21						

1st Date	2nd Date	Actual Day Difference
3/1/2016	3/15/2016	14
2/28/2016	3/15/2016	15
2/28/2017	3/15/2017	15
1/1/2016	7/1/2016	181
7/1/2016	7/31/2016	30
7/1/2016	7/30/2016	29
7/30/2016	8/1/2016	2

7. a. 1600 is a leap year.
   b. 1607 is not a leap year.
   c. 1712 is a leap year.
   d. 1774 is not a leap year.
   e. 1800 is not a leap year.
   f. 1812 is a leap year.
   g. 1900 is not a leap year
   h. 1998 is not a leap year.
   i. 2000 is a leap year
   j. 2018 is not a leap year.

Section Reviews
for
Mathematics for Business
Fifth Edition

Review of Section 1.1
Signed Numbers

A number preceded by either a plus sign (+) or minus sign (–) is called a **signed number**. The positive sign indicates the number is a positive one, while a negative sign indicates the number is a negative one. An unsigned number is considered positive.

Negatives: The negative of the negative of a number is the number itself.
   That is, $-(-a) = a$.

Subtraction: For any real numbers a and b, $a - b = a + (-b)$.

MATHEMATICAL OPERATIONS

Subtraction: For any real numbers a and b, $a - b = a + (-b)$.

Multiplication:

- The product of two positive numbers is positive.
- The product of two negative numbers is positive.
- The product of two different signed numbers is negative.
- The product of an even number of negative numbers is positive.
- The product of an odd number of negative numbers is negative.

Division:

- The result of a division is positive if both the numerator and denominator have the same signs.
- The result of a division problem is negative if the numerator and denominator have opposite signs.
- Division by 0 is not defined. That is, for any real number a, a/0 is not defined.
- Zero divided by any nonzero number a is 0.: $\frac{0}{a} = 0$, $a \neq 0$.

ORDER OF OPERATIONS
   1. Parenthesis – innermost to outermost
   2. Exponents
   3. Multiplication and division – left to right
   4. Addition and subtraction – left to right

PROPERTIES OF REAL NUMBERS

Commutative Laws:

Addition: For any real numbers a and b, $\ a + b = b + a$.
   Multiplication: For any real numbers a and b, $\ a \cdot b = b \cdot a$

Associative(Grouping) Laws:

   Addition: For any real numbers $a, b,$ and $c,$
$$a + b + c = a + (b + c) = (a + b) + c$$
   Multiplication: For any real numbers $a, b,$ and $c,$
$$a \cdot b \cdot c = a(b \cdot c) = (a \cdot b) \cdot c$$
Distributive Laws

   For any real numbers $a, b,$ and $c,$
$$a(b + c) = ab + ac \ \text{ and } (b + c)a = ba + ca$$

Review of Section1.2
Solving Equations Having One Unknown Quantity

An *equation* is a statement of equality between two algebraic expressions.

A *solution* to an equation is any numerical value, that wen substituted for an unknown, makes the equation true.

An equation that has a solution(s) is called a *conditional equation.*

An equation that does not have a solution is called an *inconsistent equation.*

An equation that any number is its solution is called an *identity equation.*

Fundamental Rule for Solving Equations: Whenever any arithmetic operation is performed on one side of an equation, an identical operation must be performed on the other side of the equation.

   Thus, any quantity that is added to, subtracted from, multiplied by, or divided into one side of an equation, the same operation must be performed on the other side of the equation.

   These operations are used to simplify an equation and determine all solutions to the original equation.

Review of Section1.3
Exponents

Exponents provide a simple notation for representing the product of the same number or expression zero or more times. Thus,

$$a^n = \underbrace{a \cdot a \cdot a \cdots a}_{n\, times}$$

The term a^n, is read "the nth power of a," or simply "a to the n", where a is the referred to as the *base* and n as the *exponent*.

DEFINITIONS AND RULES FOR EXPONENTS

For an exponent of 1: $a^1 = a$

For an exponent of 0: $a^0 = 1,\ a \neq 0$

For a negative exponent: $a^{-n} = \dfrac{1}{a^n},\ a \neq 0$

The Product Rule: $a^n \cdot a^m = a^{n+m}$

The Quotient Rule: $\dfrac{a^m}{a^n} = a^{m-n},\ a \neq 0$

The Power Rule: $\left(a^m\right)^n = a^{m \cdot n}$

Raising a product to a power: $\left(ab\right)^n = a^n b^n$

Raising a quotient to a positive power:

$$\left(\frac{a}{b}\right)^n = \frac{a^n}{b^n},\ b \neq 0$$

Raising a quotient to a negative power:

$$\left(\frac{a}{b}\right)^n = \frac{b^n}{a^n},\ a \square 0 \ and \ b \square 0$$

Review of Section 1.4
Solving Quadratic Equations
using the Quadratic Formula

The solution(s) to an equation in the form: $x^n = c$ depends on the following:

If n is even, then the solutions are

$$x = \pm c^{1/n} \ \ or \ \ x = \pm \sqrt[n]{c}, c \geq 0.$$

If n is odd, then the solution is

$$x = c^{1/n} \ \ or \ \ x = \sqrt[n]{c}.$$

The solutions to the quadratic equation $ax^2 + bx + c = 0$ are

$$x = \frac{-b \pm \sqrt{b^2 - 4ac}}{2a}$$

where a, b and c are real numbers.

If $b^2 - 4ac > 0$, there are two distinct real solutions.

If $b^2 - 4ac = 0$, there is one real solution, specifically $x = \frac{-b}{2a}$.

If $b^2 - 4ac < 0$, there are no real solutions.

Review of Section 1.5
The Cartesian coordinate system

A **Cartesian coordinate system**, also referred to as a **Rectangular coordinate system** is a coordinate system that specifies each point uniquely in a plane by a pair of numerical coordinates, (x, y), which are the signed distances to the point from two fixed perpendicular directed lines, measured in the same unit of length.

The x-axis and the y-axis intersect perpendicularly to separate the plane into 4 parts: Quadrant I, Quadrant II, Quadrant III, and Quadrant IV. (See Figure 1.18 below)

- Points that are in Quadrant I have positive x-components and positive y-components.
- Points that are in Quadrant II have negative x-components and positive y-components.
- Points that are in Quadrant III have negative x-components and negative y-components.
- Points that are in Quadrant IV have positive x-components and negative y-components.
- Points that are on the x-axis have the form: $(x, 0)$.
- Points that are on the y-axis have the form: $(0, y)$.
- The point $(0, 0)$ is referred to as the origin.

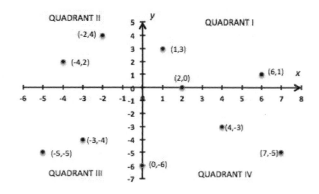

Review of Section 1.6
Graphical Solutions to Equations in Two Unknowns

The **graph** of any equation represents all of its solutions.

A linear equation in the two variables x, and y, can be written in the form $y = mx + b$, where m is referred to as the **slope** and b as the **y-interecept**.

The graph of a linear equation, is a straight line.

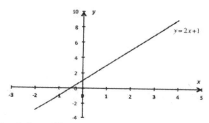

A Positive Slope with a non-zero y- intercept

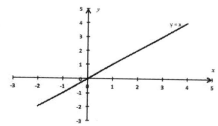

A Positive Slope with a zero y-intercept

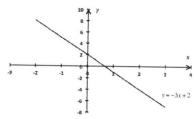

A Negative Slope with a non-zero y-intercept

For the equation $x = a$, where a is a real number, the graph is a straight line parallel to the y-axis

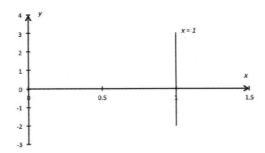

The equation y = a, where a is a real number, the graphs is a straight line parallel to the x axis

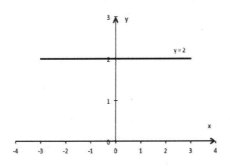

The graph of a quadratic equation, $y = ax^2 + bx + c$ or $y = a(x - h)^2 + k$ is a parabola   .

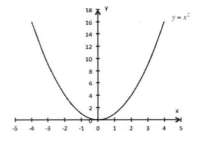   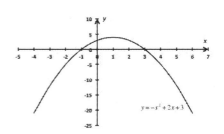

The graph of a cubic equation, $y = ax^3 + bx^2 + cx + d$, has two inflection points:

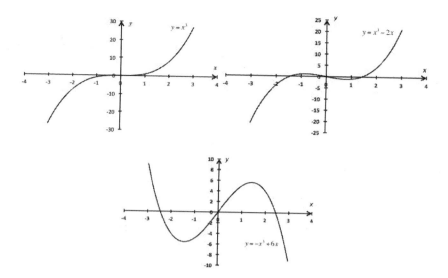

Review of Section 1.7
Sigma Notation

Sigma notation is a convenient and simple form of shorthand used to give a concise expression for a sum of the values or expressions, each of which has a repetitive form. of a variable.

Let $x_1, x_2, \cdots, x_n$ be a sequence of numbers, where x_1 is the first number, x_2 is the second number, ..., and x_n is the nth number.

Consider the expression: $\displaystyle\prod_{i=1}^{n} x_i$

The summation symbol, denoted by Σ is the Greek upper case letter S. This symbol stipulates us to add the number in the sequence. The letter i is the index of the summation, although any other letter can be used. Other commonly used indexes are j, k, m, and n. The index appears at the bottom of the summation symbol as in the expression $i = 1$. This is the starting point of the summation, and the ending value for the index is the value written above the summation symbol, in this case n.

Therefore,

$$\sum_{i=1}^{n} x_i = x_1 + x_2 + x_3 + \cdots + x_n$$

Review of Section 1.8
Numerical Considerations

- In *arithmetic rounding*, or rounding for short, when the digit you are rounding to is followed by a 0, 1, 2,3, or 4, the digit is kept and all following digits are deleted; else the rounded digit is increased by one and all following digits are deleted.

- In *rounding up*, the last digit being kept is increased by one, regardless of the following digit, and all following digits are deleted.

- In *rounding down,* more commonly known as t*runcation,* the last digit being kept is never changed, and all following digits are deleted.

- An exponential form of a number has the form:

$$a\ Eb,$$

where a is a number between 1 and 9, inclusive, and b is an integer that is referred to as the *exponent*.

Example: $2.564389\ E4$

To change a number from exponential notation to standard form, the decimal point is moved to the right the number of places indicted by the value of the exponent, b, if b is positive, or to the left by the value of b if the exponent, b, is negative.

Example: $2.564389\ E4 = 25643.89.$

Review of Section 2.1
Linear Equations

A *linear equation in two variables* x *and* y is an equation in the form
$$Ax + By = C$$
or one that can be put into this form, where A, B, and C are known real numbers and A and B are both not zero.

Solutions to a linear equation in two variables x and y are represented by all ordered pairs of numbers (a, b) in which the values of $x = a$ and $y = b$ make the equation true.

Review of Section 2.2
Graphing Linear Equations

The graph of the linear equation in two variables x and y is a straight line, and represents all of its solutions. Thus, any two solution points of a linear equation, points, represented by two ordered pairs (x, y) can be used to determine this straight line, as follows:

- Choose an x value
- Substitute the value of x into the given equation
- Solve the equation for its corresponding y
- Plot the ordered (x, y) pair on the graph.
- Repeat this process one more time to determine a second solution
- Plot this second ordered (x, y) pair on the graph
- Draw the straight line connecting the two graphed solutions that were determined above

Examples: Graphs of Linear Equations

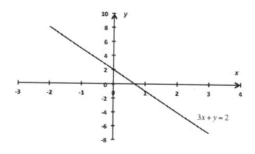

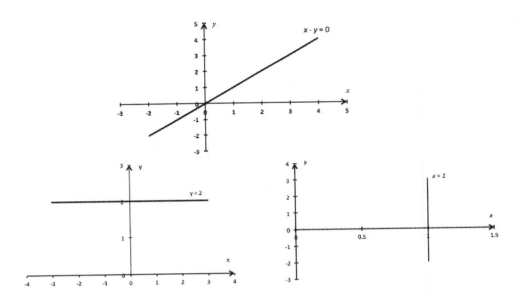

Review of Section 2.3
Properties of Straight Lines

The **slope**, m, of a straight line containing two distinct points (x_1, y_1) and (x_2, y_2) is defined

$$m = \frac{y_2 - y_1}{x_2 - x_1}, \qquad x_2 - x_1 \neq 0$$

To find the slope of a given equation:

- Choose a value for x
- Substitute the value of x into the given equation
  and solve the equation for its corresponding y
- Repeat this process for the next x value
- Use the formula $m = \frac{y_2 - y_1}{x_2 - x_1}$ to find the slope of the given equation.

The significance of the slope is that it gives us the particular ratio relating all points on a given line. As such, the slope represents the rate of change in y associated with a change in x.

If a straight line intersects the x-axis at the point $(a, 0)$, where a is a real number, then the point $(a, 0)$ is called the **x-intercept**.

If a straight line intersects the y-axis at the point $(0, b)$, where b is a real number, then the point $(0, b)$ is called the **y-intercept**.

When a linear equation in two variables is written in the form
$$y = mx + b,$$
it is referred to as the **slope-intercept form.** Here, m is the slope, and b is the y-intercept.

To find an equation of the straight line containing two points (x_1, y_1) and (x_2, y_2), first determine the slope using the formula
$$m = \frac{y_2 - y_1}{x_2 - x_i}$$
Then, using one of the points, either (x_1, y_1) or (x_2, y_2), determine by substituting the x value and y value of the chosen point and m into the equation $y = mx + b$.

Review of Section 2.4
Break-Even Point (BEP)

The *break-even point* is the point at which the income from the sale of manufactured or purchased items exactly matches the cost of the items being sold.

Revenue is the income obtained from selling items. Revenue produced from a sale, known as the *sales revenue*, is simply the selling price p of each item times the number of items sold, x. Thus, $R = px$.

The *total cost,* denoted by C, of items sold are commonly separated into two categories: fixed costs and variable costs.

Fixed costs, denoted by F, include rent, insurance, property taxes, and other expenses that are present regardless of the number of items produced or purchased.

Variable costs, denoted by V, are those expenses that are directly attributable to the manufacture or purchase of the items themselves, such as labor and raw materials. Variable costs are calculated by taking the cost per item, denoted by a, times the number of items produced or purchased, denoted by x. Thus, $V = ax$.

The **Total Cost**, denoted by C. is the sum of the variable and fixed and variable costs. Thus $C = V + F = ax + F$

The break even point occurs where Revenue equal Total Cost, $R = C$. Substituting px for R and $ax + F$ for C yields

$px = ax + F$.

Solving for x yields,
$$x = \frac{F}{p-a}$$
This value of x is the Beak-Even Point (BEP)

GRAPHICAL DETERMINATION OF THE BREAK-EVEN POINT:

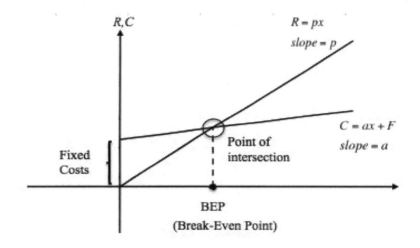

Review of Section 2.5
Quadratic Equations

A **quadratic equation** in x is an equation of the form $y = ax^2 + bx + c$, where a, b, and c are known real numbers with a not equal to zero.

The graph of the quadratic equation $y = ax^2 + bx + c$ is a parabola.

If $a > 0$, then the parabola opens upward. and the minimum value of y occurs when $x = -\frac{b}{2a}$

If $a < 0$, then the parabola opens downward and the maximum value of y occurs of when $x = -\frac{b}{2a}$.

The value $x = -\frac{b}{2a}$ is referred the parabola's *vertex*.

Review of Section 2.6
Polynomial Equations

The **degree** of a polynomial equation in x is the highest exponent on the variable x in the polynomial.

An nth degree polynomial equation in x is an equation of the form:

$$y = a_n x^n + a_{n-1} x^{n-1} + \cdots + a_1 x + a_0,$$

where n is a known nonnegative integer and

$$a_n, a_{n-1}, \cdots, a_1, a_0 \text{ are known real numbers with } a_n \neq 0.$$

$a_n x^n$ is called the **leading term** of the polynomial with a_n referred to as the **leading coefficient.**

Review of Section 2.7
Exponential Equations

An exponential equation in the variable x is an equation of the form $y = a(b^x)$, where a and b are known real numbers and b is positive.

CHARACTERISTICS OF AN EXPONENTIAL EQUATION

If $a > 0$ and $0 < b < 1$

1) The graph of the equation decreases from left to right. This means, as the value of x increases, its corresponding y value decreases.
2) The y-intercept is at $(0, a)$.
3) The graph is asymptotic. This means, as the value of x increases (larger than 1), its corresponding y value gets closer and closer to the value 0, but never equals 0.

4) $y = 0$ is the horizontal asymptote.

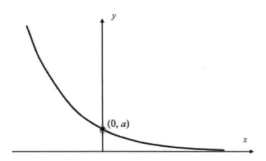

If $a > 0$ and $b > 1$

1)   The graph of the equation increases from left to right. This means, as the value of x increases, its corresponding y value increases.
2)   The y-intercept is at $(0, a)$.
3)   The graph is asymptotic. This means, as the value of x increases (larger than 1), its corresponding y value gets closer and closer to the value 0, but never equals 0.
4) $y = 0$ is the horizontal asymptote.

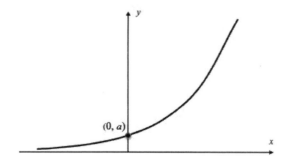

Note: The special base $e \approx 2.71828...$. e is a famous irrational number, and is known as Euler's number, named after the mathematician Leonhard Euler.

Review of Section 3.1
Compound Interest

The **Principal, P,** (also referred to as the principal amount) is the amount of money that is either deposited, lent, borrowed, or invested.

The **Conversion period** (also referred to as the compounding interval) is the time between successive interest rate applications.

The **Interest, I,** is the amount of money that is earned in a conversion period (it is obtained by multiplying the interest rate per conversion period times a principal amount).

The **Stated Annual Interest Rate, r,** (also referred to as the annual interest rate and the nominal interest rate) is the interest rate expressed on a per-year basis. It does not take into account how many times a year the interest rate is applied or compounded.

The **Effective Annual Interest Rate** is the annual interest rate that takes into account how many times a year interest is applied.

The defining property of **compound interest** is that once the *Interest, I,* is paid on a principal amount, this interest amount is added to the principle amount to form a new principal amount.

Principal Amount after nth Payment

$P(n) = (1 + i)^n P(o)$, where i denote the interest rate, n the number of interest payments that were made, $P(o)$ is the initial principal, and $P(n)$ the principle amount after the nth payment was made.

Calculating the Interest Rate per Conversion Period

Conversion Period	Conversion Periods Per Year	Interest Rate per Conversion Period, i (r = the stated annual rate)
Annually	1	$i = r$
Semi-Annually	2	$i = \dfrac{r}{2}$
Quarterly	4	$i = \dfrac{r}{4}$
Monthly	12	$i = \dfrac{r}{12}$
Daily	365	$i = \dfrac{r}{365}$

Review of Section 3.2
Comparing Investment Alternatives

$P(o)$, the initial principal, is referred to as the **present value** of the principal, or present value, for short. It is denoted by PV.

$P(n)$, denotes the value of $P(o)$ money sometimes in the future, is referred to as the **Future value** of the principal, or **future value**, for short. It is denoted by FV.

Future Value: $FV = (1 + i)^n PV$.

Present Value: $PV = \dfrac{FV}{(1+i)^n} = (1 + i)^{-n} FV$

Review of Section 3.3
Net Present Values of Cash Flow

Recall: In Sections 3.1 and 3.2, we were concerned with single sum payments which are frequently referred to as *lump sum* investments.

Cash flow consists of a set of payments from an investment due at different times.

Net Present Value $= \sum PV \ of \ all \ cash \ inflow - \sum PV \ of \ all \ cash \ outflows$

Review of Section 3.4
Ordinary Annuities

An *annuity* is a set of equal payments made at equal intervals of time.

Examples of annuities are car loans, mortgages, life insurance premiums, social security payments, and bond coupon payments.

Annuities are classified as either ordinary or due.

- An annuity is *ordinary* if payments are made at the end of each payment period.
- An annuity is *due* if payments are made at the beginning of each payment period.

An annuity is *simple* if the conversion period at which interest is paid coincides with the payment dates. In this section, we will deal with only *simple ordinary* annuity.

Present Value of an Ordinary Annuity

$$PV = R\left[\frac{1 - (1 + i)^{-n}}{i}\right]$$

where R denotes the *periodic installments* or *rents*, i is the stated annual interest rate, and n is the number of periods.

Net Present Value of an Ordinary Annuity

$$NPV = R\left[\frac{1 - (1 + i)^{-n}}{i}\right] - C_0$$

where R denotes the *periodic installments* or *rents*, i is the stated annual interest rate, n is the number of periods, and C_0 is the initial payment.

Future Value of an Ordinary Annuity

$$FV = R\left[\frac{(1 + i)^{n} - 1}{i}\right]$$

where R denotes the *periodic installments* or *rents*, i is the stated annual interest rate, and n is the number of periods.

Review of Section 3.5
Mortgages and Amortization

One of the most common types of ordinary annuities is a mortgage.

A **mortgage** is a loan used to pay for the property, with the property serving as collateral for the loan. This gives the lender, known as the **mortgagor**, a claim on the property should the borrower, known as the **mortgagee**, default on paying the mortgage.

Monthly Payment

$$R = \frac{PV}{\left[\frac{1-(1+i)^{-n}}{i}\right]}$$

where:

R = the monthly payment

PV = the original amount of the loan

i = the monthly interest rate = $\frac{annual\ interest\ rate}{12}$

n = the length of the loan, in months = 12 * (the number of years of the loan)

Total Interest Paid = $(R * n) - PV$

Amortization refers to the repayment of the loan using regular installments over a period of time.

An **amortization schedule** is a table that shows the amount of each payment, and lists the portion of each payment that goes toward paying the interest, the portion of the payment credited against the principal and, finally, the outstanding loan balance after the payment has been made. (See Below)

	A	B	C	D	E	F	G
1	Amount of Loan:	$800					
2	Length of Loan (in years):	1					
3	Annual Interest Rate:	4%					
4	Monthly Payment:	$68.12					
5							
6			Payment Number	Payment Amount	Interest Paid	Principal Paid	Outstanding Balance
7			0	-	-	-	$800.00
8			1	$68.12	$2.67	$65.45	$734.55
9			2	$68.12	$2.45	$65.67	$668.88
10			3	$68.12	$2.23	$65.89	$602.99
11			4	$68.12	$2.01	$66.11	$536.88
12			5	$68.12	$1.79	$66.33	$470.55
13			6	$68.12	$1.57	$66.55	$404.00
14			7	$68.12	$1.35	$66.77	$337.23
15			8	$68.12	$1.12	$67.00	$270.23
16			9	$68.12	$0.90	$67.22	$203.01
17			10	$68.12	$0.68	$67.44	$135.57
18			11	$68.12	$0.45	$67.67	$67.90
19			12	$68.12	$0.23	$67.90	$0.00

Review of Section 3.6
Installment Loans and Interest Charges

NOTE: Unlike mortgages that calculate monthly interest based on the unpaid balance of the loan, some commercial loans, such as, vacation loans, home improvement loans, and a host of other cash advances for specific purposes, can use two related but different interest determination methods. These are known as the **add-on** and **discount method**, respectively.

(A) Add-On Method: In the add-on method of interest and payment calculations, the total finance charge for a loan is determined by:

Total Interest Charged (Total Finance Charge)
        = (Annual Rate)*(Amount of Loan)*(Length of loan, in years)

Monthly Installment

$$R = \frac{(Total\ finance\ charge) + (Amount\ of\ the\ loan)}{(Length\ of\ the\ loan, in\ months)}$$

(B) Discount Installment Loans: In discount installment loan the installment payment, R, is first determined by dividing the amount of the loan by the number of months in the life of the loan.

Step 1 $R = \dfrac{Amount\ of\ Loan}{Length\ od\ Loan, in\ months}$

Step 2 Total Interest Charge = (Amount of Loan)*(Annual Rate)*(Length of loan, in years)

Step 3 Cash Received can be calculated by:

= Amount of Loan − Total Interest Charge

or

= Amount of Loan

− [(Amount of Loan)*(Annual Rate)*(Length of loan, in years)]

or

= Amount of Loan*[1 − (Annual Rate)*(Length of Loan, in years)]

Because the interest charge is subtracted from the original amount of the loan, if a desired cash is needed, the borrower must request a higher original amount when the loan request is made.

$$Amount\ of\ Loan = \dfrac{cash\ received\ by\ borrower}{1-rt}$$

Review of Section 3.7
Annuities Due

An ***annuity due***, which is also referred to as an ***immediate annuity***, is one which periodic payments and/or receipts begin immediately.

The Present Value of an Annuity Due

$$PV = R + R \left[\frac{1-(1+i)^{-(n-1)}}{i} \right]$$

where R is the amount due at the start of each conversion period for the next n periods.

The Future Value of an Annuity Due

$$FV = R \left[\frac{(1+i)^{(n+1)} - 1}{i} \right] - R$$

where R is the amount due at the start of each conversion period for the next n periods.

Review of Section 3.8
Effective Interest Rate

The **Effect Interest Rate** is the rate that must be compounded annually to generate the same interest as the stated rate compounded over its stated conversion period.

Effective Interest Rate

$$E = (1 + i)^n - 1$$

where E denote the effective interest rate and n represents the total number of conversion periods per year for the stated rate.

Review of Section 4.1
Concept of a Function

A **function** is a rule of assignment between two sets, which assigns to each element in the first set exactly one element (but not necessarily a different one) in the second set.

A function therefore has three components: a first set (perhaps years), a second set (perhaps numbers), and a rule of assignment between the two sets.

- This rule must be complete in that an assignment must be made to **each and every** element in the first set.
- The first set in a function is often referred to as x, input, independent variable, or domain.
- The second set in a function is often referred to as y, output, dependent variable, or range.
- The domain and range can be two sets (people, cars, colors, numbers, etc.), while the rule can be given in a variety of ways (arrows, tables, words, etc.)

Review of Section 4.2: Mathematical Functions

In business situations, the primary concern is with sets of numbers (representing price, demand, advertising expenditures, cost profit, and etc.) and rules defined by mathematical equations.

Whenever we have two sets of numbers and a rule given by an equation, where the variable x denotes an element in the domain and the variable y denotes an element in the range, we simply say that y is a function of x and write $y = f(x)$.

- $y = f(x)$ is a shorthand notation that says y depends on x in the manner that satisfies Definition 4.1; that is, it is a stand-in for a rather cumbersome statement, "We have two sets of numbers and a rule which satisfies Definition 4.1; the rule is given by the mathematical equation where x and y denotes elements in the domain and range, respectively."
Caution: The notation $y = f(x)$ does not imply "y equals f times x."

- The **domain(restrictions on the x-values, if any)** of a function is the set of allowable values from which we can select the independent variable. If the domain is not given explicitly, it is taken to be all real numbers. One exception occurs when it is clear from the given equation that certain numbers cannot be values of the independent variable. For example, $y = \frac{1}{x}$ has only one value in which the independent variable x cannot take: $x = 0$.

- The **range** is the set of all outputs, based on the domain, of the function.

- To evaluate a function at a specific value of x, substitute that value into the function.

Review of Section 4.3
Average Rate of Change

A *rate of change* measures the change in one quantity associated with a change a second quantity.

The *average rate of change* in one quantity with respect to a second quantity is defined as the ratio of two changes. Denoting the first and second quantities by y and x, respectively, we have,

$$\text{Average rate of change in } y \text{ with respect to } x = \frac{y_2 - y_1}{x_2 - x_1} = \frac{f(x_2) - f(x_1)}{x_2 - x_1}.$$

Review of Section 4.4
Instantaneous Rates of Change

Average rates of change are useful for many decision-making purposes. However, they are not always sufficient. Events sometimes change so rapidly that weekly averages, daily averages, and even hourly averages are not indicative of the actual situation. Therefore, instantaneous rates of change are needed, that is, rate effective for an instant of time.

$$\text{Instantaneous rate of change in } f(x) \text{ at any point } x$$
$$= \lim_{h \to 0} \frac{f(x+h) - f(x)}{h}$$

Review of Section 4.5
The Derivative

The derivative of the function $y = f(x)$ at the point x is $\lim\limits_{h \to 0} \dfrac{f(x+h) - f(x)}{h}$.

The derivative of a function $y = f(x)$ at the point x is denoted by y', $\dfrac{dy}{dx}$, or $f'(x)$.

DERIVATIVE RULES

RULE 1: *The derivative of a constant function is zero. That is, if $f(x) = c$, where c is a given fixed number, $f'(x) = 0$.*

RULE 2: The derivative of the function $f(x) = x^n$, where n is a real number, is $f'(x) = nx^{n-1}$.

RULE 3: *If $f(x) = cg(x)$, where c is a fixed number and $g(x)$ is a function of x whose derivative is known, then $f'(x) = cg'(x)$.*

RULE 4a (Addition Rule): If $h(x)$ and $g(x)$ both have derivatives, then the derivative of $f(x) = h(x) + g(x)$ is $f'(x) = h'(x) + g'(x)$.

RULE 4b (Subtraction Rule): If $g(x)$ and $h(x)$ both have derivatives, then the derivative of $f(x) = g(x) - h(x)$ is $f'(x) = g'(x) - h'(x)$.

RULE 5: *The derivative of the function $f(x) = e^x$ is $f'(x) = e^x$.*

Evaluating the derivative of a function $f(x)$ at $x = x_0$ is $f'(x_0)$ or $\dfrac{dy}{dx}\big|_{x_0}$

Review of Section 4.6
Additional Rules

RULE 6 (Product Rule): If the functions $g(x)$ and $h(x)$ both have derivatives, then the derivative of the function $f(x) = g(x) \cdot h(x)$ is

$$f'(x) = h(x) \cdot g'(x) + g(x) \cdot h'(x).$$

RULE 7 (Division Rule or **Quotient Rule):** If the functions $g(x)$ and $h(x)$ both have derivatives, with $h(x) \neq 0$, then the derivative

of the function $f(x) = \frac{g(x)}{h(x)}$ is $f'(x) = \frac{h(x) \cdot g'(x) - g(x) \cdot h'(x)}{[h(x)]^2}$.

RULE 8 (Power Rule): If $f(x) = [g(x)]^n$, where n is a fixed real number and the derivative of $g(x)$ exists, then

$$f'(x) = n[g(x)]^{n-1} \cdot g'(x).$$

RULE 9: If $f(x) = e^{nx}$, where n is a fixed real number, then $f'(x) = ne^{nx}$

RULE 10 (Chain Rule): If $y = u(x)$ and $u = g(x)$, and if both the derivatives $\frac{dy}{du}$

and $\frac{du}{dx}$ are known, then $\frac{dy}{dx} = \frac{dy}{du} \cdot \frac{du}{dx}$

RULE 12: *For any linear function $f(x) = mx + b$, where m and b are fixed real numbers and f(x) is a function of x whose derivative is known, then $f'(x) = m$.*

Review of Section 4.7
Higher Order Derivatives

A function is *differentiable* at a point x means that its derivative at x exists.

- Let $y = f(x)$. Then the first derivative (or just derivative) is denoted as

$$y', \frac{dy}{dx}, \frac{d[f(x)]}{dx}, \text{ or } f'(x).$$

- The second derivative of $y = f(x)$ is the derivative of the first derivative function. It is commonly denoted by $y'', \frac{d^2y}{dx^2}, \frac{d[f(x)]^2}{dx^2}, \text{ or } f''(x).$

- The third derivative of $y = f(x)$ is the derivative of the second derivative function. It is commonly denoted by $y''', \frac{d^3y}{dx^3}, \frac{d[f(x)]^3}{dx^3}, \text{ or } f'''(x).$

- Continuing in this manner, we can define the fourth, fifth, and higher order derivatives.

NOTE: Generally, only the first and second derivatives of a function have applications to business problems.

Review of Section 5.1
Optimization through Differentiation

Theorem 5.1 (First Derivative Test): Let a function be defined on an interval $a \leq x \leq b$ and have a maximum or minimum at a point c, where $a < c < b$. If the derivative of the function exists at $x = c$, the derivative must be zero there.

Maxima and minima of a function can occur at only one of three types of points:

1. points where the first derivative is zero
2. points where the first derivative do not exist
3. endpoints

To find the maximum and minimum for a differentiable function $y = f(x)$ overn the interval $[a, b]$:

Step 1: Find $f'(x)$. Then, set the first derivative to 0 and solve for x. This value, $x = c$, is called a critical point or candidate for maximum or minimum. If $a < c < b$, then c is a candidate. If not, we exclude c.

Step 2: Maximum = $\max\{f(a), f(b), f(c)\}$

Minimum = $\min\{f(a), f(b), f(c)\}$

Note: There is a "Second Derivative Test," as described Problem 28 at the end of the section..

Review of Section 5.2
Modeling

A *model* is a representation of a particular situation; the model does not reveal every aspect of the represented situation, but is meant to highlight significant elements of the situation.

The models considered in this text are mathematical models – that is, they represent the relationship between variables using mathematical equations. This type of model is very useful in dynamic situations that can change with time.

The usefulness of a model is relative to its realistic inclusion of the parameters and their relationships of the variables under investigation.

A *discrete variable* is one in which the variable can only assume finite values, usually containing two decimal digits.

A *continuous variable* is one in which the variable can contain any value between a specified interval.

Although commercial applications use discrete variables, they are generally modelled by equations that yield continuous values, with all results either rounded on truncated to the desired discrete values.

Review of Section 5.3
Maximizing Sales Profit

Method I: Maximizing Profit using the mathematical model

Profit = Revenue − Cost = $R(x) - C(x)$,

where

$R(x) = px$, p is the selling price per item

$C(x) = ax + F$, a is the cost per item and F is fixed costs

Once the profit function is defined, the value of x that maximizes profit is found by taking the first derivative of Profit and setting it equal to zero, using the steps shown in Section 5.1.

Method II: Maximizing Profit by setting $R'(x) = C'(x)$.

Marginal revenue, $R'(x)$, is the derivative of the revenue function $R(x)$.

Marginal cost, $C'(x)$ is the derivative of the cost function $C(x)$.

The value of x that maximizes profit is found by setting $R'(x)$ equal to $C'(x)$ and solving for x.

Review of Section 5.4
Minimizing Inventory Costs

Optimizing techniques are used in inventory problems for minimizing the total of storage and ordering costs while simultaneously ensuring that enough items are on hand to meet current demand.

TABLE 5.9 KNOWN INVENTORY PARAMETERS

Notation	Meaning	Comments
D	Annual demand for all of the items	A known amount.
m	Cost of placing a single ord	A known dollar amount.
k	Cost of storing one item for one year	Either given or calculated as the co financing times the cost of a single i
f	Cost of financing, as a percent	Used to calculate k, if k is not given.
c	Cost of a single item	Used to calculate k, if k is not given.
t	Lead time	The delivery time, in days, betv when an order is placed and when received.

Table 5.10 CALCULATED INVENTORY PARAMETERS

Notation	Meaning	Formula
x	Number of items to be ordered with each order	The unknown variable
N	Number of orders placed in a year	$N = \dfrac{D}{x}$
AI	Average items in inventory	$AI = \dfrac{x}{2}$
k	Annual storage cost for one item	$k = f \cdot c$, or it is given directly
TOC	Total Annual Ordering Cost	$TOC = m \cdot n = \dfrac{mD}{x}$
TSC	Total Annual Storage Cost	$TSC = \dfrac{kx}{2}$
TC	Total Annual Cost	$TC = TOC + TSC$
EOQ	Economic Order Quantity, referred to as the Optimal Order Size	$EOQ = x = \sqrt{\dfrac{2mD}{k}}$

TABLE 5.12 ADDITIONAL CALCULATED INVENTORY PARAMETERS

Notation	Meaning	Formula
d	Daily demand	$d = \dfrac{D}{Working\ days\ in\ a\ year}$
RP	Reorder Point	$RP = d \cdot t$
T	Cycle time (the time between the placement of orders placed)	$T = \dfrac{Working\ days\ in\ a\ year}{Number\ of\ orders\ placed\ in\ a\ year}$

Review of Section 5.5
Econometrics

Econometrics is the branch of economics that uses of mathematical methods to model economic systems.

An important but simple application of the derivative as a rate of change occurs in economics. By applying differentiation techniques to simplified model of a national economy, we can gain interesting insights into the effect of an increase in overall business investment on the total economy. These insights are the beginnings of **Keynesian Economic** theory.

The Simplified Model

$$T = C + B = mT + C_o + B$$

where:

T denotes total national spending
C denotes total consumer expenditures
B denotes total business expenditures

The simplified model assumes:

The economy consists of only consumers
Total business expenditure are denoted by B
Total consumer expenditures are denoted by C

Further r, assuming the portion of consumer spending on basic necessities is very small compared to the portion of consumer spending on luxuries, and that the consumer spending on luxuries is proportional to   Total expenditures,

The simplified model becomes

$$T = mT + B$$

Where m is the proportion of total expenditures made on consumer luxuriesd.

Solving for T yields,

$$T = \left(\frac{1}{1 - m}\right) B$$

The derivative of this function is

$$\frac{dT}{dB} = \frac{1}{1 - m}$$

In economic theory, the term $\frac{1}{1-m}$ is known as the **multiplier**, and represents the increase (or decrease) in total expenditures resulting from an increase (or decrease) in business spending.

Review of Section 6.1
Constant Curve Fit

The simplest curve fit occurs when the data are relatively constant.

Definition 6.1: Let a denote the average value of a set of data. The line $y = a$ is the average-value, straight-line fit for these data points.

Note: A useful modification to an average-value, straight-line fit is the concept of moving averages. Here several averages are calculated for different time periods, resulting in a set of averages which "move with the data."

Review of Section 6.2
Linear Least-Squares Trend Line

Note: Although a straight line appears to be a reasonable approximation to a set of data points (x, y), no one line of the form $y = mx + b$ contains all the given points. Therefore, we seek the straight line that best fits the data.

Definition 6.2: The least-squares error, E, is the sum of the squares of the individual errors. That is, $E = [e(x_1)]^2 + [e(x_2)]^2 + [e(x_3)]^2 + \cdots + [e(x_N)]^2$.

Definition 6.3: The least-squares straight is the line that minimizes the least-squares error.

The least-squares straight line $y = mx + b$ can be found by solving the simultaneous equations (1) and (2) for m and b.

$$(1) \quad bN + m \sum_{i=1}^{N} x_i = \sum_{i=1}^{N} y_i$$

and

$$(2) \quad b \sum_{i=1}^{N} x_i + m \sum_{i=1}^{N} (x_i)^2 = \sum_{i=1}^{N} (x_i y_i)$$

Here, x_i and y_i denotes the values of the ith data point, and N is the total number of data points being considered.

Linear least Squares straight line equations and graphs can be determined using Excel's Insert and Scatter menu options.

Quadratic and Exponential Trend Lines

Definition 6.4: The *least-squares quadratic curve* is a quadratic curve of the form $y = ax^2 + bx + c$ that minimizes the least-squares error (see Definition 6.2).

Definition 6.5: The *least-squares exponential curve* is an exponential curve of the form $= e^x$ that minimizes the least-squares error (see Definition 6.2).

Quadratic and exponential least squares line equations and graphs can be determined using Excel's Insert and Scatter menu options.

Review of Section 6.4
Selecting an Appropriate Curve

Guidelines to select the best fit curve to a given data set:

Step 1: Plot the data points on a graph by hand or by Excel.

Step 2: Examine the trend that the plot follows.

Step 3: If the trend of the data approximately resembles Figure 1, Figure 2, Figure 3, Figure 4, Figure 5 or Figure 6, use its corresponding best fit curve equation. Then, use Section 6.1, 6.2, or 6.3 to find the missing coefficients to the chosen equation.

Average-value, straight-line: $y = a$

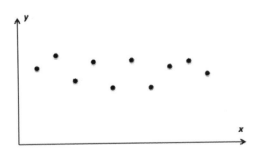

Figure 1

Straight line: $y = mx + b, m > 0$

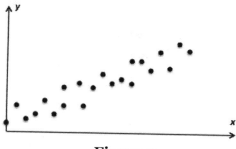

Figure 2

Straight line: $y = mx + b, m < 0$

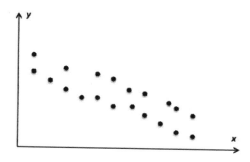

Figure 3

Quadratic Curve: $y = ax^2 + bx + c, \ a < 0$

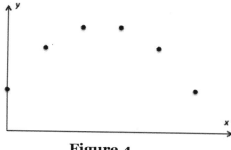

Figure 4

Quadratic Curve: $y = ax^2 + bx + c, \ a < 0$

Quadratic Curve: $y = ax^2 + bx + c, \ a > 0$

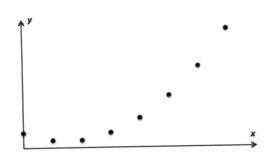

Figure 5

Exponential Curve: $y = e^x$

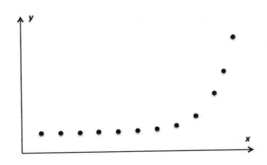

Figure 6

Step 4: Once a selection is made in Step 3, the final step is to test whether nor not the resulting curve does indeed model the data adequately. Such tests fall under the areas of statistical inference and hypothesis testing, which are both beyond the scope of this book.

INDEX

ABOUT THE AUTHORS

Gary Bronson is a Professor in the Information Systems and Decision Sciences department at Fairleigh Dickinson University, where he was twice voted the College's Teacher or the Year and received the University's Distinguished Research award. He has worked as a senior engineer at Lockheed Electronics, an invited lecturer and consultant to Bell Laboratories, and a software consultant to a number of Wall Street financial firms. He is the author of the highly successful, *A First Book of C*, and has authored several other successful programming textbooks on C++, Java, and Visual Basic, in addition to a number of journal articles in the fixed-income finance and programming areas. His Excel Primer, *Practical Excel® for Business Applications*, is also available from this publisher.

Richard Bronson is Professor Emeritus in the Mathematics department at Fairleigh Dickinson University, where he has won the University's Distinguished Teaching, Research, and Faculty Service awards, including the Distinguished College or University Teaching award by the New Jersey Section of the Mathematical Association of America. He has authored several successful texts in Matrix Methods, Differential Equations, Linear Algebra, Finite Mathematics, and Operations Research. He has also published a number of journal articles in mathematics and system simulation. His latest publication is a political thriller named *Antispin*.

Maureen Kieff is a Clinical Assistant Professor in the Information Systems and Decision Sciences department at Fairleigh Dickinson. She has received 12 awards during her career for outstanding teaching and service to students, the latest being the 2014 College Teacher of The Year. She has co-authored ten research articles published in academic journals, primarily addressing mutual fund performance.

Natalie Yang is an instructor in the Information Systems and Decision Sciences department at Fairleigh Dickinson University since 2015. Prior to that she has taught mathematics and statistics at community colleges and universities where she earned many teaching awards. She holds a B. S. degree in Mathematics from University of Alabama at Tuscaloosa and an M. S. degree in Operations Research from University of Kentucky at Lexington.

85990610R00203

Made in the USA
Middletown, DE
28 August 2018